BOOK OF
SKY SPORTS

Collier Books

Collier-Macmillan Ltd.,

London

The Macmillan Company
866 Third Avenue, New York, N.Y. 10022
Collier-Macmillan Canada Ltd., Toronto, Ontario

First Collier Books Edition 1970
The Complete Book of Sky Sports is also published in a
hardcover edition by The Macmillan Company

Printed in the United States of America

THE COMPLETE
BOOK OF
SKY SPORTS

THE COMPLETE

LINN EMRICH

CONTENTS

2 SOARING | 55

4 GYROCRAFT | 123

5 POWER PLANE | 164

PREFACE

WHY THE SKY?

This is a basic book about the sports of the sky. Its primary purpose is to teach the beginner the fundamentals important to safe, enjoyable flight.

If you have never tried a sky sport, this book will help you choose one and give you a foundation for good judgment in that sport. If you have tried a sky sport but have become discouraged and quit, this book will help you remove the stumbling block. And if you are already proficient in one sky sport, this book may stimulate you to try another.

In the discussion of each sport, I have tried to give suggestions on where to go to learn the sport, and some idea of the cost of equipment and training. These matters are, of course, subject to change. They are true now; they may not be a year from now. But the techniques and skills described will not change. They have been proven over the years, and they are the essentials of the sport. No matter what the change in planes or equipment, the basic, fundamental instructions for soaring, sky-diving, and flying are instructions which you can always use—now and ten or twenty years from now.

In the text, I dwell a great deal on the evils of overconfidence and the virtues of good judgment. This is because I want you to live to appreciate the pleasures of the sky. Every flying machine has its own set of rules to make it safe, but safety can be truly achieved only by the individual. His good judgment, his care, and his knowledge are far more important than any other safety factor. "Pilot error" in judgment accounts for almost 100 percent of sport flying and jumping accidents. A plane or parachute may be as safe as a tricycle when used sensibly.

I have not included any description of the flying sports where the participant does not himself make an ascent. Kite flying, radio-controlled model flying, and model balloon flying are all great fun, but the pilot remains on the ground.

Eliminated, too, is a discussion of flying in homebuilt aircraft. Such planes offer great sport flying rewards, but are single-place (one passenger) designs and intended for use and construction by experienced pilots.

Why try a sky sport at all? I cannot give you a definitive answer, but I can tell you why I started and what sport flying means to me.

When I was about eight I played hooky from school one day and was fishing on a dock when I noticed a gaggle of gulls flying in circles nearby. They weren't flapping and yet they kept going up. More gulls joined the throng and they became a climbing, spiraling tower of gulls emitting their laughing sounds all the while. Boy, what a great way to fly, I thought. If I could do that, they'd never get me to go to school. Well, I kept going to school. Then I went to Air Force flying school, then to an airline flying school. In spite of this promising career my thoughts remained troubled and restless. Flying just didn't seem to be as much fun as it ought to be.

In 1960 I first watched some of those daredevil skydivers plummeting themselves toward the ground, and soon I came face to face with the question: "I wonder if I could get away with that just once?" I did, and one jump led to another until soon I was literally jumping for joy.

Things began to come into focus. Here was a way to "fly" which was strictly for fun. I became more and more disenchanted with my flying job: eventually I quit. With my jump instructor as a partner we started a sport parachuting school near Seattle. He did the training and I flew the jump plane. Soon our little school expanded into its own airport and I expanded into sailplanes.

Here I discovered another dimension in sport flying. This truly was the ultimate way to fly! The sailplane is so clean and perfect in design that the air lets you pass by unnoticed. There are no rude sounds or vibrations; only a faint whisper of wind is audible. As you ghost through the sky the sailplane becomes part of you. The long, tapered wings are embraced and caressed by a rising thermal current and you begin circling upward. The pressures of competitive living in a crowded society drop away as the altimeter winds past 6,000, 7,000, 8,000 feet.

There is enchantment to such graceful, effortless flight. You will finally have discovered what those gulls were laughing about. The sky is a marvelous place to be!

There are many ways beyond skydiving and soaring to embark into the sky which I can teach you. Recent advances in man's original mode of flight, the hot air balloon, has stimulated new interest in this sport. Tethered flight in a gyroglider offers a brief, but exciting, glimpse of the pleasures of the sky. Or a gyrocopter may be your answer if you're set on having an engine to push you aloft. They are especially good for the person who has mechanical aptitudes and enjoys building.

There are many hundreds of power plane flight schools in the United States where you can learn the rudiments of pleasurable, safe flying.

Whatever mode of flight you choose I urge you to join me in the sky. Your spirit, too, will soon soar with the laughing gulls.

THE COMPLETE
BOOK OF
SKY SPORTS

1 PARACHUTING

Anyone, man or woman, over sixteen years old who is normally healthy can learn to be a sky-diver. The sport seems to have its greatest appeal to young men between the ages of twenty and thirty, but if it were more commonly known that you don't need to have an athlete's physique to be a good skydiver, there would be a greater diversity in the jumpers' ages.

I have trained many men in their fifties who became real enthusiasts of the sport. And there are records to prove that men in their sixties and seventies have made successful jumps.

Age is therefore a minor factor in determining whether to take up the sport. However, there are some physical requirements you should meet before contemplating a jump. You need two normal arms, at least one leg, and one eye correctable to 20/20.

If you are an amputee with one leg you may still sky-dive, but remember that you must never jump with your artificial limb attached.

Eyesight requirements are not as rigid as for flying, and there are many excellent jumpers with effective vision in only one eye.

Two normal arms are important for handling the canopy steerage toggles or using a reserve chute. However, there are modifications to equipment which have made it possible for some one-armed persons to jump.

People with serious physical handicaps such as heart disorder, very high or low blood pressure, stiff arm or leg joints, or joints that dislocate easily, should not consider jumping without first consulting their physcians and a jump instructor. For your own safety you should be honest with your instructor about your handicap. It may be one which can be dealt with by special training techniques or a simple modification in equipment. One helpful jump instructor once modified a chute for an amputee so that he could manipulate both steering toggles with one hand. Another time a paraplegic with an insatiable urge to make a jump was equipped with a life vest and made a successful static line jump into the water.

Sport parachute jumping is not really very demanding from a physical aspect. It doesn't take much strength to pull a ripcord or make a PLF (parachute landing fall). One of our women pupils weighed only 90 pounds when she started jumping. She was so small that the parachute harness had to be adjusted to its limit to provide a satisfactory fit, and she needed some assistance in strapping on the forty pounds of parachute equipment. She said it required a determined effort for her to keep her feet planted on the jump step. As she got into position to jump I always reduced power and slowed the plane to forty miles per hour so that she wouldn't be swept away by the prop blast. But her size didn't interfere in the least with the functioning of the chute, and the thrill of the jump experience was just as big for her as it was for another of my students who stands a full head above me—and I'm six feet tall.

He has no trouble with prop wash while getting out on the jump step. He does have some difficulty getting his 230 pounds into the small cabin of a Cessna jump plane, especially since his dimensions are exaggerated by parachutes on both his front and back sides.

He needs an oversized chute; most people don't. Twenty-eight feet in diameter is the proper size for the main parachute for anyone under 180 pounds and under thirty-five years of age. Thirty-two feet is the proper size for someone over 180 pounds or over thirty-five, or for anyone interested in a softer landing. If you weigh over 250 pounds, I would recommend a thirty-five-foot surplus T-10 chute for training.

Most clubs and training centers have a selection of chutes which would be appropriate for you.

Girls who wish to make a jump should bear a few facts in mind. Statistics show that girls have a greater chance of sustaining a fracture than men. Those ankles of yours are pretty, but they are also delicate, and many clubs would rather have you around as a nonparticipant than have you jump and perhaps break a leg. Also, there is the matter of overcoming butterflies, which is difficult for anyone, but especially for girls. The fear reactions, or butterflies, are usually not too severe on the first few jumps, but they get much worse before they get better. Around the sixth jump the butterfly attacks may become so severe that the student must have a serious talk with himself before he can muster the courage to board the plane. Girls usually lose their courage altogether during this period of training, and decide not to jump again. I have trained and helped train many girls who were extremely enthusiastic after their first jump. They could hardly wait until the next day to make another. Each time I would think that finally our club was going to have an active girl skydiver. On her third and fourth jumps the prejump anxieties would become more acute and the girl's courage would weaken. In spite of encouragement and pep talks from instructors and friends there would always come a next jump which she couldn't make.

If you are a girl who wants to jump you would be wise to analyze your motives beforehand. If you are doing it to please your husband or boyfriend who is a jumper, or to attract attention to yourself, stop! The odds are against you ever becoming a skydiver. Instead try one of the other sky sports such as soaring where girls can easily excel. If you are a girl who is motivated by a genuine desire to participate in the sport for its own sake, then you should press onward. Spend several hours or days on the drop zone watching landings. Take a ride in the jump plane and watch some exits. This may dampen your spirit. If you're still enthusiastic, sign up for a first jump. Take your training seriously and pay especially close attention to the exit and landing techniques. Practice PLF's and exits at home. A description of how to do these comes later in this book. When you jump, do not make another jump the same day. Wait at least one day because you are more tired than you realize after that first jump. Follow all the other rules outlined for male students.

COSTS

Parachuting is the most attractive sky sport from the cost standpoint. The initial training and associated fees vary greatly throughout the United States, but in most areas it will cost about $30 to $40 for the first jump, with all training, clothing, and equipment furnished, or a total of less than $200 for the first dozen jumps at a commercial training center. At a club facility the instructors are usually nonprofessionals and the student pays only for club membership and aircraft lift. Many clubs offer excellent training and supervision, and the first dozen jumps will set you back less than $100. Don't expect red-carpet service at club facilities, however, and you may have to buy your own chute. Jumpers who volunteer their services as instructors are entitled to satisfy their own jump desires first, and students must wait. I spent three weekends at a club packing loft and drop zone before getting to make the first jump.

The time was not wasted, however, as I learned by keeping my eyes and ears open during waiting periods.

After the training period a jumper may pursue the sport for a lift fee of $2.50 to $5.00 depending upon area and altitude of the lift. A fee of $3.50 is about average for a thirty-second delay jump lift.

Gear, of course, is extra. But don't equip yourself as a parachutist before you have had some experience. Don't rush out after your first jump and splurge your entire savings account on jump gear. The first jump often has a tendency to set you afire with enthusiasm. Buying equipment may be a strong temptation at this point, but take my advice. Wait until you've made a dozen jumps. Make at least one jump on a high-performance chute such as a paracommander. If you just can't help yourself, and must buy something, get a good pair of boots. The French ParaBoot for $30.00 is excellent and so is the Telsan boot for about the same price. If $12.88 is all your budget can stand, you can still fly. Get a pair of surplus combat boots slightly oversized and cut an insole from $3/16$-inch to $1/4$-inch foam neoprene, which is available at any skin diving supply house. Don't jump with hiking boots, ski boots, cowboy boots, zipper side boots, oxfords, or tennis shoes. You'd be better off in bare feet. Your feet and ankles are the most vulnerable part of your body during your training jumps and they deserve the protection of an eight- or ten-inch top boot with full lacing and plenty of toe room.

A word of caution about where to shop for parachute equipment. The worst mistake you can make is to buy a surplus chute from the local surplus store. Seldom is this type of chute worth anything to a sport jumper. I remember one of my students who came out to the loft the weekend following his first jump, and proudly displayed the "fantastic deal" he got at a surplus store. "Only $25 for this beautiful, like-new parachute! Would you believe it?" he expostulated.

"Yes," I said. "It sure is a nice looking canopy. Too bad the suspension lines have been cut at the links." "Oh, that's okay," he said. "I'll just tie them back on." Many surplus chutes have had their suspension lines severed to put them permanently out of service. It's a pitiful waste of a good chute because they can't be simply retied. "You'll have to have them resewn, and the only fellow around here with the special sewing machine required for the job charges $35 per chute," I told him. "You'll need a sleeve, of course, for $16, and the modification to make it steerable is another $20.

His face lost its gleam as I continued.

"The harness has no D rings, either," I observed.

"What are D rings?" he asked.

"D rings are two steel rings sewn to the front of the harness for attaching the reserve chute," I explained. "They require a special sewing machine, too, and the services of a master rigger who usually charges $8 to $12 for the job."

A quick tally of the costs showed it would cost Bob $106 before his chute would be ready for use. For less money and a lot less fuss and bother he could have purchased an excellent rig ready to use from a reliable firm which specializes in sport jumping equipment. Several are listed at the end of this chapter. Any of these firms would be glad to send you a catalog.

After you have passed the early training phase of a dozen jumps and feel firmly hooked on the sport, you may wisely consider an in-

Figure 1. Paracommander.
The Paracommander has been the most popular sport parachute since it was introduced by Pioneer Parachute Co. in 1964. The many slots or louvres give the chute a good forward glide and slow rate of sink.

vestment in a chute of your own. There are many varieties, but most will fall into three categories:

LOW PERFORMANCE. Surplus twenty-eight-foot and thirty-two-foot chutes modified for sport use. This type is used for training when modified into a double L or double T pattern. A good chute for the budget-minded; they cost $40 to $70 used, or about $100 new, complete and ready to jump.

MEDIUM PERFORMANCE. The same twenty-eight-foot and thirty-two-foot circular design chutes as above have been manufactured by Pioneer for sport jumper use in a special low porosity nylon, commonly called LoPo's. LoPo's have a slightly slower descent rate and better forward speed because less air leaks through the material during descent. A new twenty-eight-foot LoPo with quality harness is $300. Used, it should cost about $200. The thirty-two-foot size costs about $40 more. Low porosity chutes have suffered a decline in popularity with the advent of the high-performance chutes.

High-performance, or super canopies. Paracommander, or P.C., made by Pioneer, is the biggest seller and probably the best chute money can buy. Its forward speed is twice that of a LoPo and the rate of descent is very slow, a 170-pound jumper will sink at about fifteen feet per second, and glide forward at about 10 mph. The principal advantage to this type of chute lies in the fast forward glide, quick turning response, and slow rate of sink. Persons up to 220 pounds may use this type of chute and still enjoy gentle landings. A standard parachute is just a drag surface, but the high-performance sport chute is a crude airfoil which develops lift as it glides forward. A new P.C. complete with a quality harness is $400. About $100 of this price is for the deluxe harness and container and the cost is then reduced to about $325. The Crossbow is similar in design and performance to the P.C. It costs $600, but comes complete with a deluxe harness and reserve parachute which is mounted on the back above the main chute. If you want to use a Crossbow canopy in a B-4 harness, it will cost about the same as a P.C.

The Irvin Parachute Company and Steve Snyder Enterprises have developed and marketed an interesting chute called the Delta II Para Wing. This chute has a gentle rate of descent of about fourteen feet per second. The forward glide speed is an amazing 20 mph, or twice as fast as the para-commander or Crossbow, with a glide ratio of two to one. Spotting and wind shifts become less critical because the chute's performance will extend the jumper's area of maneuverability. Price of the Para Wing is $320 and it will fit into any standard harness and container.

The Para Wing is not packed in the conventional manner because it won't fit on a packing table. The entire canopy must be spread flat on the floor or ground.

For the jumper who is on a slim budget I suggest a used surplus double L or double T chute. After you've made thirty jumps or more you can improve the performance for a few dollars by having it modified into a TU. Have a licensed rigger examine the chute to be sure it is airworthy before you buy it. Don't worry if the date stamped on the canopy shows it was manufactured ten years ago. A nylon chute does not deteriorate with age. Jumping a chute doesn't wear it out either. Some have been jumped over 1,000 times and are still airworthy. Be careful of a chute which has been dyed, inked, or painted. Sometimes this can damage the nylon. Test the fabric by trying hard to poke your finger through it. If you succeed, the canopy is still good for making flags, but it isn't safe for jumping.

For the jumper who is on a firmer financial footing the super canopy is definitely the way to

Figure 2. Para Wing

go. The superior turning response, the fast forward glide, and the gentle, comfortable landings make these chutes a real pleasure to use. The super canopy also maintains its resale value if given reasonable care.

A reserve chute is a $40 to $70 investment. It must be repacked every 60 days by a rigger, which will cost from $2.50 to $4.00. Many clubs have reserves which you can use and will save you this investment and packing upkeep.

The only other personal jump equipment you will need is a helmet, a pair of coveralls, gloves, and goggles. An $8.95 football helmet is satisfactory. The fiberglass Bell model 500 TX for $37.00 has become the jumpers' status symbol. J. C. Penney markets a good coverall in white for $4.95. Sears or Montgomery Ward coveralls at $8.95 are good and come in various colors. If you want the type with double ankle-to-neck zippers, especially designed for jumpers, you'll spend $23.50.

Goggles are useful for freefall jumps over twelve seconds and cost $1.50 for the popular bubble type. If you wear glasses, you'll have to experiment with goggles to find a pair which will cover your glasses and still be comfortable while you're wearing a helmet. The full-face shield which snaps onto a helmet is fine for motorcycles and sport cars, but it won't work for jumping. It fogs up in the airplane and blows off in freefall.

There are many items of jump gear such as instruments, sentinels (automatic reserve openers), boot brackets, etc., which are all non-essentials. Their usefulness will be discussed later.

I would like to stress the fact that by getting economy equipment, that is, surplus chute and boots, football helmet, and coveralls, you will not have sacrificed safety. This gear will cost you under $100 total and you are ready to try the sky. No other sky sport can equal that price.

STATIC LINE JUMPS

A static line jump is, simply, a jump whereby the parachute is opened automatically by an eight- to twelve-foot cord attached to the plane on one end and to the chute on the other. As you drop away from the plane the static line comes taut and pulls the chute open. It is the easiest jump to make, but you should know the fundamentals because all other jumps share them. True, many hundreds of emergency bailouts have been made by pilots who know nothing about how to jump, except "you must pull the ring or you won't feel a thing"; but these *are* emergency jumps. If you jump for fun, you should start with static line jumps, and I suppose the best way to explain the fundamentals is to tell you what goes on in a preliminary jump class at my school.

First we take a close look at the parachute itself. We stretch it out on a table forty feet long and three feet wide.

When the parachute is stretched out we find it divided into three main parts: the development device, which consists of a pilot chute and sleeve; the canopy, which isn't called an umbrella but looks like one when inflated; and the harness that secures the parachute to your body. The container, or pack tray, is a rectangular bag which closes up with four flaps around the parachute after it has been folded into place. Each time you pack a chute you inspect it for tears, holes, frays, or broken stitching. That's one thing I like about jumping. The chute gets looked over thoroughly before each use.

PACKING A CHUTE

To pack the chute it is best to stretch it or give it tension by pulling it from both ends. This makes it easier to check the lines and pleating. A parachute will probably work effectively even when the suspension lines are twisted or tangled. In the days of barnstorm- and batwing jumpers one famous jumper would drag his chute up to the grandstand after a jump, call down a volunteer out of the crowd, and have him stuff the chute into a bag. He would then strap it on, board the plane, and proceed to make another jump. This was not a phony stunt. Chute packing really can be just that simple. But believe it or not, we jumpers

Figure 3. Packing Sequence

(left) 1. Straighten Lines

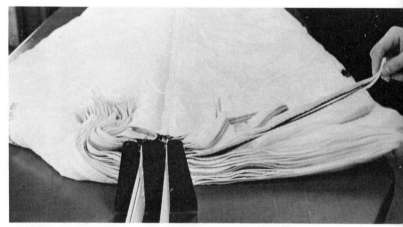

2. Straighten Apex

3. Inspect and Pleat Gores

4. Straighten Skirt Band

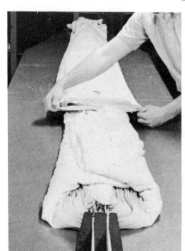

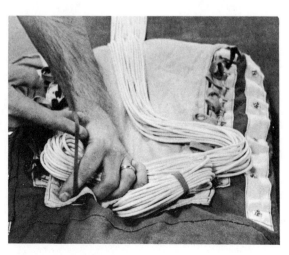

5. Pull on Sleeve

6. Form Locking Stows

7. Stows Completed

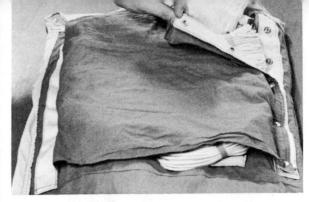

8. Snap Cover Flap

9. Loop Retainer Line and Stow Inside Sleeve

10. Inspect Harness

11. Attach Harness to Risers

12. Lay Risers and Chute in Container

13. Fold Sleeve into Stack

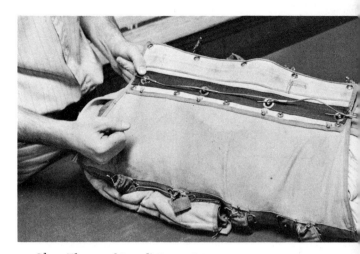

15. Close Flaps and Install Ripcord Pins

like to play it extra safe, so we go through a little ritual of straightening the lines and laying out the pleats just as the book of instructions from the manufacturer shows.

Every part of the parachute is designed to be many times as strong as it needs to be. For example, the suspension lines (sometimes called "shroud lines") have a tensile strength of 550 pounds each. On a standard size chute, which is twenty-eight feet in diameter, there are twenty-eight suspension lines leading from the harness to the canopy. Each line starts at a case-hardened steel connector link, passes up one side, over the top and down the other side to another connector link. To break away from the parachute you would have to exert a load in the neighborhood of seven tons on the lines.

After pleating the canopy the sleeve is pulled down from the apex, or top of the canopy. The sleeve was developed to reduce the opening shock, which it does very successfully. The suspension lines are now grouped together and stowed zigzag fashion into the stowing rubber bands. The first two stows are called "locking stows" because they anchor a flap shut over the open end of the sleeve. This is to prevent the canopy from inflating until all the lines are pulled out straight. Keep stowing the lines until only about eighteen inches are left between the end of the sleeve and the links. Now the sleeve is folded back and forth into a neat stack on the container. If a sleeve retainer line is used, it will prevent the pilot chute and sleeve from drifting free after the opening. Attach a six- to twelve-foot length of scrap suspension line between the apex of the sleeve and the apex of the canopy. Coil it into loops and stuff it inside the top of the sleeve, or stow it in rubbers attached to the sleeve bridle. Coil the

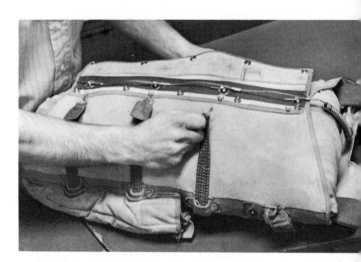

16. Attach Pack Opening Bands (bungees)

pilot chute bridle cord on top of the stack and stand the pilot chute on top of everything. Until you've seen it done you would swear an act of God couldn't get that heap of material squashed into the skimpy square container. It does take a bit of squashing, I'll admit, and sometimes it even takes a husky friend to help with the tugging and pulling. The container is held closed with four ripcord pins inserted into small, horizontal holes in the ends of brass cones that are sewn to the flaps of the container. These cones mate with grommets on the opposing flap. The final step is to attach the eight spring steel bungee straps (also called "pack opening bands") to their respective eyelets.

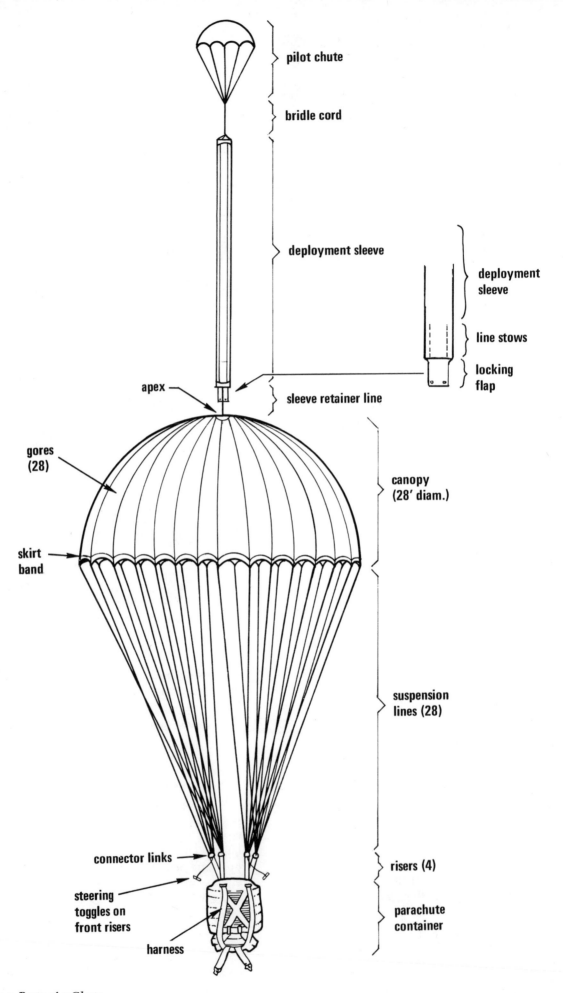

pilot chute

bridle cord

deployment sleeve

deployment sleeve

line stows

locking flap

apex

sleeve retainer line

gores (28)

canopy (28' diam.)

skirt band

suspension lines (28)

connector links

steering toggles on front risers

harness

risers (4)

parachute container

Figure 4. Parts of a Chute

At this point in one of my classes a student named Joe shook his head and said, "I hope you don't expect me to jump with that thing." "Why not?" I said. "It'll never work . . . you've got that parachute locked inside that sleeve thing and I don't see how it will ever get out." This was a good excuse for a demonstration to show the opening sequence, so I laid the chute on the end of the table and pulled the ripcord. The pins need to move only about one inch, but you have to pull the ripcord handle out several inches because of slack in the cable. When the cones are released, the pack bands pull the container flaps back and the spring-loaded pilot chute leaps into the air. I had my skeptical student take the pilot chute and walk down the table with it. The sleeve unfolded until it was straight, and then the stowed suspension lines began popping out of the rubber stows. When the last two stows pulled out, the locking flap was released and continued tension from the pilot chute caused the sleeve to slip nicely off, exposing the canopy. "Okay. I'm convinced," said Joe. "Let's jump." "Not so fast. You've got to know a few other things," I replied, "such as how to exit."

EXITS

There are an infinite number of wrong ways for students to exit the airplane, and only one proper way. This is with the body arched from head to toe and from finger tip to finger tip. This position gives your body a shape which will cause it to fall belly toward the ground. You will not tumble if you execute your push-off from the plane properly and hold this arched or "stable" position.

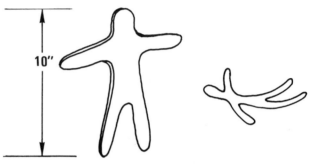

Cut doll from stiff paper. Bend into arched shape and drop from 6 feet high. It will always fall curved side down, or stable.

Place kink or bend in center of doll and drop again. Pattern of fall is random and tumbling. This is unstable and happens when jumper bends forward at waist during free fall.

Figure 5. Paper Doll

A very simple device can serve as an illustration. Cut a paper doll as shown from heavy paper or thin cardboard. Bend it into an arched shape and drop it from arm's length overhead. It will always fall curved-side down. Although your body is not cardboard it is responsive to the same aerodynamic forces.

Figure 6. Static Line Exit.

1. At the jumpmaster's command, "Put your feet on the step," student positions himself in the doorway, guarding the reserve ripcord handle with his left hand all the while.

2. At the command, "Get out there," student grasps wing strut and pulls himself forward to crouched position leaning well forward.

The most common error in exits comes when the student bends forward at the waist. This throws a reverse arch into the body no matter how well the chest, arms, and legs hold an arch. The result is usually an out-of-shape tumble.

Take the paper doll again and fold a kink at the waist as diagramed. When you drop it there is no stable pattern to its fall. It tumbles randomly through the air. If you want to fall stable, you must hold the arched body position.

As a student you will be sitting on the floor with your static line attached to the plane (usually the pilot seat) and your left hand protecting your reserve ripcord. As you approach the drop zone on a jump run at 2,500 feet the jumpmaster will tell you to "put your feet on the step." At this signal you should sit in the doorway facing forward on a 45° angle with knees close together and feet on the step. Do not lean out into the prop blast, but place your right hand at the lower door frame and left hand on the wing strut next to the fuselage. The jumpmaster will spot from behind you and at the appropriate moment say to the pilot, "Cut." Don't let this command trigger you into action because it is a signal for the pilot to cut the engine in order to reduce the wind blast past the door. Your next command will be, "Get out there," and you should lean forward, reach your right hand out and grasp the wing strut about two feet from the fuselage and pull yourself out to a semi-crouched, standing position. If the plane is of a tricycle gear design, your right foot will be on the wheel, and left foot on the step. Be sure to bend forward at the ankles with knees bent and support much of your weight on your hands, which are still gripping the wing strut. Your head should be in front of the wing strut. When the jumpmaster slaps you firmly on the left thigh, kick your feet up and then push off with your arms, sending you back and down the plane in a horizontal, belly-down attitude. It is very important to kick the feet off the step before pushing away with the arms. If you push off simultaneously with feet and arms, or release hands first, you will probably do a backward somersault off the step. This is not the recommended exit procedure. See photos at page 38.

3. At the slap on the thigh student jumps backward and begins to spread out into an arched body position.

4. With body nicely arched, parachute begins to deploy. His arms are held a little too high. They should be straight out from the shoulder.

5. Pilot chute pulls free from the static line. Jumper's position keeps him stable with no tendency to tumble or roll.

(right) 6. He is pulled to an upright position as the chute fills with air.

Figure 7. Practice Exit

You can practice coordinating the exit by standing two feet back from a sturdy table. Place hands on the edge of the table and lean forward in the semi-crouch as you would on a jump step. Raise your feet about six inches from the ground by pivoting your weight forward onto your arms. Then push away with the arms. You should land on both feet about two feet behind your original position. Throw your hips and chest forward into an arch, hold your head and arms arched backward from your shoulders and count out loud, "Arch thousand, two thousand, three thousand, four thousand, check canopy."

I recommend you practice this exit pushoff until you can do it mechanically without thinking. You might do it ten times and say to yourself, "It's so easy, how could I forget?" You'd be surprised how many things you will forget the first time you lean on that wing strut at an

Figure 8. Practice Table Exits

lean on hands   pivot forward   push off   land

As your feet touch the ground, catch your balance and arch your body.
Then count out loud "arch thousand, two thousand, three thousand, four thousand."

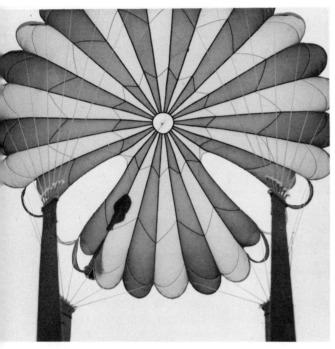

Figure 9. Checking Canopy

altitude of 2,500 feet. I forgot everything on my first exit and didn't even count. My first perceptions after feeling the jumpmaster slap my leg were those of seeing the bright colors of the open parachute canopy and thinking, "My God, that's beautiful." I went back up for the second jump simply because I felt cheated and wanted to find out what an exit was really like.

I've seen lots of students forget the pushoff sequence when their minds were foggy with fears. Practice the exit exercise with perseverance and be sure to sing out, "Arch thousand, two thousand, three thousand, four thousand, check canopy." The words, "Arch thousand," help you remember to arch the back and arms immediately after pushing away from the plane. You say "Check canopy," to remind yourself to look overhead at the chute. You do this to determine that it is properly and fully opened, and because it is a beautiful sight which you will always remember, and I don't want you to miss it.

If you do the exit jump and push with

proper timing and lock into a good arch for the count of four, you will be stable and your chute will deploy cleanly from your backpack. As the chute blossoms you swing smoothly from a horizontal to a vertical position about 100 feet below the plane.

An alternative exit procedure commonly used in some areas is the one-legged pushoff. Stand on the left foot and dangle the right foot free behind you. Keep weight on the arms in the forward crouched position exactly as in the two-legged exit stance. Jump up with the left leg and push away with the arms exactly as before. The advantage to this type of exit is that it places the legs in an already spread-out position.

Usually the chute will blossom open and you will feel the harness snug up around you

Figure 10. One-legged Exit Position

before you reach the count of four. If you get to four and haven't felt anything except the thumping of your heart, then you may have counted as some students do who say, "One thou . . . gasp, FOUR THOUSAND." Or you may have had a pilot chute hesitation. This occurs when the pilot chute doesn't get well anchored in the airflow, but instead it flutters about for a moment in the turbulence behind your back. This may delay the opening for a few seconds. A pilot chute assist system now used throughout the country eliminates the possibility of the pilot chute hesitation on static line jumps. See exit photos at page 12.

Don't try to analyze a slow opening. A normal opening takes just two and a half seconds, and if nothing has happened after you have held your arched position for a moment, then you should proceed with the reserve chute opening procedure which I will explain later.

After a normal opening, and after you have inspected the canopy, take a few seconds to look around and appreciate the unrestricted view. Then proceed with the canopy steerage portion of the jump.

CANOPY STEERING

Steering is accomplished with little wooden handles, called "toggles," which you will find on the back side of each rear riser. They may be hard to see when you're suspended in the harness, so I suggest running your hands up overhead along the risers until you get a grip on the handles. To make a turn pull down on one handle for a distance of three to four feet. The handle connects to a line which connects to a suspension line, which goes up to the canopy skirt at one of the open or blank gores.

These open gores are on the back side of the chute and they allow a certain amount of air to spill out, creating some forward thrust. You will need to keep a steering toggle pulled for about four seconds to make a 180° turn, seven seconds for a 360° turn.

By pulling down on the left toggle you distort the shape of the canopy. The air spilling out of the blank gore which is generating forward thrust suddenly is diverted sideways and becomes a weak but effective turning thrust. The canopy begins to rotate slowly to the left. The jumper suspended twenty feet below turns with the canopy. A right turn works the same way. If you pull down both handles simultaneously, the forward thrust is eliminated and the turning thrusts cancel themselves out, so your chute begins to sink vertically through the air. This simultaneous use of the toggles is called "braking." Brakes are useful in target accuracy, but until you've made several jumps, you should avoid experimenting with brakes while approaching for a landing. You might instigate an oscillation or pendulum-swinging motion which would lead to an uncomfortably harsh landing.

The toggles should always be used with smooth, deliberate strokes. Don't snatch them up and down like a yo-yo; you'll only succeed in setting up an oscillation.

When to steer is a matter of judgment and it takes a few jumps to get the idea of controlling your turns and landing somewhere near the target. Usually you are assisted from the ground on the first jump and told either by radio or by a large pointer which way to steer. You will catch on to the steering, or navigation, of chutes much quicker if you study the following principles and diagrams.

If you jumped with a chute which had no

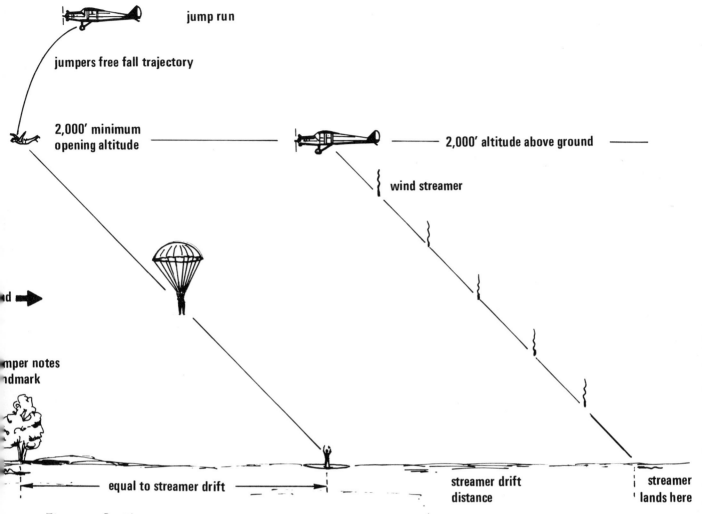

jump run

jumpers free fall trajectory

2,000' minimum opening altitude

2,000' altitude above ground

wind streamer

d ➤

mper notes
ndmark

equal to streamer drift

streamer drift distance

streamer lands here

Figure 11. Spotting

modification and therefore no forward speed, you would be at the mercy of the wind. You would drift with the wind according to the following simple formula:

Distance = Time × Speed
Distance = Horizontal distance across ground
   Time = Number of minutes of descent under the canopy
  Speed = Average wind speed in feet per minute

*Example*s An average descent takes two minutes from 2,000 feet. A wind of 8 mph will convert to about 700 feet per minute. Two minutes × 700 = 1,400 feet horizontal drift. This jumper would land 1,400 feet downwind from the spot on the ground over which he jumped, hereafter called the "opening point."

Predicting the wind is fairly simple. It doesn't even require any mathematics. You cast a wind drift streamer out of the plane at 2,000 feet directly over the intended landing point, or target. This is a weighted sheet of yellow crepe paper which descends at the same speed as a jumper. Watch it as the plane circles and note the point on the ground where it lands. Imagine a line running along the ground from that point to the target and extending on past it. This is called the "windline" and represents the average direction of the wind. Look at that drift distance from the streamer to the target. Shift your eyes to a point on the opposite side of the target and an equal distance from it. That is the proper opening point. If the pilot maneuvers the plane so that you can exit and open directly over that chosen opening point,

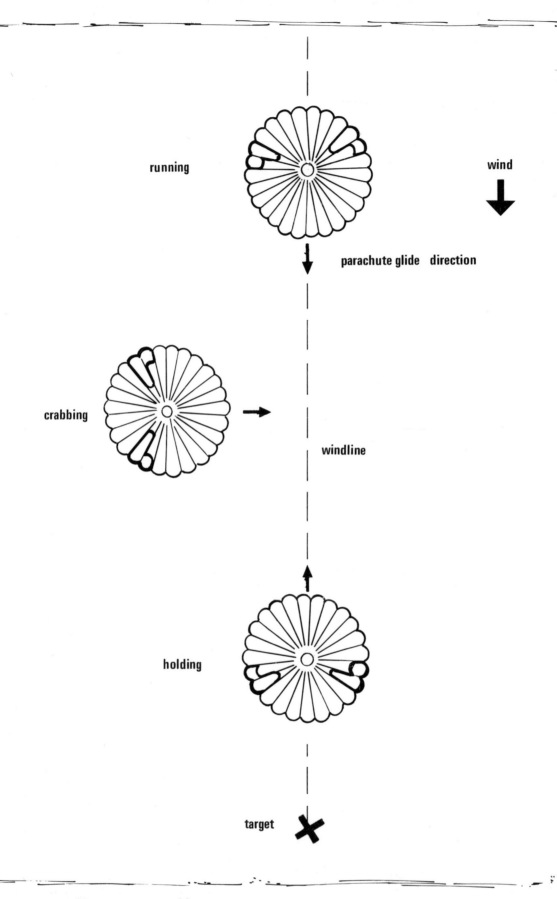

Figure 12. Holding. Running. Crabbing.

you will likely drift back to a landing in close proximity to your target. This is providing the wind doesn't change, which the wind has a habit of doing.

There are a few other variables, too. The wind downstream from the target must be the same average speed and direction as it is on the upwind side. Also, you must open your chute at the precise altitude that you threw the streamer. In sum, target jumping a nonsteerable circular chute is just a little too much of a challenge for the beginner.

Most modified sport-type chutes have a forward glide speed in calm air of 8 mph, or 700 feet per minute. This means you could miss your opening point by a quarter of a mile and still make the target. Or you might use the forward glide to correct for shifting winds or improper opening altitude.

Here is another way to look at it. As you descend with a modified chute in perfectly still air you can glide to any point on the ground within a circle with a diameter of 2,800 feet and a center directly below your opening point.

We seldom encounter conditions of absolutely no wind, so a wind drift check is made before the first jumps of the day or anytime a wind shift is suspected.

If the wind is less than 8 mph on the ground, it is considered safe to jump students.

Usually the wind aloft is stronger than at lower altitudes and it is not uncommon to see the wind drift streamer land a half mile or more from the target. This puts the exit point upwind an equal distance and after your chute is open and you've checked the canopy, you must look around and locate the target.

If you didn't turn during the exit or opening, you will be facing upwind, or away from the target. There are three terms which refer to the direction you are facing in relation to the wind:

HOLDING means facing into the wind. This way your canopy's forward glide helps to offset the wind drift. While holding, you will progress slowly forward or backward across the ground depending upon the wind velocity. If the wind velocity is 8 mph, your ground speed will be nonexistent while holding. If the wind is 12 mph, you will drift slowly backward at about 4 mph. If the wind is less than 8 mph, you will advance slowly against the wind.

RUNNING means the wind is at your back. Downwind is the direction to face if you really want to cover the ground. When facing with the wind you compute your ground speed by adding wind speed to canopy speed. While running with an 8 mph wind you will move along at a healthy 16 mph, or 24 feet per second.

CRABBING is facing sideways to the wind and may be either a left crab or a right crab. It is used when you are off the windline due to a bad spot or because the wind shifted.

On a normal descent you will spend about an equal amount of your two-minute descent time running and holding. Hold for about a minute and then run for an equal time. Look down at the ground and notice your horizontal progress while running. It will surprise you.

The imaginary point on the ground below your body moves along as you drift. This is called your "track line." It should be on the windline and if it isn't, you should crab over toward the windline.

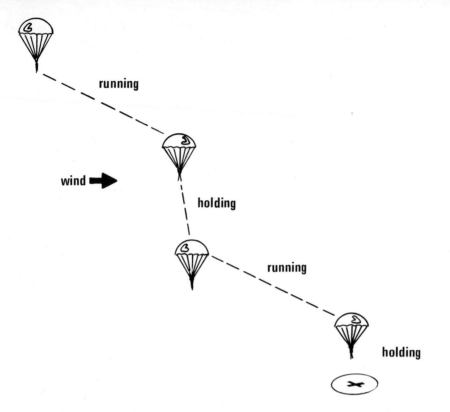

running

wind ➡

holding

running

holding

✈

Figure 13. Typical Descent

If you were put out short, that is, not far enough upwind, you will need to spend more time holding than running. Conversely, if you were put out long, or if the wind suddenly diminished, you would have to spend most of the descent facing the target, or running.

At about 300 feet high verify the direction of the ground wind by flags or smoke on the ground and turn to a holding position and prepare to land. It is very important to hold while landing. You could be in for a rude shock if you land heading downwind. (Remember that 16 mph ground speed while running with a mere 8 mph wind.)

At most training centers you will get some assistance from the ground if you become disoriented and don't know which way to turn. Some places have a small radio receiver mounted on the reserve chute or in the helmet. One good way that we have found to assist a student is by using a simple ground pointer made from an old scrapped white canopy. Three panels are cut from the chute. Spread out on the ground near the target it becomes a gigantic arrowhead pointer to tell the student which way to face.

The success of this system depends upon the student jumper making frequent visual checks of the ground indicator and responding by making turns to the directed heading. When holding with back to the target, you may have to make some partial turns every few seconds and look over your shoulder to check for new heading commands.

THE LANDING

The Parachute Landing Fall

The parachute landing fall, commonly called PLF, is the method of landing whereby your descending motion is cushioned to a halt by a progressive fall. Most parachuting injuries result from improper PLF technique.

The speed of the descent depends on many variables such as weight of jumper, size of canopy, type of modification, and density of the air. It is commonly thought that the landing shock is equivalent to dropping from ten feet high or more. If this were so, the only practical place to land would be in a lake. The normal descent rate of fourteen to eighteen feet per second is equivalent to a drop from about four feet.

You may think, "Gee, I could land standing up from only a four foot jump." Maybe you can, but don't try it on your jump. As you watch the ground approach from the harness you may be impressed with the slowness of the

Figure 14. Expert Jumper Landing

descent and be tempted to land as if you were jumping a fence.

Experience has proven that if you want to land safely, you had better do it according to proper student PLF technique. After you have made thirty jumps you will have some judgment, which will allow you to deviate from student technique and make flashy landings in the manner of the pros. See photos of students landing as compared to instructors.

The PLF is accomplished from an upright position with legs and feet together. The hands should grasp the front risers high above your head, with elbows close together in front of your face. During the last fifty feet of the descent keep the eyes looking straight ahead at the horizon. Do not lock your legs into a rigidly straight position, but keep them very slightly bent and with just a little tension in the calf and thigh muscles. If you land with legs relaxed, you will collapse in a heap and could be injured. The whole secret to a comfortable, safe parachute landing lies in the way you position your body before you touch down. This is called the "Prepare to land" position.

The prepare-to-land position and subsequent landing roll may be practiced at home until perfected by referring to the following description and photos.

Put on a pair of old trousers which won't be damaged by grass stains on the knees, and retire to a patch of backyard lawn. Memorize and practice the prepare-to-land position before going on to the landing roll. Stand erect with legs touching at the knees, ankles, and balls of the feet. Place arms overhead with backs of the hands forward and elbows close together, or touching, if possible. Eyes should look straight ahead.

Now go over this check list to be sure you haven't overlooked something. Are your legs touching each other at the knees? Press them

Look at your elbows. There should be six inches or less distance between them and they should be level with, or above, the nose. Now stand at ease for a moment and recheck the accompanying photographs.

The legs are kept pressed together during a landing to make them be like one single, super-strong leg. You get many times the strength against injury or fracture than if you landed with legs separated.

It is easy to land in a bent, or piked, position because the parachute harness supports you

(above) Figure 15. Student Landing Position. This student is approaching the ground for landing with good form except that his elbows should be in front of his face and his eyes should look at the horizon, not at the ground.

(right) Figure 16. Student Prepare-to-land Position

together a little to be sure they are actually touching. If you are bowlegged, you will have to bend slightly more at the knees to bring them together in contact. It is very important that your knees and ankles remain together throughout the landing roll. Now check your feet. They should be in contact at the ankles, heels, and toes. Do not raise up onto the toes because a flat-footed landing is preferred to a toe-down landing. (I know this isn't what they teach at military jump school, where they recommend toe-down landings. However, we jump chutes with a forward glide and toe-down landings often result in broken toes. Flat-footed is correct. Don't land heels first, either.)

under the hips and tends to push your legs forward. This piked position puts you in good shape to land on your tailbone, which is not recommended. Your legs, when properly positioned, act as shock absorbers and help reduce the momentum left for the balance of the landing roll. Eyes are kept up for landing because if you watch the ground approaching on your first few jumps, there comes a moment just before your feet touch that you will impulsively thrash your legs out of proper landing position. It is called "anticipating the ground" and it invariably happens when a student sneaks a look at the ground just before he touches down. If he's lucky, he is able to get up, but all too often a sprain or fracture will result from anticipating the ground. Arms are held overhead and elbows together in front for a couple of good reasons. Your arms and hands do not assist in any way with a parachute landing. In fact they can only get in the way and perhaps get hurt. Grasping the front risers will help keep your arms out of the way during your landing. Holding your elbows in front of your face protects them in case you fall sideways, and they protect your face if you should land in a tree or wires.

Try popping into the "prepare" position as though a drill sergeant had just said, "Atten-Hutt!" Now run through the checklist from the feet up. Feet touching, pressure between the knees, body erect, eyes up, elbows in and level with nose. If you are having trouble getting your elbows close together, check to be sure the forearm is rotated so that the backs of the hands face forward. When your "prepare" position is perfected, you could probably make a safe jump. If you are faced into the wind and hold that prepare-to-land position right down to the ground, you will have made a good landing.

The Landing Roll

Don't let me discourage you from learning the landing roll, however. You will have to perform it properly for your instructor before he will let you jump.

Draw an imaginary cross on the ground and stand at the center facing out toward one of the arms of the cross, hereafter called the "center line." We will first practice the right-hand PLF. The contact points for this will be knees, right hip, and left shoulder. Look down at your feet and find a spot on the grass at a 45° angle out from your toes to the left of your center line. The distance should be your toe-to-knee distance. This is where your knees should contact the ground on a right hand PLF. Your next contact point is your right hip on the center line about thirty inches out from your toes. The balance of the roll is accomplished by straightening out the bent legs and letting the feet follow a rainbow-like arch as you maintain a pike in the waist and roll from right hip to left shoulder. You should now be lying on your left side with elbows and arms still in the original positions. Legs should be semi-straight and held together throughout the roll. The pike at the waist should approximate 120°.

The PLF will work smoothly only if you use a smooth and continuous shoulder rotation during the landing. During a right-hand PLF the shoulder rotation is to the left and begins as you start bending the legs to drop to your knees. When your knees touch the ground your shoulders and head should face directly out the left-hand cross arm, or 90° from where you started. Keep the shoulders rotating so that when your hip touches the center line your head and shoulders are facing out the opposite center line, or 180° from starting posi-

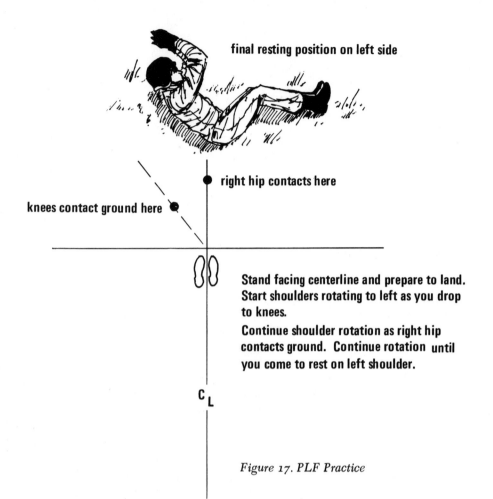

final resting position on left side

right hip contacts here

knees contact ground here

Stand facing centerline and prepare to land. Start shoulders rotating to left as you drop to knees.

Continue shoulder rotation as right hip contacts ground. Continue rotation until you come to rest on left shoulder.

C L

Figure 17. PLF Practice

tion. During the roll to your left shoulder the final 90° position of shoulder rotation will be completed. If you're completely confused by this time, try again. Stand up facing the center line and prepare to land. Rotate shoulders left as you drop to the knees. Stop there and maintain your balance. Check to be sure your knees are 45° off the center line and your shoulders have rotated 90°. Now keep the shoulders rotating left until the hip contacts the ground and stop. I know it seems impossible, but you can balance there if you lean away from the direction you are falling. Now continue the shoulder rotation as the legs are straightened at the knees, and as the feet prescribe the arc up to the left, and down.

Don't let the knees or ankles lose contact any time during the landing. Rehearse this technique step by step until it is right, and then try it without stopping at the knees and hip. It now becomes a continuous falling, rotating action which starts from a standing position

and finishes in a piked, prone position on your left side.

As a check to be sure you are not letting your knees come apart during the landing, put a $1 bill between your knees at the start of the PLF. Pretend it's a $100 bill and you'll be even less likely to drop it.

When the falling roll is practiced until it is smooth, you can reverse and practice left-hand landings. The sequence is the same except that your shoulders will rotate right and your knees will contact the ground 45° the right of the center line. To finish, you will lie prone on your right side.

The most common mistake is failure to get the hip down as a positive contact point. This leaves you going from the knees to the back or shoulder with a temptation to jab an elbow into the ground to help you rotate. Keep the landings slow until the proper sequence is mastered. Then you may try it from a two-foot platform with a forward pushoff. You will im-

Figure 18. Daisy Chain Lines.

1. *After landing, back away from the chute until the lines are straight and bunched together.*

2. *Twist a loop in the lines next to the connector links.*

3. & 4. *Reach through the loop, grasp the lines and pull them through the first loop to form a new loop.*

mediately determine whether or not you have grasped the fundamentals because if you haven't, the landing will smart. You will feel as though you are shaped like a block with all the pointy corners jamming into the ground.

If the roll is properly coordinated, you can do it on concrete and not get a bruise. I suggest you stay with grass, though, until both left- and right-hand landings feel smooth from the two-foot platform. The younger set may then step up to a four-foot platform as an optional challenge.

As the final step in PLF practice, make fifteen or twenty jumps from the platform without falling and rolling. In other words make a standup landing. This will cause you to put the right amount of tension in your legs for the actual jump landing. You aren't expected to make a standup landing on the jump, but you shouldn't land with relaxed legs, either.

This question may occur to you: "How do I know whether to do a right or a left PLF on my jump?" You won't know and shouldn't try to predict or determine your direction of fall. The actual parachute landing takes only about one second from start to finish. The direction of fall is determined by your direction of drift across the ground. If you are drifting to the left slightly, you will do a left PLF, and no amount of forethought or rotating could make it into a right PLF.

On your jumps the landing roll will develop as a natural product of your prepared position and your drift across the ground. The most difficult PLF is accomplished when your descent is straight down with no drift in any direction. You must divert this vertical descent into a horizontal roll, or you may wind up with a knee in the face.

If you are holding into a wind which exceeds

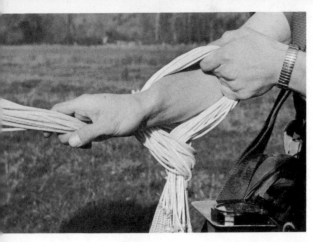

5. & 6. *Reach through this loop, grasp the lines, and pull them through to form a new loop. Continue chaining in this manner until you are about two feet from the skirt of the chute. The bundle of lines 20 feet long has now shrunk to a 4-foot chain.*

9. *Pull the slack out of the final loop to secure the bundle. Disconnect the parachute from the harness.*

7. *Make the final loop a large one.*

8. *Pick up the center of the chained bundle and thrust it part way into the final loop.*

10. *Pull the sleeve down over the canopy (an assistant is helpful when available).*

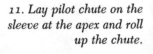

11. *Lay pilot chute on the sleeve at the apex and roll up the chute.*

12. *The rolled chute may be carried easily or strapped onto the parachute harness until repacked for use again.*

your canopy speed, you will be drifting backward on ground contact. Falling under this condition is easy as you simply roll from feet to hips and over your shoulder like a backward somersault. Often the momentum of the landing will not carry you through a complete roll and you will be stopped at about the time your hip contacts the ground.

You may spend some time on the drop zone watching experienced jumpers land, and be perplexed at the unusual sight of a fellow running downwind all the way to the ground. Just before contacting the ground he swings his body to a near horizontal postion and lands on a heel, a hip, and an elbow. He gets up smiling as though it didn't hurt a bit. You have just witnessed the target approach of an experienced jumper who performed the accepted style for an accuracy approach. He wasn't concerned with contact points or PLF's because his experience of 100 jumps or more gave him the judgment to land safely in an unusual position.

Hazardous Landings

If the student jumper is thinking, he will probably never encounter a landing on an obstacle such as a road, tree, power line, or fence. If you find yourself above some obstacle, you can best avoid it by turning downwind and running past the obstacle. While running downwind in even a light breeze you can cover ground at a surprising rate, and when in the clear again, turn upwind and hold for the landing. The secret is to make all downwind runs while above 300 feet high. If you wait until you are very low, below 100 feet, there will not be sufficient time to complete a run and another turn upwind.

The prepare-to-land procedure I've described will successfully protect you from in-

Figure 19. Pro Landing. Jim Cone.

jury even when you land on a tree or power lines *if* you don't deviate from the position in a moment of last-second panic.

For example, the jumper prepares to land with legs together, body erect, and arms overhead with elbows in. If his descent carries him into power lines, this position will allow him to slide between them without touching two wires simultaneously. If a tree landing is encountered, the arms protect the face from branches and the feet and legs together will prevent straddling a branch. Do not cross the legs because there is no assurance in a tree landing that the chute will catch and stop your descent. It usually will, but sometimes you will crash right to the ground and a PLF is called for. There have been many jumpers who have come away unscathed from landing on hazards because they locked into a good prepare-to-land position.

Unintentional water landings can be very dangerous and drownings have resulted from them. If you see you are going to land in water, loosen the chest strap and one side of the reserve, land facing into the wind, and get clear of your harness. It will sink, but that's better than being pulled under. Don't attempt to drop out of your harness before you touch the water. It is very difficult to judge altitude over water—there are statistics to prove it.

Another type of unusual landing obstacle that you may encounter some day is the sudden wind which keeps your chute inflated. You may be dragged along so fast that you can't get up and outrun the drifting chute. The solution is simple in this matter. Just undo one canopy release fitting (also called "capewell fitting"). The chute will collapse immediately.

Don't ever tamper with a capewell during a descent. They have a safety lock which prevents inadvertent release, but for some reason an experienced jumper one time released a capewell 200 feet in the air. The canopy collapsed immediately and he had insufficient time to open a reserve.

Night jumps may look like an interesting challenge, but they should be avoided except under carefully planned circumstances. A good prerequisite for night jumping is a full moon.

Suffice it to say that jumping is a sport where, for safety, you need to see what you are doing, and you cannot see on a pitch-black night.

Treat Your Reserve Chute with Caution

Treat the reserve chute with the same degree of precaution that you would if it were a hand grenade with the pin pulled. It is up to you to keep the handle covered with your fingers. The ripcord is not spring-loaded to open when you let go of it; however, it is amazing how easily it can be jarred loose by catching it when you move about. Although the handle is on the right side of the reserve, it is afforded the best protection with your left hand. (See photo.) If you encounter an accidental reserve opening in the plane, you keep it under control with both arms and don't let it spill out the door. Either detach the open chute from your harness or keep all your hands, arms, elbows, and chins wrapped around it so it doesn't get into that windstream by the door. If it starts flowing out the door, you have an immediate state of *Emergency*. Don't wait to assess the situation. Don't wait to unhook your static line, or ask any questions. *Jump immediately*. It will take less than two seconds for the reserve chute to inflate behind the plane, and if you are still inside the cabin, the chute will assist you out of it, and you may lose your favorite head on your way past the stabilizer.

If you lunge out the door before the reserve

Figure 20. Equipment Check

inflates, you will safely clear the plane and descend under the reserve. If the main chute also deploys during your hasty exit, then you may ride down with both chutes open.

Accidental reserve openings have caused several parachuting injuries and fatalities. *Guard that reserve handle.*

You should also be careful how you handle the reserve chute on the ground after your landing. Often you will find it convenient to remove the reserve chute while you are gathering your main chute together. When you pick up your reserve chute, hold it by a web strap, not by the ripcord handle. It will probably open accidentally if you try to pick it up by the ripcord handle. Spectators are often guilty of this mistake. In their desire to give you a hand with your gear they pick up your reserve by the convenient metal handle, and kerplunk! You suddenly have an open reserve which will cost several dollars to be repacked.

HOW TO DEAL WITH AN EMERGENCY

The dependability of the modern sport-type parachute is very, very high, but it is not perfect. If you inspect your chute carefully each time you pack it, use the packing method recommended, and have your equipment checked before boarding the plane, you can still expect to encounter a malfunction once during your first thousand jumps. Jumpers who experiment with packing methods, or who seem to be racing the clock as they haphazardly throw the chute together, will have a higher percentage of malfunctions.

Malfunctions come in two categories: partial and total. Occasionally a chute will open with one or more suspension lines draped over the top. This restricts the full rounded inflation of the canopy and is called a "partial malfunction," or "line over." The rate of descent with a line over will be faster than normal, although many jumpers have landed safely under a partial malfunction. There have also been a number of jumpers who did not land safely, so the rule for dealing with a line over is to open the reserve chute. After it has blossomed, the main chute may clear itself because of the reduced pressure in it, or it may remain constricted throughout the descent.

Another form of partial malfunction happens when one or more gores or panels are blown out of a chute during the opening. This may result from jumping a chute which has become weak or rotten due to extended exposure to sunlight, or from foreign matter such as dyes. You can also succeed in blowing panels in a healthy parachute by accelerating past normal terminal velocity in a streamlined head-down position. You can achieve speeds approaching 200 mph this way, and an opening at such speeds may result in a "blown" chute. Deploy the reserve if this happens to you.

When the reserve chute is open you have lost virtually all of your horizontal steering control. The main chute cannot be effectively manipulated when the reserve is out.

The rate of descent when both chutes are open is about the same as with only the main chute properly blossomed. This is because two chutes will position themselves at an angle so that much air spills out of each and effective support is lost.

A total malfunction occurs when the backpack doesn't open at all, or when the canopy does not inflate. Total malfunctions are extremely rare. I have personally observed over 50,000 parachutes open and have witnessed only three total malfunctions, and these really couldn't be blamed on the parachutes. One resulted when the static line was inadvertently disconnected from the plane as the student exited. Another happened because the jumper had attached his backpack bungees to the wrong flap so the container couldn't open when the ripcord was pulled. The third was caused again by the jumper himself who experimented with a technique of tying a heavy rubber band around the suspension lines at the skirt of the canopy to assist in packing. The only trouble was that he forgot to remove it before closing up the container.

The pilot chute or sleeve will occasionally catch in one of the blank gores. This may interfere with steering but is not considered a malfunction. Another discrepancy occurs when during packing the jumper inadvertently reverses the risers as he connects them to the harness. The risers should always be marked "L" for left and "R" for right with a felt marking pen to help prevent this mistake. Usually the jumper who finds himself with risers reversed spends the two-minute descent trying to figure out how to steer.

You cannot predict a malfunction, but you can minimize the chances of it happening by exercising care in the packing and inspection of your chute.

An important thing to remember about a malfunction is that it will be detected immediately after it occurs. After pulling the ripcord you should allow not more than four seconds to elapse before suspecting a malfunction. After you feel the chute open, *always* look at the canopy to be sure you don't have a line over or other discrepancy.

I watched nervously one day as a jumper came down from 2,000 feet with a line-over malfunction on his main chute. He was obviously unaware of his problem and was snatching first one steering toggle and then the other, trying to make the chute respond. Our group on the ground began hopping around and shouting and pointing, but he just looked at us and wondered what all the turmoil was about. At about 500 feet high he finally discovered the malfunction. Acting hastily he put his legs together, pulled the reserve ripcord handle, and threw the reserve out. It floated upward and inflated a few seconds before he touched the ground, thus saving him from a harsh landing and probable injury. If he had looked at his canopy in the approved manner immediately after opening, he would have detected the malfunction while still over 1,500 feet in the air.

He would have been able to open the reserve chute without such a last-second panic effort, and without scaring himself and all of the spectators who were observing from the ground.

If I live to 105 I will never forget the following example of a student jumper who waited too long for comfort before detecting a total malfunction. It was a girl student on her second static line jump. The jumpmaster inadvertently stepped on the static line hook and it become detached from the plane. This was in the days before our jumpmaster hand-deployed the static line chutes by looping it around the hand and manually jerking the chute open as the student dropped away.

I was piloting and watched in horror as she pushed away in a perfect stable exit with the white static line fluttering freely behind. There was absolutely nothing the jumpmaster or I could do except pray she would utilize the reserve opening procedure promptly. From a 2,500-foot jump altitude it takes eighteen seconds to freefall to the ground. She freefell for twelve seconds before reaching for the reserve chute. The ripcord was tight and it took her another three seconds to get a two-handed grip on the handle and make a successful pull. Her speed was up to terminal velocity now and the reserve chute took less than a second to blossom from the container, once the handle was pulled. Ground observers calculated her opening altitude at 450 feet, which allowed her a little over two seconds of freefall time at her terminal speed of 176 feet per second. The point this example emphasizes is that in order for jumping to be safe, we must recognize a malfunction or other hazard immediately and take remedial action. If the jumper just described had counted to four and deployed her reserve, she would have been hanging safely in the harness about 1,800 feet in the air. This particular "near miss" is especially impressed upon my mind because it happened to be my wife I was watching.

How to Deploy the Reserve

Reserve chutes, or chest packs, are usually mounted on the front of the harness at waist level. The reserve chute may be used either with or without a pilot chute. A pilot chute will spring from the pack as soon as the ripcord is pulled, and definitely gives a quicker and more positive reserve chute opening. However, there is always the small, but significant, chance that the pilot chute will entangle with a partially opened main canopy. This rarely happens, but it has led to one popular concept that the reserve chute should not have a pilot chute attached.

To deploy the reserve you follow these simple steps: (1) Place the legs together. (2) Place left hand on the front of the container with hand open and fingers down. (3) Look at the ripcord handle and grasp it securely with right hand. (4) Pull handle with brisk tug, using arm *and* shoulder muscles (it could require a twenty-pound pull to actuate the handle). (5) The left hand holds the expanding bundle of nylon in place while you discard the handle and bring the right in to help throw the reserve out. (6) Throw chute in a downward and sideways direction with all the thrust you can muster. If you give it a good strong throw as you would bounce-pass a basketball, the canopy will stream out and float upward as it inflates.

You should place the legs together as a precaution in the event you forget Step 2 (covering the chute with the left hand). If the ripcord is pulled without holding the chute in with the left hand, it may drop as a bundle between the legs and float up behind you. It is nearly impossible to get a reserve chute open if you once straddle it. By placing the legs and feet together you avoid any chance of straddling it, even if you should drop it accidentally before throwing it.

Throwing it downward gives the chute an extra moment to spread out and begin inflating before getting overhead near a malfunctioned main chute. Do not throw it straight ahead because if you have some forward glide it may blow back into your face.

Also remember that if your main has malfunctioned in a way that is causing you to spiral downward, always throw the reserve into the direction of the spiral. For example, if you have detected a line over, and when you look down at the ripcord handle you notice the world below going around as though you were on a merry-go-round, then notice also which direction you are turning. If it is left, then you should throw the reserve in a downward thrust to the left. This will reduce the possibility of the reserve spiraling around your main chute suspension lines as it is inflating overhead.

Follow the same reserve opening procedure even if you have encountered a total malfunction. Your position with the legs together, left hand and forearm on the chest pack, and eyes on the ripcord handle, will cause you to rotate from a stable position with chest to the ground to a back-to-the-earth, or "rocking chair," position. Back-to-the-earth is the best position for enduring the reserve opening shock, which is quite brisk if you are traveling at terminal velocity.

Chest packs which have the pilot chute installed should be used only by experienced jumpers who can handle the responsibility of dropping away from the main chute before opening the reserve. This prevents any chance of interference between the main and reserve chute. It is called "cutting away" the main, and is an emergency measure which should not be used by the novice. Whenever a reserve is used with the pilot chute installed, the old style capewell fittings should be replaced with "cable releases," also called "shot and one halfs." The cable releases are a quicker and more efficient device for cutting away the main chute.

Some reserve chutes are mounted on the back above the main chute. This leaves the jumper's front side completely clean and improves ground visibility for accuracy jumps. This design is called the "piggyback reserve" and utilizes a ripcord handle mounted on the shoulder straps.

If you are descending under a chest pack-type reserve, your body position will be in a backward slanting position because your suspension points are a little above the level of the waist. This is not the recommended prepare-to-land body position. You may improve this position before landing by keeping the legs together and arching them backward slightly, so that you land feet first instead of fanny first. Don't try to cushion your landing with your arms.

On two occasions I have seen jumpers who thought they could improve on the PLF technique when making reserve chute landings. They held their arms behind them to help soften the landing. They both sustained fractures of the forearm.

WHAT TO EXPECT AFTER THE FIRST JUMP

The first jump is quite an emotional experience. Before the jump the fears and anxieties begin a crescendo which reaches a climax of bone-chilling tension in the moment of pushing away from the plane. Immediately upon realizing that the chute is open and you are safe, there is an unbelievably rapid reversal in emotions. The fears and tensions are supplanted by euphoric joy.

Most first jumpers are so overwhelmed by their first feelings of well being and achievement that they want to make another jump right away. The next jump should be delayed until the next day. Some of that enthusiasm is false and will wear off after a sobering night of sleep. It is not unusual to have some stiff muscles or bruises after the first jump. These are most likely to come from the prejump training, and not the jump itself. If your prepare-to-land position is executed properly, there is little danger of injury. Many first jumpers ignore the recommended PLF technique and land with reckless abandon. As I said, the first jump is an emotional experience and sometimes the jumper develops feelings of omnipotence during the descent.

It is a mistake to let your emotions replace the judgment of your instructor. The jumper who ignores the proper landing technique and approaches the ground with eyes down, body piked, or legs apart, has a good chance of injury.

FURTHER TRAINING TO BECOME A SKYDIVER

If your enthusiasm is still prevailing on the day after your first jump I suggest making another. It should be a simple static line jump from 2,500 feet above the ground, just like the first. Strive to make a perfectly poised exit and show the instructor that you know how to arch from head to feet, and from finger tip to finger tip. Sing out the count loudly from One Thousand through Four Thousand. Check your canopy immediately after it opens, and then steer for the drop zone. If your exit was good, the jumpmaster who "put you out" will make a note in your log book "OK for DRCP" (dummy ripcord pull). This means that on your next jump there will be a ripcord handle in place on your harness, but it will not be connected to the chute. There may be a piece of red or yellow material attached to the handle to help the instructor observe your successful pull.

Before making a dummy ripcord pull you should rehearse on the ground for at least ten minutes. Stand in the practice exit position leaning on a table as previously explained. Make your jump and push off from the table exactly as before. As you plant your feet on the ground and assume the arched position, count as follows: "Arch thousand, look thousand, reach thousand, pull thousand." Counting in this manner gives you a verbal cue to help prompt your actions. On "look thousand" you should drop the chin far enough to look down across your cheek at the ripcord handle. Glue your eyes on that handle, but don't alter your head-back position more than necessary. "Reach thousand" means to grasp the ripcord handle with your right hand while reaching the left hand in to a position behind or above the head. "Pull thousand" means to pull the ripcord handle out as you return to the original arched position with head back and both arms spread.

Rehearse the steps slowly at first, taking several seconds for each count. Gradually work up to a normal count speed, which means four seconds for the entire routine. Practice the pull

Figure 21. Dummy Ripcord Pull   1. Arch, Thousand   2. Look, Thousand

sequence until it is thoroughly memorized. You have to be able to perform it perfectly by mechanical reflex because during these early jumps the thinking processes are usually handicapped by fear. If you have to think your way through the pull sequence, then you will probably muff it on the jump.

If your DRCP timing is good on the jump, you will be executing the last step, "pull thousand," about the time the chute begins to blossom. Don't be discouraged if you miss the handle or if you reach in for it a moment too late and find your arm pulled back as the harness tightens up. You should make three properly executed DRCP's before the jump-master will insert a real ripcord into the chute and make a logbook entry, "OK for freefall." The first ripcord pull may come on the sixth jump, or may be delayed as late as the sixteenth if you're having some serious problems with stable exits and the pull sequence. Your last dummy pull and first freefall should come on the same day. This helps prevent the build-up of too many butterflies before your free fall.

You will find that the first time you pull your own ripcord will be the biggest thrill since your

first jump. It is very inspiring to progress to this stage of independence whereby you are truly as free as a bird for that brief, matchless moment before pulling the ripcord. Don't get too wrapped up in the rapture, though. The first freefall is only at 2,800 feet, and a properly timed pull will be four seconds after your exit.

Be sure you always reach in with the left hand behind the head as your right grasps the ripcord. If you leave the left arm out, you will be starting a bad habit that will be hard to break. On longer delays an outstretched left arm will cause you to roll to the right during the pull.

Occasionally the student will fail to get results from his first yank on the ripcord. This is definitely not a time to become discouraged. The four ripcord pins need to move only a little over an inch to release the cones and allow the pack to open, but, as noted, it may require a twenty-pound tug to accomplish this. If the ripcord does not come freely out of the housing on the first tug, place your left hand promptly together with the right on the handle and press firmly away from the body with both hands. This is called the "two-handed pull" and is

3. Reach, Thousand

4. Pull, Thousand

used effectively any time you encounter a re-luctant ripcord.

During the first half dozen jumps you will develop your judgment in canopy steerage. You will be particularly impressed to learn that each jump is unique and different. The wind is never the same twice and just a few jumps will develop your appreciation and desire to meet the challenge of manipulating your chute toward the target area. You will learn to judge your rate of drift and when to run, hold, or crab.

In your eagerness to land near the target you shouldn't sacrifice good PLF technique. When you reach an elevation of about 300 feet you should always verify the direction of the ground wind, hold into it, and prepare to land as previously described. After six jumps you may alter your form by dropping the chin and watching the approach and touchdown and keeping your hands on the steering toggles. This will allow small last-minute turning cor-rections. Maintain every other aspect of your landing position, especially the body-erect, legs-and-feet-together part.

Be wary of overconfidence in landings. It

takes only one-tenth of a second to break an ankle and it hurts just as much if you do it on the tenth jump as it would on the first. By the time you have thirty jumps you will have suf-ficient landing judgment to allow feet apart or downwind landings. These are discussed later on under "Competition."

Prejump Jitters, or How to Conquer the Butterflies

It is a strange and curious thing, but undeni-ably true, that prejump feelings of fear and anxiety get worse instead of better as you progress through your training jumps. I have trained or supervised the training of hundreds of skydivers, and so far there have been no exceptions: Everyone has gone through a period of increasing anxiety with each jump.

At some point between the sixth and twelfth jumps the prejump jitters reach a peak and from there on they gradually subside. Seldom does a student achieve complete relief from butterflies until he has made thirty or more jumps.

It would seem more reasonable that the worst

fears would occur before the first jump, and I have attempted to determine why this delayed action occurs. One psychiatrist explained that we are born with only two fears. These are loss of support (fear of falling), and loud noises. The jump experience involves both of these. There is a lot of noise and racket from wind, engine, and the jumpmaster shouting commands at you as you prepare to jump, and as you release from the plane you experience an undeniable falling sensation.

The innate fear of falling was awakened in me on my first jump to a degree I will never forget. With determined cool-headedness I positioned myself for the exit. As I leaned forward into the propwash I planned the next moves. I would push off, arch, and count exactly as instructed. I jumped at the signal slap on the thigh, but the downward acceleration forces triggered an immediate panic feeling, and my only thought was, "I'm falling!" The next thing I was aware of was the tightness of the harness and I was looking at the most beautiful sight I had ever seen—a great lovely orange and white flower blossoming overhead. The two or three seconds between the push off and opening are a blank memory except for the terrible falling sensation. Many, many times I have listened to students relate a similar lack of perception of their surroundings during the seconds the chute is deploying. The psychiatrist explained that under severe stress, such as that moment of dropping away from the plane, the mind plays a trick whereby perceptions of sight, sound, and hearing are blocked or intercepted before they get to the recording or memory area of the brain. Therefore, you can't remember every perception.

Many students have said to me, "I've got to do that again. I can remember everything ex-cept the exit, and I've got to find out what it was like."

Further jumps teach you what the exit was like. Each time you jump, a little more information feeds into the recording area in the mind and by the fourth or fifth jump the memory becomes complete. The whole terrifying picture is indelibly recorded. It is terrifying, however, only in relation to the innate fear of falling. Intellectually you are convinced that it is a great and wonderful thrill, but it takes time and a certain number of jumps to overcome the instincts of self-preservation.

During the fear-reaction period of the training the jumper finds himself in a dilemma as he puts on his equipment and rides aloft. One part of his mind is speaking thoughts such as, "Come on, Charlie, this is the greatest thrill going and it's absolutely safe." At the same time another part of the mind is shouting, "I'm not convinced. Falling through the air is dangerous. Don't do it." The conflicting thoughts grapple about while the adrenalin builds up in your blood and your pulse accelerates and your legs get weak and your mouth dry, etc.

It is a real test of your courage to push on past these butterfly attacks. Many jumpers reach a point where they simply cannot make that next jump. Girls usually succumb to the anxiety and quit trying; men may utilize their masculine powers to rally in the face of fear and press onward.

An awareness of some of the following facts and suggestions about jump fear may help give you the determination to make the "tough ones," or "butterfly jumps."

1. The condition is temporary. You are merely re-overcoming an instinctive fear.
2. Talk freely about your butterflies. It helps

to discuss your fears with someone else, but be sure to include experienced jumpers in your audience. They have been where you are and will lend you a sympathetic ear and encouragement.

3. The only sure cure is to make that next jump. The butterflies are always instantaneously obliterated the moment you make your exit.

4. Avoid letting too much time elapse between jumps. Two or more jumps per week are much better than one jump every two weeks.

5. Be careful to avoid injury. Pay strict adherence to safe landing techniques. An injury during the "butterfly phase" will put you out of training for weeks or months, and your chances of winning the battle with anxiety after a long layoff are slim.

6. Cultivate a mind-over-body attitude. Remind yourself that the greatest achievements are those that you have to work for. Make the jump, even though you'd rather be doing anything else.

Some of the "butterfly washouts" are found at almost every drop zone. These are the jumpers whose courage failed at a critical time and they quit. They hang around the clubhouse with numerous petty excuses of why they can't jump. "My ankle still hurts." (I've seen this one used long after he has forgotten which one he sprained.) "It's too cold today." (A favorite of the gals.) "I don't have time today." (He promptly forgets why he doesn't have time and spends the rest of the day at the drop zone.)

Sometimes one of the butterfly washouts will rally after several weeks or months. He will begin to make sounds of positive thinking about

making another leap. The courage curiously is found for strange reasons and in strange places.

One jumper was inactive for six months. He turned up one day in a highly polished pair of new French jump boots. He jumped that very day and showed perfect form as he exited the plane. He had apparently found his courage in his feet.

The Six-Jump Slump

At some point during early jump training the student may come to a plateau of learning during which he will repeat a mistake for several consecutive jumps. We call this the "six jump slump." It may occur as early as the third, or as late as the twelfth; most commonly it begins with the first ripcord pull.

The butterflies which we have discussed contribute to this slump or lack of learning progress. The anxieties interfere with both thinking and physical coordination so that a mistake or combination of mistakes will be repeated over and over. Some common examples follow.

HASTY PULL

One student progressed normally through the static jumps and made three successful dummy ripcord pulls. During the plane ride to 2,800 feet prior to his first clear and pull, he was quite nervous and preoccupied with the responsibility of actuating his own ripcord. At the signal from the jumpmaster, he made his exit. As he pushed up with his legs his chin dropped so he could see the ripcord. As soon as his fingertips left the wing strut, both hands flashed to the handle, snatched the ripcord out of the pocket, and before he had dropped four feet the pilot chute was in the air.

Figure 22. Out-of-Position Pulls.
Here are some good pictures of a bad exit example.
1. A girl student pushes off hands first and topples backward off the step.

2. As she rolls to a face-down position, the static line pulls the main chute from its container. (Note static line attachment to pilot chute with velcro tape.)

The normal ripcord pull sequence requires four seconds and you will be 100 feet or so below the aircraft when the chute deploys. The student accomplished the pull on his sixth jump in about two-thirds of one second. The same thing happened on his seventh, eighth, ninth, and tenth. No matter how strongly he resolved to make a properly timed pull, it was always the same story. As he pushed clear of the plane the impulse to "get that thing open" would overcome him and the lightening pull would follow.

FAILURE TO ARCH

Immediately after the exit the body should assume an arched contour from head to toe and fingertip to fingertip. One student would exit the plane properly, but fail to push his belly out. Instead, he would push out his fanny and thus create a reverse arch. This is a sure way to get turned over on your back, which is what happened to the student on every jump for a dozen or more consecutive jumps.

These early freefall jumps are a fairly tense sort of experience, even when performed in perfect form, but when you get "out of shape" such as on your back, the tendency is to lose your composure completely and struggle, kick, squirm, and finally fumble your fingers onto the handle and pull.

OUT-OF-POSITION PULLS

The reverse arch example just given is the most common type of mistake observed in training students. There are many other ways of improperly executing the freefall position.

Joe was good at arching and timing his pull, but he invariably left his left arm flying as he reached his right in for the ripcord. The left should reach in toward the body with the hand behind and above the head. By leaving his left arm straight out to the side, an unbalanced condition existed and a roll to the right developed with each ripcord pull.

Jim would hold his arms in a slight sweepback position which, together with a failure to hold the head back, resulted in head-down openings. They are less comfortable because the body must make a 180° swing during the opening G forces.

Topper developed one of the wildest and most unique habits I've ever seen while working

3. This is called a "reverse arch position." Body is piked at hips with legs extending forward. Suspension lines are deploying from the sleeve.

4. As lines continue to deploy she holds her awkward position, but remarkably remains face down.

(above) 5. As the parachute begins to open she feels the harness tighten snugly about her. Even when body position is wrong, there is rarely any discomfort felt as the chute opens.

(right) 6. As though suddenly remembering the technique she had rehearsed during training, the student spreads into a good arch with head back. Note canopy is inflating from the top. This entire sequence took only 2½ seconds.

through a jump slump. On his ninth through his fourteenth jumps he would bounce on the jump step a couple of times. At the slap on the leg he would spring into the air, but not clear the aircraft. Instead, he would fling his whole 220-pound barrel-built self back through the open jump door. Then he'd flop his red-faced head against the wall and pant. It takes the airplane about one and a half minutes to make a circle over the target. During this time Topper would regain his composure and on the next jump run he would again be bouncing with anticipation on the step. This time he would push off on a nice stable exit when slapped on the leg.

The six-jump slump will usually cure itself as confidence develops and the butterflies decrease. Having your exit and opening technique observed is very important. It is difficult to analyze your own mistakes, so be sure to get a briefing from your jumpmaster after each jump when working through a slump.

Sometimes a definite remedy will be called for to break a slump. "Lightning Pull George," for example, was finally cured by putting him back on the static line for a couple of jumps. On the static line he was relieved of some emotional pressures and was able to make properly timed dummy ripcord pulls. Then he went back to freefall and progressed normally.

Freefall Time vs. Altitude

Before discussing the techniques used for longer freefalls, I would like to explain the facts about the distance you fall as the seconds tick by during freefall. The following chart tells how far you fall during each second of freefall up through twelve seconds. The figures are computed for a 170-pound jumper wearing two chutes and using a stable spread position.

DISTANCE FALLEN IN FEET EACH SECOND TO TERMINAL VELOCITY

Second	Distance
1	16
2	46
3	76
4	104
5	124
6	138
7	148
8	156
9	163
10	167
11	171
12	174

You will note that the first second you fall only 16 feet, then 46 feet the second, 76 feet the third, and 174 on the twelfth. After the twelfth second your rate of fall is a constant 176 feet per second, which is terminal velocity. The next chart shows the *total* distance fallen after a given number of freefall seconds.

There are variables such as other body positions, higher than normal temperatures, and lower than normal pressures that could affect the accuracy of these figures.

To find a jump altitude for any certain number of seconds of freefall, add 2,500 feet (opening altitude) to the distance figures in the right column. For example, to make a five-second delay add 366 feet to 2,500 and your jump altitude will be 2,866 feet. A ten-second delay should be made from 3,638 feet. These are altitudes above the ground. Remember, aircraft altimeters, including the one in the jump plane, are set to show altitude above sea level. Therefore, to

Sec.	Distance	Sec.	Distance	Sec.	Distance	Sec.	Distance	Sec.	Distance
1	16	13	1657	25	3745	37	5833	49	7921
2	62	14	1831	26	3919	38	6007	50	8095
3	138	15	2005	27	4093	39	6181	51	8269
4	242	16	2179	28	4267	40	6355	52	8443
5	366	17	2353	29	4441	41	6529	53	8617
6	504	18	2527	30	4615	42	6703	54	8791
7	652	19	2701	31	4789	43	6877	55	8965
8	808	20	2875	32	4963	44	7051	56	9139
9	971	21	3049	33	5137	45	7225	57	9313
10	1138	22	3223	34	5311	46	7399	58	9487
11	1309	23	3397	35	5485	47	7573	59	9661
12	1483	24	3571	36	5659	48	7747	60	9835

compute the altimeter reading for a ten second delay you must add field, or drop zone, elevation to the 3,638-foot figure.

In practice the jump pilot will usually level the plane for a jump run at the nearest 100-foot level. The most frequently used jump altitudes at our drop zone, which is only fifty feet above sea level, are as follows:

5	3,000'
10	3,700'
15	4,500'
20	5,400'
30	7,200'
45	9,800'
60	12,300'

Longer Delayed Falls

Most jumpers feel that the most exciting part of the jump is the freefall, and the longer the freefall, the more gratifying the jump experience. But like many good things you can't achieve it all at once. You have to build up to longer freefalls gradually. Different schools use different techniques for advancing students to higher altitudes. Some stand on the firm rule of a minimum of three five-second delays, three ten-second delays, three fifteen-second delays, etc. At our school whenever a student demonstrates good control and opening altitude judgment, he may add two seconds to the freefall on the next jump until he reaches fifteen-second delays.

Beginning with your first five-second freefall you should start learning two new things: the frog position and opening altitude judgment.

THE FROG POSITION

The frog position is very easy to do and more comfortable to hold than the extreme arch of the stable spread position. As soon as you exit the

Figure 23. Frog Position

plane, arch the back with the hips well forward. Relax the neck so your head comes to a face-to-earth position. Relax the arms. They will bend at the elbow and your hands will float about 18 inches out from your head. Relax your legs below the knees and your feet will float upward until your lower leg is vertical. This position affords comfort, but still allows excellent stability and control in freefall.

OPENING ALTITUDE JUDGMENT

Hereafter called "OAJ," your visual judgment of opening altitude is equally important to your freefall safety as your PLF's are to landing safety. When developed properly, your OAJ will tell you better than an altimeter when you have reached 2,500 feet. Beginning with your first five-second delay you should avoid timing your ripcord pull by a verbal count. Instead, you should visually observe the ground and make your ripcord pull when it looks as if you have reached 2,500 feet. Your instructor will time you with a stopwatch and tell you if you pulled early or late. Don't be tempted to start wearing an altimeter. If you do, you will develop a dependence upon it and will never have confidence in your eyeball. At our club no students are allowed to wear an altimeter until they have fifty jumps. By this time they have good OAJ and can wear an altimeter without becoming a slave to it. The problem with altimeters is that they are a mechanical device which can malfunction, and the jumper who always relies on the instrument could fall dangerously low. I was eyewitness to a jumper whose chute deployed 200 feet from the ground. A stuck altimeter was his alibi. Your eyes can be trained to judge altitude, and they won't ever fail you. If you learn to jump at a club where an altimeter is required,

use it only as a reference after your chute has opened.

You might consider fifteen-second delays as your threshold to achievement. You reach terminal velocity of 120 mph after twelve seconds, and if your body position is not correct you will have stability problems on fifteen-second delays. You must master lateral control before making longer delays. This means you should be able to start and stop a turn in both directions.

HOW TO TURN

To turn in freefall you bend or arch your body at the waist in a sideways direction and simultaneously rotate the shoulders. The shoulder you wish to turn toward should go forward. After exiting, relax into the frog position and freefall for six seconds to build up some vertical speed. Observe your heading with a ground reference, such as a road. To make a right-turn, bend to the right and rotate the right shoulder forward (toward the ground). When the ground is going by from right to left, your turn is in progress. Once started, the turn will continue even if you straighten out your shoulders and sideways bend in your body. A turn can be stopped only by aerodynamic forces, so bend left and rotate the left shoulder forward exactly as you would to make a left turn. Watch the ground closely, though, as you must straighten out as soon as the turn stops.

SPINS

The first few times you attempt turns you may find they start all right, but when you try to stop turning, your turn only continues or perhaps even accelerates. This uncontrolled turn is called a "spin." You can overhear many interesting gymnastics and body maneuvers claimed to be sure cures for the spin. Don't listen to any of them. When you are out of control, whether spinning or tumbling, pull your ripcord. Your parachute is the most stabilizing influence at your command. Practice your turn and stop-turn positions on the ground before each jump. Have your instructor check your positions, or stand in front of a mirror.

BUFFETS

As you approach terminal velocity you may find yourself pitching back and forth from a slightly head-down position to a feet-down position. This oscillation, or teeter-totter effect of your body, is called "buffet" and may occur when your arms are extended too far forward. If you encounter a buffet, glance momentarily to the side and you will see your arms reaching forward with hands well above the head. If you pull them back even with your head and bend a little at the knees, the buffet will stop immediately and you will resume a smooth, stable, vertical descent.

Spotting and Judging the Streamer

While making your fifteen-second delays you will at last sever the final dependence upon your jumpmaster. You will learn to choose your exit point from watching the wind drift streamer and direct the pilot to fly you over this exit point. This is called "spotting," and you can expect to make some long walks back to the DZ when first learning to spot yourself.

You should study the diagram on spotting on page 17 and note that your exit and opening point will vary by about 500 feet when you make an eight-second or longer delay. This is because

Figure 24. How to Turn Right

Figure 25. Buffets

you leave the plane with a horizontal speed of 50 to 70 mph. During the ensuing eight seconds you prescribe a curving path, or trajectory, to the vertical fall. This trajectory will carry you about 500 feet horizontally across the ground. You must anticipate this and "lead" (get out early) your opening point by this distance.

Remember also that the drift streamer will tell you the average of the wind between opening point upwind from the target the same distance that the streamer drifted downwind.

Verbal signals are commonly used, such as "Right five," meaning turn right 5°, but the hand signal is less strenuous on the vocal cords and there is no chance of misinterpretation. Use a clenched fist with thumb extended in the direction you want to turn. Move the hand in a

continuous side-to-side motion and the pilot will keep feeding in rudder until the plane is on your desired heading. At this instant you should spread your hand out flat and hold it in a vertical plane. The pilot will hold that heading unless you call for another turn with your thumb. Be sure to hold your hand well forward near the windshield so that the pilot can see it. When you are over the exit point you can call, "Cut," if you want the throttle chopped, place the right foot on the jump step, step out, and make a poised exit. If you prefer to make a door exit, you simply swing your head and shoulders until you are facing straight out the door, brace your feet, and launch yourself through the doorway.

Spotting is best accomplished from a kneeling

Figure 26. Spotting

position facing forward inside the airplane. This allows you to look at the ground from two angles: head forward (lined up with the longitudinal axis of the plane), and head toward the wingtip (90° from the longitudinal axis). Swivel your head back and forth between these two positions and you will see on the ground a more accurate perspective of the track line of the plane. The pilot will make the initial lineup, but it is up to you to tell him verbally or with hand signals what corrections you would like him to make in the plane's heading.

When spotting, always be sure the area below you is clear of other aircraft before making an exit.

Making a door exit (also called the "lump-out") marks the third major stepping stone to becoming a proficient skydiver. The first step is the first jump. Second is the first ripcord pull. Third is the lumpout, which proves to you that you can dive away from the plane in any old form and recover stability at will. The final step is freefall contact or relative work, which will be discussed later.

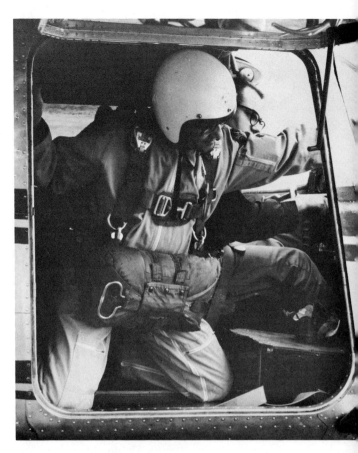

Figure 27. Hand Signals

FREEFALLS OVER 15 SECONDS

When ready to progress to longer delays you might make two or three twenty-second delays from 5,500 feet just to build further confidence. There is really nothing different about these longer falls except the duration of freefall time. You do the identical thing in body coordination to maintain stability as at the lower altitudes. The relaxed frog position will give you good stability and turning response.

As you begin your spotting lineup on your first jump from 7,200 feet you will see the ground in a new perspective. It is almost a mile and a half away and your spotting judgment will be

given a good test. You have no bombsight to assist in lining up the airplane. You're depending entirely upon your eye to follow that imaginary track line of the plane and launch yourself into the sky at the exact moment the track line intercepts your chosen exit point. Be sure to use the head-swiveling technique during spotting, and keep your feet and legs inside the plane until you're ready to exit. The pilot may still be climbing that last few hundred feet while on the jump run, and if you are hanging halfway out the doorway, the plane's climb is virtually stopped.

The thirty-second delay is proving altitude for your equipment, too. If you are using goggles, they must be fitted very snugly, or you will find them oscillating about, and within seconds your eyes will be flooded with tears from the irritation of the intermittent wind blast. Don't make a habit of making long delays (over ten seconds) without goggles because the 120 mph freefall wind blast can damage your eyes.

A loose jumpsuit collar can drive you crazy at terminal velocity. It sometimes lies against your neck and buzzes against you with such speed and force that you may develop a red welt after the jump. I tuck my collar underneath the top of the suit to prevent this from happening.

If you have learned your fundamentals properly on the fifteen-second delays, you should not encounter any spin or buffeting problems at the higher altitudes. If you do lose stability, remember the most stabilizing influence of all is the open canopy. Whatever you do, don't adopt the attitude of the lad who was overheard to say, "If I get into another spin, I'll break it or else. . . ." Well, he spun all right, all the way to the ground! The point is, you shouldn't get out of control if you know your fundamentals, but if you do, pull your ripcord without further hesitation.

10,000 feet of altitude will allow you forty-five seconds of freefall time. 12,300 feet of altitude will allow you sixty seconds, 15,000 feet will allow one minute fifteen seconds of freefall if your DZ is at sea level, and this is the highest you can safely jump without oxygen in the jump plane for breathing up to the moment you jump. 18,000 feet above sea level is the highest you can jump without carrying an oxygen bottle and mask for use during freefall.

Better Freefall Control

After a dozen or so thirty-second delays you may want to experiment with upsidedown freefall, loops, rolls, and tracks.

The back-to-the-earth freefall is quite a novel sensation. It is best accomplished immediately after exit on fifteen-second or longer delays. Make a door exit or fall backward off the step, and reverse your arch as though you were hugging a big barrel. You'll get a unique view of the plane as you drop away.

A loop is accomplished by first accelerating to terminal velocity, then holding your arms in a swept-back or delta wing position for just long enough to drop slightly head down. Now, simultaneously thrust your arms forward well ahead of your shoulders, and fold your knees up to your chest. A rotation will begin which will carry you through a complete airborne backward somersault.

A barrel roll may be done by starting from the frog position. Fold one arm to the chest. The roll will begin. Straighten your legs as you roll to your back and keep the other arm close to your body. The rotation will continue until you are face down again, at which point you should resume the frog position.

Some horizontal travel across the ground may be accomplished during freefall by using the delta position. With arms held in a swept-back attitude, and legs close together and rather straight, you will skid forward through the air. It's not too efficient, but you may cover 1,000 feet or so of horizontal travel during 5,000 feet of descent.

The "max track" is the only way to go if you really want to cover ground horizontally. If it is properly executed, you can achieve over 40 mph of horizontal ground speed by tracking. This would give you nearly half a mile of travel during a thirty-second delay. The max track is very useful when you discover after exiting that your spot was bad. You simply track to your chosen opening point. The max track may also be used to offset strong winds aloft which are sometimes encountered. A 40-mph wind can blow you 2,000 feet from your intended opening point unless you track against the wind.

Figure 28. Delta

Figure 29. Max Track

The max track requires good balance and free-fall control because it utilizes a slight reverse arch, but you must remain face down. Start from a delta position. Then close your arms tightly against your sides with hands open and palms to the front. Press the legs tightly together with toes pointed. Drop your chin against your chest —and now comes the tricky part. Hump the shoulders forward and at the same time, pike slightly at the waist. This position makes a crude airfoil of your body. You become a piece of wing with a six-foot chord and an eighteen-inch span, and you start to fly. You can actually feel the forward acceleration as the lift develops above your back. It's a rather crude wing, I'll admit, but it works. Champion ski jumpers use it to extend their jumps.

Relative Work

After you have made thirty to fifty jumps and are relaxed in freefall, you should ask an instructor or other advanced jumper (meaning 200 jumps or more) to make a relative work jump with you. It used to be called "baton passing," but now is more commonly done without a baton and is called simply a "hookup."

Always make your first few hookups with an expert. Nothing could be more hazardous than careening through the air with another novice. This is like the blind leading the blind.

You need at least a thirty-second delay for the attempt. You exit first and hold a stable frog position without turning. Your partner will follow you out and work down in front of you. Don't hold your head back too far, or your arms in front of you. This will have the effect of a reverse delta position and you will slide backwards away from your partner. When he stabilizes on your level, you both make minimal corrections to your body positions to close the gap ever so slowly. The good clean hookup is not a slamming together of two bodies, nor is it a grasping at each other's arms or legs as you shuss by on a near collision course. A mid-air collision is not fun, and it can be, and has been, fatal to one or both jumpers. Closing the gap from ten or fifteen feet apart should be slow and smooth, and should take at least five seconds. For large horizontal corrections, such as forty to one-hundred feet, use a delta or even a track. For small corrections use just the forearms and hands. Point hands and forearms slightly down to move forward and slightly upward to brake or back up. If there is a vertical distance between you, the upper jumper should contract slightly (called a "tight frog position") to drop a little faster, while the lower jumper spreads out to slow his descent slightly. An effective technique for slowing your descent is called the "bear claw" and consists of spreading as wide as possible with arms and legs, then reversing both the body and arm arch. It takes delicate balance, but you can stay stable during this reverse arch after some practice.

After the first fifteen to twenty seconds of free-fall, you must divide your attention between your partner and the ground. Never become so preoccupied with a freefall exercise that you ignore the ground. It takes only a fraction of a second to look down and check your altitude. If you're still well above opening altitude, proceed with the minor body movements to bring you together with your partner. Always break away or terminate efforts to hook up at or above 3,000 feet. You need those last few seconds to clear yourself before opening. Never allow yourself to get directly above another jumper when near opening altitude. Falling into a deploying or

open parachute means almost certain disaster.

After a couple of successful hookups as first man out, try it with your instructor jumping first. The secret here is to let go of the plane as close as possible to the same instant he jumps. If you wait just one second, there will be almost 200 feet of separation between you when you reach terminal. With a half-second interval you will still need to close a gap of ninety feet. If you can time your exit to be within one-tenth of a second of that of your partner, you'll have a pretty good chance of making a successful hookup.

Jumpers with much relative work experience can achieve three-, five-, and even ten-man hookups. Jumpers have even hooked up after exiting different airplanes flying in formation.

One final word of caution about relative work or group exits. Avoiding a freefall collision or a collision during opening is important. It is also important to avoid bumping canopies with another jumper during the canopy descent. The forward glide speed of modern chutes makes this a real hazard. Keep alert and avoid collisions. The sky is a big place, but it can become conjested enough over a drop zone for a crash to happen.

Competition

Sport parachute meets are held all over the country. They present a grand opportunity for enthusiasts to socialize and match their skills with others. Most meets have novice and advanced events, so you don't need more than fifteen or twenty jumps to get into the fun.

Accuracy events, where you are scored by the distance between your point of landing and the target center, dominate most meets. As a novice you should place a safe measure of caution ahead

Figure 30. Mass Hookup.
This unusual photo was taken by Carl Boenish of Hawthorn, California.
This mid-air rendezvous demonstrates the maneuverability of experienced
freefall jumpers.

of desire for points. Don't make last-second low-altitude turns or radical departures from good landing technique.

The upper class jumpers will usually make downwind or running approaches to the target. The descent is adjusted so that a "key" position is reached upwind of the target and 300 to 500 feet high. The distance out depends upon wind velocity. If you are flying a P.C. and the wind is 10 mph, your key position should be about twice as far out as you are high. The 300-foot-high key should be 600 feet out and directly on the wind line. You descend facing the target with half brakes (toggles pulled about halfway to the full stall position). Minor corrections to your heading may be made by gentle use of the toggles. Always release one slightly when pulling the other toggle down. Adjustments in the glide angle are made by using more or less brakes. Just before impact swing the feet as far as possible toward the target disk. Be sure feet touch before your hip, or the fichet (official marker) will score you where your fanny hit.

Smoothness and relaxation in use of the toggles are important to consistent accuracy in spot jumping. The jumper who flails the air with arms and legs, snatching and jerking at the toggles all the while, puts on a terrific show, but seldom carries home any trophies. In contrast the real professional will drift gracefully down the wind line hardly moving a muscle. It appears almost as though he were riding a wire from the target through an eyelet on his helmet.

Freefall or style competition consists of judges scoring your form and speed in performing the international series of maneuvers. This series is a 360° turn followed by a back loop, another 360° followed by another back loop, then the whole sequence repeated with turns in the opposite direction. Style jumps are made from 7,000 feet and good competitors can complete the entire sequence of four 360° turns and four loops in ten seconds or less.

Overconfidence

The biggest threat to your safety is your own willingness to ignore the known standards of safe behavior. The troublesome aspect of overconfidence is that it is like halitosis . . . you can't recognize it yourself. You have to rely upon your friends to tell you, and often they won't.

Parachuting has a unique way of dealing out punishment to the overconfident. If you should develop the idea that landings don't require care and judgment, your misconceptions will soon award you a "cement foot" (plaster cast). If you think your parachute will work no matter how you throw it together, you shall one day be thankful for the custom of wearing two chutes because you'll have to use the second one to save yourself.

People who become overconfident usually do so before they reach the 100 jump mark. If you have had more than one sprain or fracture with less than 100 jumps, or more than one malfunction, you probably have too little respect for your own safety, and I strongly recommend taking up another line of recreation before you become a statistic.

Three-hundred jumps seems to be another likely time for overconfidence to undermine one's humility and safety standards. If you pass the 300-jump mark with no more than one injury and/or malfunction, you can consider yourself a safe jumper and should continue using that same good judgment.

United States Parachute Association

The United States Parachute Association was organized in 1957 to help promote jumping as a safe recreational sport. It is a national organization and is affiliated with the Fédération Aéronautique International (FAI), which is the world aviation coordinating body.

In its efforts to encourage safety the United States Parachute Association has published a set of Basic Safety Regulations and a Doctrine, which are used as a valuable guide to safe jump activity throughout the country.

Membership cost in USPA is currently $12 per year, which includes a membership packet, a monthly magazine, and public liability insurance. You may join USPA without having any jump experience.

I recommend membership in USPA for everyone with a serious interest in parachuting. Their excellent monthly magazine keeps you informed of what is new in training, equipment, techniques, and competition. It is also the organization which sponsors the regional and national jump contests. The jumpers who place highest in the national meet are selected as U.S. Team members for the international jump meets.

Parachutists who meet certain jump qualifications may obtain an internationally recognized license through the USPA as follows:

Class A	10 jumps
Class B	25 freefalls
Class C	75 freefalls
Class D	200 freefalls
Instructor	Must be D-license holder and pass written exam.

Each license rating (except Class A) also has performance requirements for duration of freefall, ability to maneuver in freefall, and target accuracy.

Holding a jump license is a good way to verify your experience and ability if you go to another club or another country to jump.

Where to Go for Training

For a current list of jump clubs and training centers which are recognized by the USPA send 50¢ to United States Parachute Association, P.O. Box 109, Monterey, California, 93940, and request their latest directory.

There are also several hundred clubs in the United States which, for various reasons, are not affiliated with USPA. These may be good clubs with high safety standards, and there may be one active at your nearest airport.

Before you take training anyplace, find out how many jumps your instructor has. It's only a rule of thumb, but I would not take instructions from anyone with less than 100 jumps. A USPA Class D license holder or Instructor rating would be preferred experience qualifications.

Parachute Equipment and Supplies

McElfish Parachute Service, 2615 Love Field Drive, Dallas, Texas 75235. $1 for catalogue—94 pages.

Para Gear Equipment Co., 5138 N. Broadway, Chicago, Illinois 60640. $1 for catalogue—130 pages.

The Chute Shop, P.O. Box 445, Highway 202, Flemington, New Jersey 08822.

Strong Enterprises, Inc., 542 E. Squantum St., N. Quincy, Massachusetts 02171. Free catalogue.

Midwest Parachute Co., 46091 Grand River, Novi, Michigan 48050.

Parachutes Incorporated, P.O. Box 96, Orange, Massachusetts, 01364.

Brown Engineering Co., P.O. Box 1436, Patterson, California 95363.

Sport Chute and Co., 139 Millicent Ave., Buffalo, New York 14215.

Rhode Island Skydivers, 40 Waldron Avenue, West Barrington, Rhode Island 02890.

Parachuting Publications

Australian Skydiver, 291 Senate Rd., Port Pirie 5540, S.A. Australia

Canadian Parachutist, 42 Manor Drive, Brockville, Ontario, Canada

CASPA Newsletter, Charter House Motel, 1917 Blandensburg Rd., NE, Washington, D.C. 20002

Colo SPC Newsletter, P.O. Box 9225, Denver, Colorado 80209

CPC Newsletter, 2706 Dry Creek Drive, Huntsville, Alabama 35810

CPI Newsletter, P.O. Box 953, Manchester, Connecticut

DZ-USA ($4 per year), P.O. Box 2131, Wichita, Kansas

MEPA Newsletter, W. H. Ottley, Suite 610, 806 15th St., NW, Washington, D.C. 20005

Mid-State SPC Newsletter ($1 per year), 125 Knox St., Millinocket, Maine 04462

Midwest S.P.S. Newsletter, 2631-B Summit Rd., Columbia, Missouri 65201

NCC Newsletter ($2 per year), 4120 Nevada #12, Minneapolis, Minnesota 55427

OPA Newsletter: Static Line, Cliff Davis, 1346 SW 74th St., Apt. 706, Oklahoma City, Oklahoma 73159

Parachutist ($5 per year), P.O. Box 109, Monterey, California

Skydiver Magazine ($5 per year), P.O. Box 44, Buena Park, California

Skydiver Southern Africa (free), P.O. Box 4758, Johannesburg, South Africa

Sport Parachutist, British Parachute Association, Artillery Mansions, 75 Victoria St. SW1, London, England

The B.C. Para News, 7471 Kingsway #4, South Burnaby, B.C., Canada

The Cross Winds ($1 per year) 117 E. Alice St., Phoenix, Arizona 85020

The Link (free), Denny Morse, MRC, USS Kittiwake ASR-13, FPO, New York, N.Y. 09501

The New Para-Flyer, 82 E. Pleasant, Hamburg, New York

The Pilot Chute, P.O. Box 1834, Cincinnati, Ohio 45201

The Spotter ($2 per year), P.O. Box 172, Orange, Massachusetts 01364

The Windline ($2 per year), P.O. Box 1283, Richardson, Texas 75080

The Wing ($2 per year), Box 4333, CSE, US Strike Command, McDill AFB, Florida 33608

PARACHUTING GLOSSARY

ACCURACY JUMPING—Guiding the chute so jumper lands as close as possible to selected target. Also called Spot Jumping.

ALTIMETER—An instrument with a clock-like face which indicates altitude above sea level. Sometimes used by parachutists.

APEX—Top center portion of canopy where suspension lines cross.

BACKPACK—Same as main parachute.

BATON PASS—Same as Relative Work and Hook-up.

BLOWN CHUTE—When one or more gores, or panels, are ripped during the parachute opening.

BRAKING—Holding both toggles down to slow canopy forward speed.

BREAKAWAY—Intentional releasing and dropping away from the main parachute. Same as Cutaway.

BUFFET—Longitudinal oscillations of the body during freefall caused by holding arms too high and legs too straight.

BUNGEES—Spring steel elastic bands which assist opening of parachute container.

CANOPY—The umbrella-like portion of the parachute, usually made of nylon, which supports the parachutist during his descent.

CANOPY RELEASE—Same as Capewell.

CAPEWELL—The hardware fitting on the harness at the shoulder which attaches the parachute to the harness. Also called Canopy Release.

CHEST PACK—Same as Reserve Chute.

CLEAR AND PULL—Opening the chute immediately after exiting the plane.

CRABBING—Facing your chute on a diagonal to the wind or crosswind, similar to tacking in a sailboat.

CUTAWAY—Intentional releasing and dropping away from an open parachute, and then opening another chute.

DELAYED FALL—A freefall of more than three seconds before parachute opening.

DELTA—A freefall position where arms are held in a sweptback position from the shoulder. Used for horizontal travel.

DEPLOYMENT—The unfolding and opening of the chute. Normally requires one to three seconds.

DOOR EXIT—A quick method of leaving the aircraft by diving out the door.

DRIFT—Horizontal movement across the ground due to wind. Term applies to jumper, parachute, airplane, and wind streamer.

DUMMY RIPCORD PULLS (DRCP)—A training technique where static line student pulls an inactivated ripcord.

EXIT—Any of the varied ways of departing the jump craft.

FICHET—The person who marks the jumper's landing point during accuracy or spot jumping competitions.

FREEFALL—Any jump whereby the parachutist pulls his own ripcord.

FROG—A relaxed freefall position commonly used by skydivers.

GLIDESLOPE—The descent angle through the air along which the parachute descends.

GORE—A pie-shaped area or segment of a parachute. A common twenty-eight-foot diameter chute is made up of twenty-eight gores.

HARNESS—The network of webbing or straps which secures the parachute to the jumper.

HOLDING—Facing your chute into the wind to reduce groundspeed.

HOOK-UP—Same as Relative Work.

HOP AND POP—Same as Clear and Pull.

INFLATION—Expanding of the parachute canopy as it fills with air.

JUMPMASTER—The man designated to supervise student exits from the plane.

LINE OVER—A parachute malfunction where one or more lines fall over the canopy during an opening and restrict its full inflation.

LUMPOUT—See Door Exit. Usually used during group exits.

MALFUNCTION—Any improper opening of the chute.

MAXIMUM TRACK (MAX TRACK)—A freefall position with reverse arch, arms at sides and legs together. Allows horizontal component speeds of up to 40 mph.

OPENING—Same as Inflation.

OPENING ALTITUDE—Usually 2,200 feet above the ground is used as the accepted minimum.

OPENING ALTITUDE JUDGMENT (OAJ)—The jumper's ability to open his chute at 2,500 feet high by visual reference to the ground.

OPENING POINT—The reference point on the ground selected before jump. Jumper opens his chute over this point.

OPENING SHOCK—Decelleration forces experienced during parachute opening.

OSCILLATION—Pendulum-swinging motion of jumper beneath open canopy.

OUT OF SHAPE—Losing stability in freefall.

PACK—The canvas or nylon enclosure which contains the parachute canopy and sleeve and is attached to the harness. Also called Container.

PARACHUTE CLUB OF AMERICA (P.C.A.)—National parachuting organization. P.O. Box 409, Monterey, California.

PARACHUTE LANDING FALL (PLF)—A method of falling which distributes the landing momentum over the entire body. Alternate definition: A method of landing whereby the descent is cushioned to a halt by a progressive fall.

PILOT CHUTE—A small parachute which ejects itself with an internal spring and pulls out the main parachute.

POISED EXIT—Method of exiting plane utilizing step and wing strut to achieve maximum balance and stability.

RELATIVE WORK—An advanced skydiving technique whereby two or more jumpers exit close together and maneuver to close proximity or actual contact. Also used for freefall photography.

RESERVE CHUTE—A spare or emergency chute worn on jumper's chest or sometimes piggyback style above main parachute.

RIGGER—A person qualified and licensed by Federal Aviation Agency to maintain and repack parachutes. Reserve chutes must be rigger-packed.

RIPCORD—The steel handle and cable which is pulled to open a chute.

RISER—A two- or three-foot length of webbing attached to harness by capewell fitting and to suspension lines by connector link.

RUNNING—Facing your chute downwind and running with the wind.

SLEEVE—The sleeve-like cotton sack which pulls over the canopy and slows deployment to reduce opening shock.

SLIPPING—Pulling down risers or suspension lines during descent to cause increased glide of chute.

SPOT JUMPING—See Accuracy Jumping.

SPOTTING—Selecting an opening point and directing the pilot in flying over it.

STABLE EXIT—Leaving the plane in poised belly-down position without tumbling.

STABLE SPREAD—A belly-down position with body arched, and arms and legs extended.

STATIC LINE—A length of webbing attached to aircraft and parachute. It starts parachute deployment as jumper exits plane.

STOWS—The zigzag loops of suspension lines which are held in place on the sleeve by heavy rubber bands. Sometimes the rubbers themselves are called stows.

STUDENT PARACHUTIST—Any jumper who has less than twenty-five freefalls.

STYLE EVENT—Jump competition where turns and loops are performed in freefall.

SUSPENSION LINE—The 550-pound test nylon lines which connect the canopy to the risers. There are twenty-eight on a twenty-eight-foot chute.

TARGET—Point selected by jumper for a landing target.

TERMINAL VELOCITY—The greatest speed a body will reach in freefall in a given body position. Approximately 120 mph, or 176 feet per second in the frog, or stable-spread, position.

TOGGLES—Small handles (usually wood) grasped and used for turning and braking chute.

WIND DRIFT STREAMER—A length of crepe paper (usually yellow and slightly weighted) dropped at opening altitude from the plane before a jump to detect direction and speed of wind.

2 SOARING

WHAT SOARING IS LIKE

The sport of soaring lives up to the first impression one gets when looking at a sailplane in flight. The craft itself is a joy to behold. The long tapering wings and smoothly contoured fuselage have a great aesthetic appeal. The design makes you think of speed, and in flight you have a definite feeling of high speed, especially when flying near a cloud or ridge. The speed sensations are partly an illusion, however, created by the feel and sound of the wind. Soaring speeds are usually under 50 mph.

It looks like a quiet and graceful way to fly, and it is. The only manner of flight which gives you some of the same sense of smoothness is when you take the controls of a jet. The sailplane has other advantages which make it much more appealing than flying a jet.

Once you have released the tow line a contest begins. You match your wits, coordination, and judgment against the force of gravity pulling you gently earthward. You attempt to fly within the areas of ascending winds which will allow you to remain aloft; the challenge lies in finding the upward currents and avoiding the downward ones. You win when you remain aloft as long as you wish.

When I am aloft in a sailplane I have a sense of calm, well being, and detachment. I become absorbed in concentration as my attention jumps from airspeed to altimeter to variometer to horizon. A good effort in judgment and coordination combined with "workable lift" will result in an upward gain in altitude. A spirit of exuberance and glee wells up within me as I circle skyward. Altitude is like wealth when soaring. As I go higher I become rich with potential to travel and explore through the streets of clouds.

The altimeter creeps upward past 8,000, 9,000; finally at two miles up, I abandon the dwindling updraft and survey the world from my orbit. I feel a great sense of achievement, for no booster rocket or power plant brought me to this height. I can remain airborne for an hour even if further thermals elude me. In a straightaway glide I could travel sixty miles across country. On this flight I choose to squander my wealth of height in a frivolous cavorting of loops and wingovers. A landing at the takeoff point saves the work of a retrieve. As I climb from the cockpit I am convinced that of all the wondrous variety of adventure sports which are available to us, soaring is supreme.

FAMILY ASPECTS OF SOARING

The sailplane, more than any other flying machine, is attractive to women. Perhaps its appeal lies in the graceful, delicate design; perhaps it is because the plane is so clean. There is no vibration during flight, no smell of gasoline and exhaust fumes, and you can even perform a preflight inspection on a glider without getting oily and dirty.

Many sailplanes are utilized by both husband and wife. Still, a two-place glider is *not* like a family boat. Only on rare occasions do husband and wife make a soaring flight together. We know several couples who both fly their glider, and even when there are two seats available, they usually choose to take turns. This is because a soaring flight is a very personal experience wherein the individual becomes attuned with nature.

The contest to remain aloft requires great concentration, and suggestions or outside influences

from another could easily lead to emotional conflicts. And the sky is no place for emotional conflicts.

The two-place design is most useful for introducing newcomers to the sport and for dual training. But for enjoyment of the real art of soaring you need a single-place ship. It is cheaper to buy, lighter to handle and assemble, more responsive and pleasurable to fly. You can avoid another pitfall by *not* trying to give your wife dual instruction. This would be a good way to break up the marriage and/or the sailplane. Besides, the FAA has a requirement that training must be given by certified instructors.

When only the husband soars there are still enjoyable opportunities for the rest of the family in acting as a support crew. There is a lot of adventure and suspense in crewing, especially when cross-country flights are made to unknown destinations. It's not at all uncommon for the retrieve crew to find the glider parked in a cow pasture, the pilot engaged in keeping the livestock from molesting the ship.

If your family has teenagers who show an interest in flying, they can begin training in gliders much younger than in powered flying. Our daughter, Leslie, was twelve years old when she first began taking instruction in gliders. She was so little we had to prop her up with stacks of cushions so that she could reach the controls, and we added a parachute for ballast so that the glider wouldn't be tail heavy.

Physical requirements for soaring are less rigid than for almost any sport outside of chess. The person of light or small stature actually has an advantage in gliders because the ship flies better with less weight in the cabin. However, there

is a minimum weight specified for the pilot seat of any glider to assure proper balance.

No medical certificate is required to fly gliders, and there are many heart patients, diabetics, and amputees who are active in soaring.

If you are 6′ 4″, you will have room for only one thin cushion under you when you fly the Schweizer sailplanes, which is the most common American-built design. However, some of the European designs will comfortably accommodate very tall persons in a semi-reclining position.

Women make very proficient sailplane pilots. They often catch on to using proper control pressures more quickly than men who are inclined to use too much force in control movement. The ladies have a more sensitive touch and frequently excel in their coordination and in perceptions of upcurrents.

My wife and I were flying together above a 2,000-foot ridge one day. The wind was very light, and by being very cautious I was able to maintain altitude at 2,200 feet. After about ten minutes of soaring at this constant altitude, Marian took the controls. Five minutes later we were at 2,400 feet and I thought it was due to an increase in wind. I took over and flew the same figure-eight pattern she had. We began to settle right away and were soon back at 2,200 feet. We repeated the cycle again, and this time I had to face it. My wife had a better "feel" for the controls, could utilize the lift more efficiently, and eke out that extra couple of hundred feet of altitude.

Power Plane Pilots

Power plane pilots find sailplanes very challenging and rewarding to fly. They represent about one-half of the newcomers to the sport. The soaring flight helps them to recapture some of that original thrill of flying which has

Figure 31. SHK V-Tailed Sailplane

been lost or obscured by the melee of speed, power, and an overwhelming battery of FAA regulations and required radio procedures.

Sailplane experience is also valuable to the power pilot in teaching refinements of control feel and understanding of air currents. I know an airlines copilot who is also a skilled glider guider. He often dumbfounds his captain by predicting weather phenomena from studying cloud formations. "We better slow down, it's going to get turbulent," said Carroll on one flight across the Rockies. "What do you mean, turbulent?" scoffed the captain. "This air is as stable as last week's dishwater." "We're headed right for a rotor area," said Caroll, and sure enough, in a moment the DC-6 was bouncing around and shaking like a small ship in a choppy sea.

The power-off landing experience which one gets in gliders is excellent for developing judgment in case a pilot should ever have to make a forced landing in his power plane. A pilot ran out of fuel directly over the Skyport one day at several thousand feet high. He misjudged his landing approach and fell short of the field. If he had simply made a glider-type approach, he would easily have made a safe landing.

WHERE YOU CAN SOAR

Good soaring conditions are encountered over all of the land masses in the world. However, I don't recommend trying a glider flight across the polar ice cap. Hilly or mountainous territory is good for ridge and wave flying, but don't discount soaring in the flatlands. The world's sailplane distance record is held by Alvin Parker, who made a 646-mile cross-country flight starting at Odessa, Texas, and ending at Kimball, Nebraska.

Eastern Washington and central Nevada are examples of arid regions in the lee of mountain ranges where soaring conditions are especially good. You should think of soaring conditions as being related mostly to the condition of the air mass. Air masses shift about daily and with the seasons, and periodically good soaring conditions will develop almost every place. It is true that the topography and nature of the ground surface have something to do with the lift conditions. However, if you have a good unstable air mass with fairly low humidity, thermals will develop even if the ground is covered with snow.

There are many soaring clubs and commerical glider ports around the country where you can take glider training. A list of these is given at the end of this chapter.

Even though sailplane flight has been going on since the early part of the century, it has only recently started to expand into a popular sky sport. There are many regions in the country where no gliders are flown, and you might be able to introduce the sport in one of these areas.

You should try to gain some sailplane experience at a glider port even if it means spending a few days of your vacation time to get checked out. If you have a power plane license, you can qualify for a glider rating in just a couple of days. It is often possible to get an instructor to come to an area complete with glider to train a nucleus for a new club. All you need to start a glider operation is an airplane for towing, an airstrip (an unobstructed road or 2,000-foot smooth field will do), a glider, and an instructor. Almost any light plane of 100 horsepower or more will do for a towship. The Super Cub is commonly used and so are the Champion Sitabria, Cessna 150, 170, or 172. The Model 180 and larger Cessnas are a little too fast and expensive to be used as tow ships. Normal tow rates of $1.50 per 1,000 feet provides good earning power for a tow plane, and local private plane owners or fixed-base operators are often willing to equip their planes for towing.

An FAA-approved release hook is available from Schweizer Aircraft Co. for under $10, and any A & E mechanic can install it.

COST OF SOARING

Training Phase

If you go to one of the glider training centers, your financial outlay will be under $200 to get a glider rating added to your pilot license. A beginner with no previous experience will need forty or more flights, and the cost will be approximately $450.

Costs include instructor fees and use of both a two-place training glider and a single-seat craft for your solo work. The figures also include the cost of the tow plane and pilot which pull you aloft on each flight. Also furnished by most glider schools are the books and training which prepare you for passing the FAA written exam.

A training flight lasts about twenty minutes including the tow to 3,000 feet. You may be discouraged if you relate these costs to an hourly cost figure. Your training time will come to something like $30 per hour, which is considerably more than power plane lessons. Bear in mind, however, that it requires two airplanes and two professional pilots to make your glider flight possible. Also, it requires fewer flights to qualify for a glider rating than a power rating, so the total cost is only about two-thirds the cost of a license to fly power planes. If you have ambitions to get both a power and glider rating, by all means get the power rating first. Very little glider training may be credited toward your power license, but, as the above costs reflect, a rated power

plane pilot may obtain a glider rating for a very nominal fee.

Club Training

In many areas the cost of training is less at a club facility where instructors are volunteers and the students pay only club fees which reflect the basic airplane operating costs. The Boeing Employees Soaring Club in Seattle is partially subsidized by the company, and newcomers pay an average cost of $75 for a private pilot, and $200 for a beginner.

When training with a club, you are expected to devote a fair share of your time to helping with club duties, and training progress may not be as fast as you would like from the volunteer instructors.

Cost After Training

After training, when you have developed some soaring proficiency, the cost figures for gliding look more favorable. When weather conditions are good, a single aero tow costing $3.50 to $5.00 will allow you a flight which may last for several hours. If you are renting the sailplane, $9 to $10 per hour is the average rate.

During your first few weeks of enthusiasm after being first "kissed by a thermal," the temptation to rush out and buy a sailplane is very strong. I suggest waiting until you have logged at least fifty flights or thirty hours of glider time. This will give you time to observe the selection of ships available and weigh the financial picture carefully. The lure of ownership is strong, but not financially practical unless you fly more than fifty hours per year. A medium-performance Schweizer 1-26 costs $4,000; in kit form, where you assemble the plane yourself, you will spend $2,500. If you have a gourmet's taste and budget, your outlay will approach $6,000 to $8,000 for one of the fine high-performance designs. Some of them are of all-fiberglass construction with fantastic aerodynamic efficiency.

If you don't live near a glider site where rentals are available, you may have to make a purchase outright or form a partnership or club in order to spread the investment.

Sailplane Kits

Several good sailplanes are available in kit form for enthusiasts who have a talent in the shop. The 1-26 kit mentioned for $2,500 has a completely welded steel tube fuselage. The builder's job is mainly drilling, bolting, and riveting, plus some covering and painting, of course. The factory predicts about 500 hours are needed to complete assembly.

Briegleb offers a nice design in kit form, or it can be built in a couple of years from plans. Some of the good European ships, such as the K-7, can be ordered in kit or plan form at nominal costs. Your time investment for building a wooden ship will tally upwards of 2,000 hours.

You have to enjoy your work when building or assembling a glider in order to justfy the time invested. It is easy to become a slave to the construction job and spend many frustrating weekends in the shop sanding or riveting when you could be aloft in a rented ship. I know one local chap who frequently was seen circling a rental ship in the skies over Issaquah, Washington, until he began assembling his 1-26 kit a little over two years ago. Since then he hardly ever flies, and has obviously become enslaved by the building project. On the other hand, another friend who is a gifted craftsman assembled his 1-26 with a little help in two weeks.

If you choose to build a 1-26 from a kit, don't yield to the temptation to alter the design. You must follow the plans exactly if you want your glider to have a Standard Airworthiness Certificate, which is issued by the FAA after an inspection of your craft. Any alteration will place it in the experimental category, and you may experience problems in getting it licensed to fly.

Ready-Built Sailplanes

There is only one United States sailplane production manufacturer. The Schweizer Co. at Elmira, New York, has been turning out gliders for over twenty years. They have five models in current production with prices ranging from $3,995 for the 1-26 to $10,000 for the 2-32, a two-passenger, high-performance, all-metal ship. One of the advantages to a domestic built sailplane is the availability of parts. A friend of mine was once on his way to a glider contest trailering a Schweizer model 1-23. In a moment of sleepiness near Reno, Nevada, he bumped the glider's tail on a motel neon sign and damaged the rudder. A panic phone call to the factory brought the assurance that a replacement rudder would be shipped on the next westbound jet to San Francisco. The rudder arrived in San Francisco about the time my friend did. He made the return trip to Reno, installed the new rudder, and was flying over the ridge before sunset of the same day that the accident occurred. I doubt if this type of service could be duplicated if you needed a wing or a fuselage, but it certainly is a secure feeling to know that your glider can be serviced with factory parts without waiting six weeks or six months, which is not uncommon in the case of foreign ships.

Probably the most fascinating and exotic designs in sailplanes come from Europe, where

Figure 32. Two Libelles

soaring has been exploited since the early 1920's. Most imported ships are single-place, high-performance designs.

The great interest and activity in soaring in recent years has stimulated European designers and factories to produce more and better ships at an astounding rate. Improvements in design, performance, and construction are coming very fast indeed. So fast, in fact, that the buyer often finds himself in a very frustrating position. The new fiberglass "exotica" which he ordered a year ago has just been delivered. It is now out-of-date while still in the crate. The factory is already producing an improved version.

There are consoling facts, however, such as the excellent market for used sailplanes in the United States. Unlike automobiles and other types of airplanes, gliders depreciate very little in value when maintained in good condition.

Other Expenses

Although the glider itself is the biggest expense associated with soaring as an owner, there are several other sizable costs you should understand before buying. A trailer is a necessity and will cost $300 to $600. You may resolve to do without, and never land away from your base field, but the day will surely come when you will qualify as a "sod buster" and find yourself parked in a field which is too small from which to make an aero tow. Flatbed trucks big enough to accommodate a glider are rare, so a trailer is a must. It should be outfitted with mounting brackets designed to fit your glider so as to hold it securely during transport.

If you have a large carport or covered storage area at home, you may keep your ship there and save the expense of hangar storage at the airport. However, the convenience of keeping the ship assembled and ready to fly may be worth the extra $20 to $30 per month for a hangar at the glider port.

Plenty of soaring enjoyment may be experienced with the minimum of instrumentation. An airspeed, altimeter, and variometer are usually installed in the ship at delivery. The temptation of luxuries such as additional variometers, compass, oxygen system, and two-way radios may be hard to resist, and it is not uncommon to find $1,500 worth of these niceties in a sailplane.

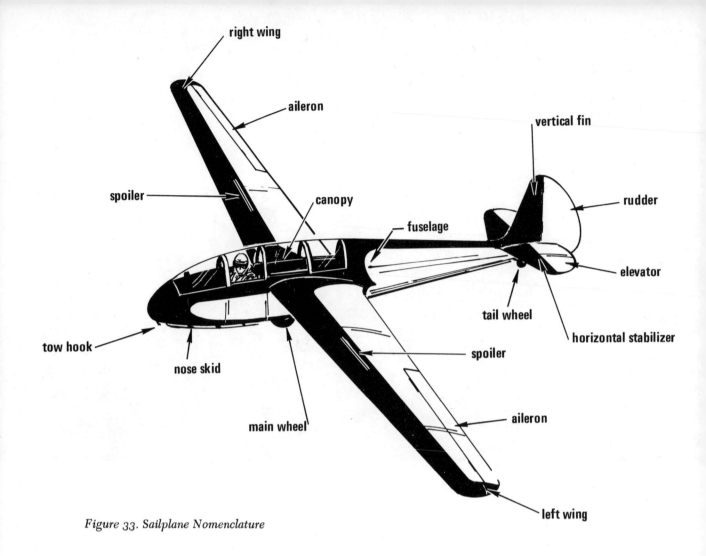

Figure 33. Sailplane Nomenclature

Maintenance is a nominal expense because gliders have so very few moving parts. The all-metal and fiberglass ships are especially easy to keep up. The ship needs to be washed and waxed occasionally for best performance, and a little oil on control cable pulleys and hinge points will save you from the distractions of squeaks in the rigging when soaring.

Liability insurance for your ship is a small cost unless you carry passengers for hire. Hull insurance to protect your investment is another story. Many underwriters are charging ten percent per year of the ship's value, which is unreasonably high for most private owners. Few owners carry this type of insurance and simply assume the risk of damage. In the partnership or club ownership of a glider the hull insurance cost can be spread among the members, and it becomes practical again. If you are sharing ownership of a glider, you should have either insurance or partners who are financially responsible. In either case an agreement is called for in advance of flying the ship.

HOW TO FLY A GLIDER

If you are a beginner I suggest you read the later chapter on power plane flight. It will acquaint you with the basic principles of flight and the fundamentals of coordinating the controls. This chapter will deal with how to fly a glider and will explain what is unique and different about them.

Probably the first thing you will notice as you approach a glider is that it looks as if it has a collapsed landing gear, for one wing tip lies on the ground. This is how a glider stands because it has only one wheel in the fuselage, located at the center of gravity. Sometimes a small wheel about four inches in diameter is located at the tail and on each wing tip to make it easier to move the glider on the ground. The absence of the engine makes possible a smoothly contoured nose section, and I'm sure you will be impressed by the length of the wings. A sailplane wing may have a fifty-foot span and average width, or chord, of less than three feet. This long-span,

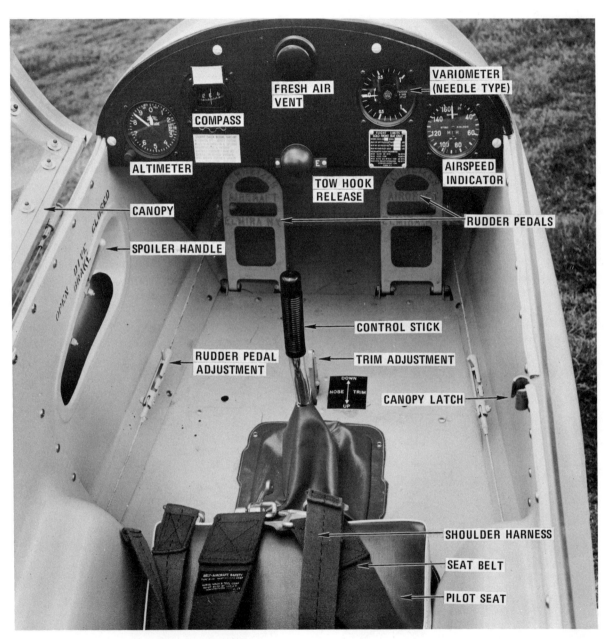

Figure 34. Sailplane Controls and Instruments

narrow-chord design is called a "high aspect ratio," and it is used in gliders for maximum flight efficiency. The wings have large control surfaces called "ailerons." On top of each wing is a panel which will open against the airflow during flight when the spoiler handle is pulled. This effectively "spoils" the lift over a section of the wing and allows the pilot to increase his descent rate without building up airspeed. You might consider the spoiler as an airbrake which is most commonly used during landing approaches.

The tail is of a conventional design with a horizontal stabilizer, large elevator, and a large vertical fin and rudder. The device for gripping the towline is usually located on the underside of the glider's nose. A few gliders have the tow hook placed a little ahead of the wheel near the ship's center of gravity. This latter type, called a "C. G. hook," has no advantages for aero towing, but is more efficient than the nose hook for winch or auto launches.

A look at the cockpit will reveal a very simple set of instruments and controls. The stick and rudder pedals are the primary flight controls. In addition there is a spoiler handle which will also apply the wheel brake if you pull it all the way back. The only other controls are the towline release handle, the trim adjustment, and the cabin vent. Some of the more sophisticated high-performance designs have a lever for retracting the wheel.

The instrument panel in a training glider will have an airspeed indicator, altimeter, and a

Figure 35. Sailplane Ground Handling

Figure 36. Aero Towing

variometer usually of the Robinson or "pellet" design. In addition to the above, the connoisseur will often have two or more variometers, a turn and bank or attitude instrument, a compass, a G meter, a radio, and an oxygen system with gauges.

Ground Handling a Sailplane

Although a sailplane is incomparably graceful when airborne, it is probably the world's most awkward bird on the ground. One person can move it a few feet by opening the canopy and pulling forward on a sturdy structural part of the cockpit. To move it any distance over 100 feet you need a couple of energetic hands, or a tow vehicle. When using the latter, be sure to have a twenty-foot or longer line, tow slowly, have one man carry the glider's wingtip, and

don't stop suddenly or the glider could coast forward into the tow vehicle.

When hand-moving, the tail-first technique works well on Schweizer designs with one person on each side of the fuselage facing aft, carrying and supporting the stabilizer very close to the fuselage.

Glider Launching

The safest way to launch a glider is by towing it into the air with a powered plane. Aero towing places the minimum in stresses upon the sailplane and offers good possibilities for soaring flights because your tow pilot can help you explore for lift during the climb to altitude.

There was a time in the early 1930's when gliders were launched by catapulting them down a slope from a hilltop with a huge rubber band

Figure 37. Tow Hook on Tow plane

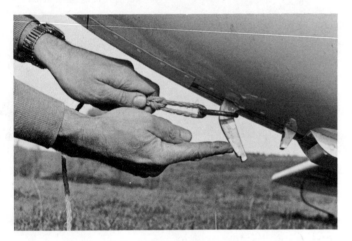

Figure 38. Tow Hook on Sailplane

called a "bungee," made from automobile inner tubes. This technique has been abandoned because you can't buy natural rubber inner tubes anymore, and the tow plane or winch will launch you much higher.

Winch and auto towing are still used in a few areas, and each offers an economical launch method. They are most practical when soaring is done on a ridge very close to the launch site.

Since aero towing is the most commonly used method of launch, I shall describe in detail the techniques you should know as a student glider pilot. The towline which links the tow plane to the glider is made from ¼-inch nylon or polyethylene and has a two-inch welded steel ring tied to each end. The ring engages the release hooks on the tow plane tail and glider nose. The glider pilot normally releases the towline when desired altitude is reached. The tow plane pilot would release the glider only in case of emergency.

On rare occasions the glider may get so far out of position that the tow pilot can no longer control his airspeed. If the glider is too high, the upward pull may nose the tow plane toward the ground. If the glider gets very low the tow plane tail will be pulled downward and a stall may result. When this happens, the alert tow pilot will pull the towline release. I will discuss the details of how to fly a glider during aero tow in a later section.

Hook-up and Takeoff

Your position as a student will be in the front seat; your instructor will ride in back. Be sure you are properly cushioned to be able to reach the rudder pedals and control stick. Experiment with cushions until you can push each control to the full extent of its travel. Now if the canopy will close without hitting your head, you can secure the shoulder harness and seat belt around you.

It takes two people to connect a towline properly. One should be in the cockpit, the other slips the ring into the tow hook. It is taboo to connect a towline to a glider before the glider pilot is strapped into position. If the pilot gets out of the sailplane cockpit he should release the towline. This is a rule that will prevent the inadvertent towing aloft of a pilotless glider.

Double-check the canopy to be sure it is

Figure 39. High Tow Position

securely latched. On some gliders you need outside assistance to get the canopy properly latched.

Sometimes one or more helpers are used to relay your signals to the tow pilot. If you have a wingman, give him a nod and he will pick up your wing and hold it level. The signalman standing by the tow plane will swing his extended arm back and forth and the tow plane will taxi forward and take up slack in the towline. Waggle the rudder with full deflection both ways and the signalman will swing his arm in a full circle; then the tow pilot will begin the takeoff.

At our school and others such as Les Arnold's at Fremont, California, the instructors like to minimize the chance of crossing up signals through middlemen. The tow pilot observes the glider directly and tightens slack upon seeing the glider's first rudder waggle and pours on the power at the second waggle.

If nobody holds your wings level at the start of the takeoff, you will have to deflect the aileron on the low wing to a full "down" position so that airflow will raise the wing after you start forward. After the wings are level, you attempt to keep the glider fuselage level with the ground as you accelerate. If the tail is low or dragging, apply a little forward stick pressure. If the nose skid is rubbing the ground, a little back stick is needed. If a crosswind is blowing, keep the upwind wing slightly lower and keep the fuselage pointed directly at the tow plane with your rudder.

The takeoff will happen without any effort on your part when the glider reaches flying speed of 30 to 35 mph. You must use some effort now, though, to keep the glider from climbing more than ten feet while the tow plane is still on the ground. You must apply more and more forward

stick pressure as speed increases. Tow speed is 60 to 65 mph and the glider is balanced to fly at 40, so the unbalance of forces generated by the excess speed is resolved in the pilot's hand and arm as he keeps some forward pressure on the stick.

Control During Tow

I don't expect any pilot, no matter what his ability or previous flying experience, to catch on to flying the aero tow on the first try. When I first tried a glider I was amazed at how easy it was to get out of shape during tow. Every few seconds the instructor would say, "I've got it," and he would fly us back into position behind the tow plane.

Flying tow is tricky because it is like formation flying. Military pilot trainees have a lot of experience before they begin formation flight. A beginning glider student must meet the challenge of keeping the glider in a precise relationship with the tow plane.

Successful tow flight means reacting immediately to any change in your relative position to the tow plane. "High tow" is the best position and means flying the glider above the slipstream or propwash of the tow plane. Looking from the glider end of the towline you should see the tow plane's rudder lined up with the center of the wing. Some schools have a big red circle painted on top of the wing above the cabin of the tow plane. This is popularly called the "meatball," and when flying tow your job is to keep the rudder tip lined up with the meatball.

Another good way to tell if you are in proper position is to look at the tow plane in relation to the horizon. It should be right on it. If you see land above the tow plane, you are too high and should apply forward stick immediately. If

*Figure 40. Sailplane Viewed from Towplane.
High Tow Position.*

(above) Figure 41. Too Far Left of Towplane

(below) Figure 42. Too Far Right.

you see sky below the tow plane, you are too low. Apply back stick pressure.

Don't overshoot when making corrections. Every time you apply pressure to correct your position, relax that pressure when you get back into position.

Any time you fail to keep your wings level you will progress sideways until laterally out of position. This is less easy to correct, because it requires use of both aileron and rudder to get back in line. Aileron is used to keep the wings level, and rudder to skid sideways. When the tow plane's rudder is not centered in the fuselage, you are too far left or right. When left, move right with right rudder. Be sure to keep a little left-turn pressure on the aileron, or the right wing will drop when you apply right rudder. This is especially tricky because it is exactly opposite from the way you have learned to make a coordinated turn. Normally right stick goes with right rudder, but not during tow. Position corrections are done during tow with "crossed controls," such as you use for slips and skids. A coordinated turn will result in aggravating your condition. Try it once and you'll see.

Skids and *small corrections* are the rules for flying tow. "Small corrections" means applying corrective action immediately upon noticing you are out of position. Six feet too far in any direction is enough to detect, and you can begin to correct. Sixteen feet out of shape is beyond the small correction stage, but still not too far to cure with proper and positive control movement. Sixty feet is seriously out of shape and the

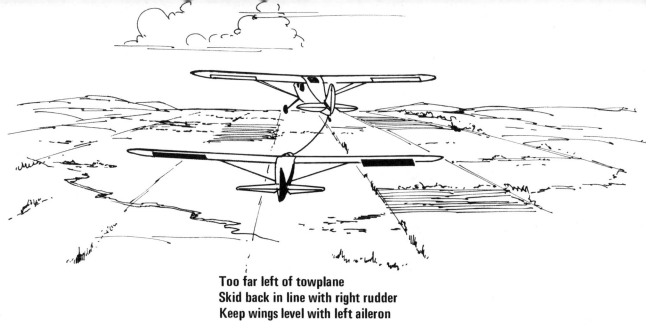

Too far left of towplane
Skid back in line with right rudder
Keep wings level with left aileron

Figure 43. Too Far Left.

student is likely to push the panic button and shout, "You've got it," to the instructor. What he will do depends on the direction of error. When way low and off to one side the chance of climbing and skidding back into position is good if the tow plane's speed isn't dangerously low. Being extremely high is more serious because you are lifting the tow plane's tail and making matters worse. A combination of spoilers and forward slip will do the most to remedy this condition.

You really don't have time to think about each correction as you make it. Your reactions must be almost mechanical, and experience is the only way to develop proper mechanical responses.

I do it this way when working with a student. During tow he takes the stick and flies until out of shape. I say, "I've got it," and fly us back into position, then say, "You've got it." He may get out of shape in five seconds or less the first few times. I keep giving verbal cues to help with corrections, but the key to the student's developing proper responses comes from the mechanical experience of feeling that stick and those rudder pedals and seeing the results of his manipulation of them. I have seen the gratifying results of this technique when the student becomes able and confident in flying tow after only a few flights.

I stated that your wings should be kept level during tow. The exception to this is when the tow plane is turning. You are permitted to bank at the same angle as the tow plane during turns . . . no more. Adjust the angle of your back to match the tow plane and keep the same rudder and horizon reference points. If you slip to the inside of the turn, your airspeed may fall dangerously low and a slack towline may develop with a subsequent jerk. If you get high and outside, you are playing a most dangerous game of crack-the-whip. Your airspeed and necessary forward stick pressures will increase. If you dive and develop slack during recovery, a severe jerk may result. Any time you have slack in the towline, see that the glider is in a yaw or skid when the line comes tight. Much of the jerk will be relieved by the cushioning action of pulling the glider out of the yaw.

It may require only two tows, or it may take twenty, but eventually you will be able to consistently maintain a good tow position. Then it is time to feel your way through the prop wash into low tow position. Forward pressure on the stick will lower you until the whole glider starts to shake and tremble as the wings buffet their way through the cone of turbulent air behind the tow plane's propeller. You will need corrective aileron pressures to prevent rolling into an inadvertent bank because that prop wash is swirling and may force a wing down.

The air will become smooth again when you reach a position about thirty feet below your normal high tow position. A little back pressure and you will climb back through the burbles to high tow. This exercise is a good confidence builder and should be done periodically along with the exercise of circling the prop wash.

To do this, skid out to the right about forty feet, then drop to low tow, and skid back to the

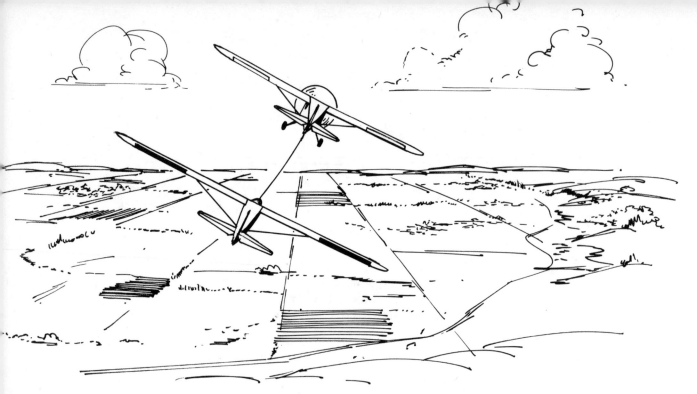

The sailplane should match the angle of bank of the towplane

Figure 44. Match Bank Angle of Towplane

left. This puts you in low tow without having to shudder through the prop wash. To get back into high tow, simply skid left about forty feet, climb until level with the tow plane, and then skid right. There is an excellent chance that the FAA flight examiner will require you to perform this same exercise when you take a glider license check flight.

Abnormal Tow Procedures

I don't like to call these "emergency procedures" because they really don't all qualify as emergencies. These are some standard signals with which you should become familiar.

If you see the tow plane rolling his wings back and forth, he wants you to release. Maybe he's trying to tell you he is low on gas or is having engine trouble. Sometimes he is saying, "We're in 1,000-foot-per-minute lift now. What more do you want?"

If you should attempt to release and find, after repeated attempts, that the hook won't work, you can convey this message to the tow pilot by skidding off to the side and rolling your wings back and forth when you get his attention. You may even point to the towline if his rearward visibility is good enough to see you. After he gets the message, he will tow you over

the glider port and pull his release. You pull yours again, but don't pressure the towline to be clear of the glider unless you bank and actually see it dropping away. A safe landing could be made with towline attached if you clear the fence with 200 feet of altitude.

If neither glider nor tow plane can release . . . has anybody got a guardian angel with a pocket knife to help cut the rope? This is truly serious, although I've never heard of it happening. However, in flying we are taught always to expect the unexpected. The accepted routine for dealing with a double release failure would be to try first to break the towline. Climb a little high, dive to develop some slack, and apply some spoiler to decelerate. Don't yaw to absorb the jerk. Try a few gentle jerks first to get the idea. Above all don't get violent. You only want to break the towline, not the equipment. If this fails and you find yourself inextricably anchored together with your tow plane, you must trust him to find the largest airport within range and make a slow and gentle letdown to it. The tow plane should not descend faster than 200 feet per minute with glider attached. On final approach, drop into low tow position. Land before the tow plane does. Don't use spoilers or brakes until he is landed, then drag the nose skid, brakes, and even your feet if you can.

TOWLINE BREAKS DURING TAKEOFF

If this happens just after takeoff and you don't have 200 feet of altitude, pick a straight-ahead or 90° landing spot. Don't attempt a 180° return to the runway. If you have over 200 feet, you could make make a 180° return to the runway, or fly a full 360° pattern and land upwind. If the towline should break or come free at either end during initial takeoff acceleration, there is no problem. Simply brake the glider to a stop. The tow plane should avoid abrupt stops in such an event. If the glider is already airborne when the line breaks, the glider should land immediately and the tow plane should fly on around the pattern.

TOW PLANE ABORTS TAKEOFF

If the tow plane has a power failure during takeoff when there is ample runway ahead in which to land and stop, the tow pilot will first release the towline and then brake to a stop on the left side of the runway. The glider pilot should pull his towline release as soon as he sees the slack line. The main problem here is to avoid overrunning the tow plane. The courteous tow pilot will use all the available runway to decelerate. If the tow plane can get himself stopped, so can the glider by touching down promptly, regardless of speed, and using brakes and nose skid to stop. It may be wise for the glider pilot to bear right during the landing to allow for coasting past the tow plane.

Remember, the glider can be landed easily even with a lot of excess airspeed. Most landings are made at 40 mph or less, but there is no reason why you can't touch down at 60 or 70. Just be sure to keep the tail high (forward stick pressure), wings level, and the nose skid dragging if you want to decelerate quickly.

I have experienced the above takeoff problems from both ends of the towline, and believe me, there is no need to panic. Just keep cool and do what looks like the sensible thing.

The Release

The procedure for releasing is quite simple. Climb about twenty feet above the normal tow position, clear yourself (look around to avoid turning into another airplane), and pull the release knob firmly. That extra twenty feet of height is to establish a firm tension on the towline. When you release on a slack towline, the tow pilot may be unaware that you have released.

As soon as you hear the "clack" of the release hook and see the towline spring away from the nose, bank to the right in a 90° climbing turn. The tow plane banks left in a descending turn.

Don't confuse the release knob with the spoiler handle. Both are normally operated with the left hand, and serious consequences can result from pulling the wrong knob. As a student on tow, I once tugged ineffectively on the spoiler handle to release. Not only had the release hook apparently failed, but the whole glider seemed to be acting strangely. I had settled into the prop wash and was shuddering and wallowing along. Just about to bail out, I gave one insightful look at what I was doing. The "release knob," which my white-knuckled fingers were clutching, was plainly labeled "spoiler."

Here is a tip which may save you the embarrassment of pulling the wrong knob. Your left hand is used to pull two different things in a glider cockpit: the tow release, and the spoiler handle. When you anticipate using either of these, grasp the handle first before you are

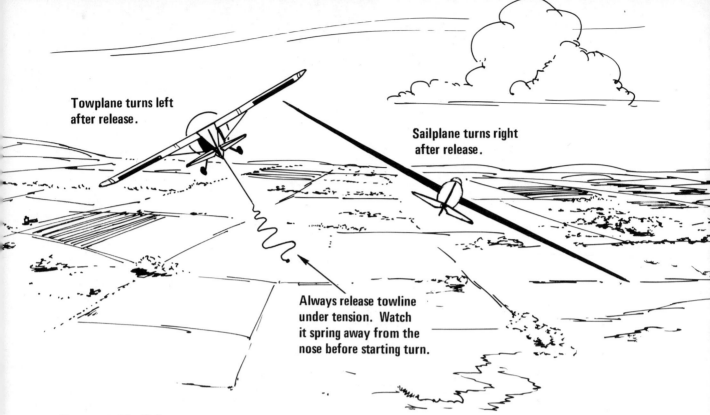

Towplane turns left after release.

Sailplane turns right after release.

Always release towline under tension. Watch it spring away from the nose before starting turn.

Figure 45. The Release

ready to pull. Feel it. Does it feel like the right handle? Now look at your hand grasping the handle and ask yourself the question, "Is that the handle I want?" Only after making both these checks are you really ready to use the handle.

One other point about releasing. After you have your glider pilot license and you may take your spouse or friend up for their first glider ride, it will save your passenger a bad moment of fright if you warn them (before you pull the release knob) about the noisy clack of the release mechanism.

Ground Launching by Auto or Winch Launch

This method of giving a glider some altitude is still used in some areas where a long runway is located near a ridge which provides dependable lift.

At Torrey Pines, California, gliders are winch-launched at the top of the seacoast bluff. On-shore winds provide great soaring for gulls and gliders alike.

A friend of mine has for years launched gliders by auto tow from the Dillingham airstrip on Oahu, Hawaii, where the 5,000-foot runway lies at the base of a mountain ridge. For a few

pennies worth of gasoline he can launch a glider directly into the lift provided by the prevailing northeasterly trade winds.

This method of launching differs from the tow-plane method because during a winch launch the glider simulates the flight of a kite. The glider is held in a very steep nose-up pitch altitude, and the flight path prescribed upward is almost frighteningly steep.

Altitude achieved during the lanuch depends upon many variables such as length of line used, power available, wind speed, type of glider, and type of tow hook. If the glider's tow hook is mounted on the underside near the center of gravity, it is called a "CG" hook, which is more efficient for ground launching.

A CG tow hook on a single-plane glider should allow launches to a height slightly better than half the length of the launch towline. When auto towing with a 1,000-foot cable the best altitude potential would be 600 to 700 feet. You should be sure to use a line length compatible with the tow distance available. On a 5,000-foot runway a 2,000-foot cable works very nicely. On a 3,000-foot runway, 1,200 feet would be a good length for the towline.

The tow vehicle should have an observer and a driver. Always tow into the wind and avoid towing under severe crosswind conditions.

Figure 46. Winch Launch

To execute a launch properly in the ground launch method you must abandon all preconceived ideas about flying your way up the flight path by using some coordinated manipulation of the controls. Auto or winch launch projects you into the sky like a kite on a string, and there is very little control movement necessary except to hold the stick back in your lap and use aileron to keep the wings level. You may need to use rudder to correct for drift from a crosswind.

To begin the takeoff you need a wingman to signal the tow vehicle when you are ready. He will level your wings for you, which tells the tow vehicle to take up towline slack. When you are ready for takeoff, wiggle the rudders or have the wingman rock your wings. That's when the excitement begins. As you accelerate, keep the glider balanced on the wheel and the wings level exactly as with an aero tow. When your airspeed shows 30 mph and you are airborne a couple of feet, it is time to apply a little back stick pressure. Climb gently to about fifty feet. This gives you a little cushion of altitude in which to recover should the towline break. Now pull the stick back into your lap to establish a

Figure 47. Auto Tow Launch Method

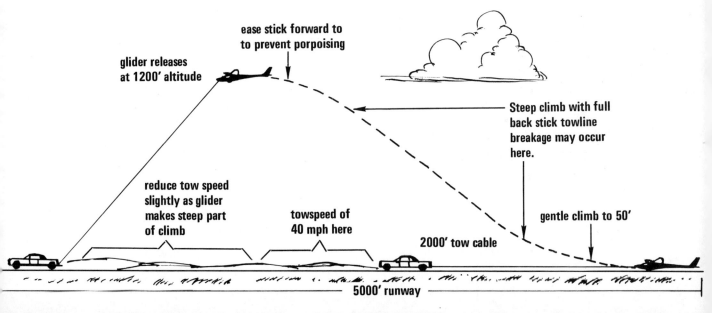

45° nose-up altitude. As the climb begins you will notice a peculiar thing. The airspeed increases. This is probably the only flying situation where you can get increased airspeed by pulling back on the stick. The increased speed comes from the upward acceleration. If you refer to the diagram (Fig. 47) you will see that your flight path covers a greater distance than that of the tow vehicle during the same span of time. The glider will show speeds of 10 or 15 mph greater than the tow vehicle during the climb portion of the tow.

As you approach the peak of the climb a peculiar set of aerodynamics comes into effect. You are offsetting the downward pull of the towline with up elevator, but a point is reached during climb where oscillations or porpoising will develop if you continue with full back stick. This is a pitching up and down of the nose and is a good clue that you have reached release altitude. Gliders equipped with a CG tow hook are less likely to porpoise. Be sure to ease the stick forward and establish a normal glide immediately after releasing, or you may stall.

Towline Breakage

During the steepest part of the climb you have no horizon reference, and a glance to the wingtip will confirm your steep climb altitude. This is the time when maximum stresses occur on the towline, and a broken towline is not an uncommon occurrence. A good rule is to begin each ground launch *expecting* towline failure because if it occurs, you must nose down to a normal glide *very* quickly to avoid a stall. Be sure to pull the tow release knob after establishing a glide to dispose of the dangling towline.

How to Fly After Release

A glider reacts to the controls in the same way a power plane does except that the glider feels a little lighter and more responsive. It takes less pressure on the stick to obtain the desired results. Also, the sailplane will bank with the same ease in either direction. (The power plane has propeller torque, which assists in left banks and inhibits right-hand banks.) Practice 180° and 360° turns in both directions using roads or fence lines for your heading references. A 30° bank will give you a faster rate of turn in a sailplane because of the slower airspeed. The only time you will bank more steeply, at 45° or 60°, is during thermalling when you may have to spiral in a very tight turn to remain within a thermal.

While practicing turns in a power plane you attempt to maintain a constant altitude, but in a sailplane you can't maintain a constant altitude, so your primary instrument reference during turn practice is the airspeed indicator. High airspeed means you didn't maintain the back stick pressure during a turn and consequently the nose dropped. Slow airspeed means you applied too much back stick and the nose is consequently high.

Accurate, well-coordinated turns are made by visual checks of the position of the wings and nose in relation to the horizon, with periodic glances at the airspeed indicator. You will never be able to make a good turn, or even fly straight and level for that matter, by concentrating your attention on the airspeed indicator and applying corrective stick pressures in response to high- or low-speed readings. This is called "chasing the airspeed" and will invariably result in porpoising. The instrument readings lag behind the pitch angle of your craft, and if the instrument reading is off, the mistake already took place a couple of seconds ago. The visual reference of ship's nose to horizon is the only way to get instant pitch information.

Overcontrolling is probably the most common error you will make during your initial flights in a sailplane. If you find yourself thrusting the stick back and forth in an attempt to stop fluctuations in the airspeed, the chances are that you are overcontrolling. Try to think in terms of stick pressures rather than stick movements. The experienced pilot can put a sailplane through a series of graceful maneuvers with hardly a perceivable movement of the stick. Your grip on the stick has much to do with how you apply the proper pressures to fly effectively. It is sometimes said that a glider talks to you. If you attune your perceptions to the glider's language, it will tell you what it needs to accomplish coordinated flight. With no engine noise to distract you, the subtle sounds and feels of the glider will communicate to you in ways uncommon to power planes. Keep a light touch on the stick and rudder pedals. Tenseness brings stiffness in the muscles and clutching of the stick. To feel what the stick is telling you, you must hold it with a relaxed grip.

If you raise the nose slightly and fly the glider under 40 mph you will notice, through a relaxed grip on the stick, that control pressures feel light. During slow flight a greater amount of movement is required of the stick to make a banking turn. This "light and sloppy" feel of the stick will always tell you that your airspeed is slow. Conversely, a stiff and heavy-feeling stick means that the airspeed is high. Lower the nose until the airspeed shows 60 and you will experience the heavier feel of the stick.

Now establish a nose-high pitch attitude to approach a stall. A gentle pulsing or buffet will be felt in the stick, which is your signal that a stall is beginning to occur. If you "feel" for it, you can always detect the turbulence which develops over the wing and tail just before a complete stall occurs. Relax your feet on the rudder pedals. Tenseness in the legs and feet may cause you to hold unbalanced pressures, and you will be unable to feel what the rudder can tell you.

Stick and rudder feel is not the only way a sailplane talks to you. Attune your ears to the gentle whisper of air around the cabin. You will notice subtle changes in the pitch and intensity of wind noise as the airspeed varies. Pull the nose up and the wind noise will decrease. Lower the nose and the wind noise increases.

Sight is of course the most important of all your senses during flight. Your eyes will tell you instantly where the nose and wingtips are in relation to the horizon. During tow your eyes are the only sense that will tell you when you are in proper tow position. Keep your eyes moving and avoid fixing your gaze on any one instrument. Ninety percent of your visual attention should be directed outside the cockpit. With practice you will be able to scan and interpret all the instrument readings in one second. The rest of the time is spent attending to visual references outside.

Besides checking your aircraft altitude your eyes should be used to watch for other aircraft. Many hours of flying may go by without encountering another plane anywhere near you; however, occasions do arise when planes pass close together and the anti-collision rule is "see and be seen."

"Keep your head on a swivel," is what my

instructor used to shout at me, and my attempts to comply sometimes resulted in a stiff neck from the exercise.

Listening, seeing, and feeling the glider talk to you are all fine, but remember that you are the pilot. You have the responsibility of directing the plane's flight, and you should never become a passenger and let the plane fly you. Women seem to stumble most often on the responsibility of controlling the plane in a positive manner. Landing in a crosswind, for example, requires the pilot to have a confident and positive attitude. During the landing it may be necessary to use considerable control pressure to make the plane respond. Ladies may be a little too delicate with the controls under such situations. "Get mad at it," is the command used by one instructor to his students who can't seem to put the needed muscle pressure on the controls.

Flying straight and level requires little or no effort by the pilot. Properly trimmed, the glider will fly by itself and maintain a normal flight attitude. It is when the pilot's will, and outside forces such as turbulent air, come into the picture that corrective control pressures are needed. The pilot must learn to apply precisely those corrective control pressures to continue his desired flight path. Sometimes proper corrective pressures may measure only an ounce or less. Side slips, recovery from steep banks, and maneuvers during tow, are situations which require control pressures that may amount to several pounds.

Stalls

A description of the aerodynamics of stalls is given in the power plane section.

Because of its lighter wing loading a glider stalls at a slower speed than a power plane. Most gliders can be slowed to 30 or 35 mph before they stall. The airspeed indicator may read somewhat less than this speed because errors develop in the airspeed readings at very slow speeds.

During a straight-ahead 20° nose-up stall the wings usually remain level, and recovery is simply a matter of releasing the back stick pressure used to hold the nose up. A glider is very stable and will make a nice recovery from any stall if you just relax stick and rudder pressures. Recovery to level flight after a stall can be hastened by a little back stick pressure when the airspeed indicates 40 mph or above.

The point to remember about stalls during turns is that stall speed increases as your angle of bank increases. This is because centrifugal force acts to increase the plane's weight during banking turns. During a 45° bank the glider's weight is doubled, and stall speed will increase by about twenty percent. In a 60° bank a glider which stalls normally at 30 mph would encounter a stall at 40 mph. Any time you feel heavy in the seat, such as during turns or maneuvers, you should be aware that the ship is heavier also and will stall at some speed higher than the normal wing-level stall speed.

Spins

A spin is a stall aggravated by the pilot continuing to hold the stick back and also throwing in rudder deflection. During a spin most planes will descend vertically in a stalled condition and rotate or spin about the vertical axis. Sailplanes, because of their design, seldom spin more than one revolution.

The stall and first-half turn of a spin can be achieved, but after that the ship starts to resist your control pressures and fly anyway. A steep spiral is invariably the result, and recovery is quick if you simply relax your pressure on the stick and rudder.

In a plane which will spin successfully the proper recovery procedure would be to apply opposite rudder to the direction of the spin and relax back pressure on the stick.

Your instructor may demonstrate some spin entries, but it is a maneuver you should never encounter in normal flight. The value of such a demonstration is to illustrate what happens when the pilot flies very slowly and applies considerable rudder pressure. The stall which occurs may involve wing rotation that will cause a considerable loss of altitude before recovery is made. You might recover from a simple forward stall with only a fifty-foot loss of altitude. The spin entry stall will take more like 200 feet of altitude. Always be aware of this fact when making turns in your landing pattern. Many pilots have made spin entries when approaching for a landing because they let their airspeed diminish to the stall point.

Glide Ratio

Every glider has an efficiency curve which can be plotted on a graph to illustrate the ship's performance at various airspeeds. Performance is measured in two ways: (1) "Minimum sink," which is the speed in feet per second at which a glider descends in calm air at an optimal airspeed; (2) Glide Ratio, or Lift/Drag Ratio, commonly expressed simply as L/D. This is the most significant performance figure because it tells you how far a glider will go forward for

each foot of altitude. A single-engine power plane with engine cut has a glide ratio of about 8/1. A Schweizer 2-22 two-place trainer will glide at 18/1. A Schweizer 1-26 single place glides at 23/1. A German all-wood and fabric glides at 32/1. A sleek Libelle all-fiberglass glides at 38/1.

The better your glider's L/D, the farther you can travel from the airport and still be within safe gliding distance of home base. You might note that even the lowest performance glider listed has over twice the performance of a gliding power plane.

Distance from Airport

A safe glider pilot must develop an awareness of where he is in relation to the airport. This awareness involves direction and velocity of the wind, altitude of the glider, and glider performance. Further considerations are the lift or sink potentials likely between glider and airport. Many glider pilots have developed this awareness, as I did, by failing to make it back to the field. Believe me, you develop a lot of awareness while carrying the parts of a disassembled glider across country. You could avoid the trouble and embarrassment of a "clodbuster" landing by always being sure you are well above your glide cone. This is an imaginary cone with its point 800 feet above the runway and its sides representing your L/D or glide ratio. The 800 feet is to give you altitude to fly a normal landing pattern. The higher your glider's performance or glide ratio, the flatter will be the sides of the glide cone. You will lose about 300 feet of altitude per mile in a Schweizer 2-22, 200 feet per mile in a 1-26.

If the wind is blowing and you are downwind of the airport, your glide ratio will be less than in calm air. For example, a 2-22 which will glide eighteen feet forward for each foot of descent in calm air, will make good only 11/1 against a 15 mph headwind.

Conversely, if you were upwind of the airport in a 2-22, you could glide at 25/1 with a 15 mph tailwind. The glide ratio figure which is quoted by the manufacturer is always based on flying in calm air, and it is up to the pilot to determine the wind's influence on glide ratio during each flight.

Wind Drift

Every skysportsman must develop an understanding of the effect of wind drift on his flight path. This is especially true for the sailplane pilot because he has no engine to help him correct for the effect of wind.

Think of wind as a mass of air moving horizontally over the ground. Your plane doesn't know when the air mass is moving, so it behaves exactly the same as it does in calm air. However, your flight path in relation to the earth below changes when the air mass you are flying in is going some place. This change is called "wind drift," and it may affect both your speed and direction of travel. When your ship is faced directly into the wind, your forward speed across the ground will be reduced by the amount of the wind velocity. When flying with the wind at your tail, your ground speed will be increased by the wind velocity. Tailwinds are handy when you are in a hurry to get some place.

Track is the imaginary line along the ground traced by a point vertically below your plane. When flying on an angle to the wind, you will have a sideways drift and you must remember to head your plane slightly more upwind than the track or course you wish to follow along the ground. This is called "crabbing."

In summary, try to remember that your ground speed and track are influenced by the wind. Flying upwind is slow, so be sure you don't get too far downwind of the airport or you may find yourself a candidate for the Clodbuster Award given by some soaring clubs for an unintended off-airport landing.

Right of Way

The official right-of-way order is ranked as follows: Balloons have the right-of-way over everybody. Next come sport parachutes, sailplanes, gyrocraft, and power planes.

I have my own way of looking at the matter of right-of-way, which I developed while watching a gaggle of a hundred or more gulls packed into a small thermal. Some were circling clockwise and some counterclockwise, but in spite of the congestion and swift converging speeds, you never see a collision between gulls. Each bird is constantly evading the others. None of them have any concept about right-of-way.

Whatever type of craft I am flying I have a certain degree of maneuverability. I keep ever watchful for other aircraft and use the maneuverability of my ship to keep safely out of everybody's way.

The Landing Patterns

Study the accompanying diagrams to become familiar with terminology for the parts of the landing pattern. Flying a consistent landing pattern is very important to your safety as a glider guider. Power planes can get away without flying a pattern because errors in the approach

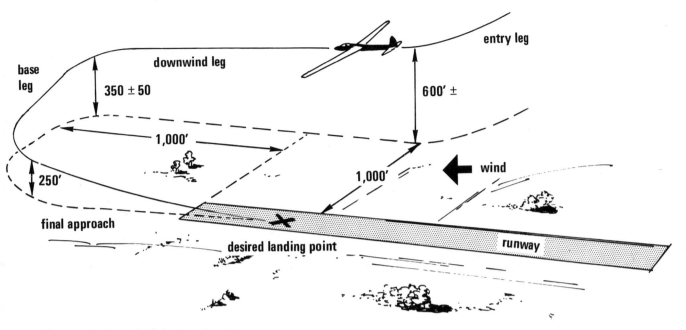

Figure 48. Normal Glider Landing Pattern

can always be corrected with the engine, and a missed approach can be done over. This is not the case with a glider. The final approach leg for a glider means exactly that, the final and *only* approach before the landing. It *has* to be right the first time. I am reminded of the alibi I've often heard from pilots who resist the idea of making a sport parachute jump. "Why should I practice something that has to be done right the first time?" they say.

I have found that practice is essential to good performance, whether it is for making a jump or landing a glider. Gliders have a generous amount of flexibility in their performance of a landing. You can land at any speed from 35 mph to 85 mph, or more. The runway also allows room for error. A glider will land nicely in 200 feet. The runway is usually 2,000 feet or longer.

Before you receive your glider pilot rating you will make not less than fifty landing approaches. The first twenty or thirty will be "dual," meaning performed with an instructor. During the dual landings you will develop judgment and awareness, which will allow you to practice more landings solo. By the time you have made sixty landings you should realize that the more practice you have, the better your landings will be. A pilot, in effect, practices landing for all his flying life. I have made over 10,000 practice landings, and I am still improving my judgment. A friend who was a pioneer in aviation

once said, "A perfect landing never happens, but some are just better than others."

As you approach the field for a landing try to determine the landing direction before you get down to pattern altitude. Landings and take-offs are made into the wind, so the wind sock and/or airport traffic will tell you which way to make your approach. Tap the altimeter frequently to be sure you are getting an accurate reading. Altimeters frequently lag 100 feet or more. Scan the area for other planes. Start an entry leg to the pattern at 700 or 800 feet high to allow your arrival at a point abeam the runway 600 feet above it and about 1,000 feet away. This is the final decision point for determining your direction of landing. Watch for other planes entering the pattern. Turn with a medium bank (20° or 30°) onto the downwind leg and fly a track parallel to the runway. Fly the pattern at least 10 mph above normal cruise speed. Fifty miles per hour is a good pattern speed for a 2-22 or 1-26. Keep scanning the sky above, below, and to the sides for other ships in the pattern.

If a wind is blowing on an angle to the runway (crosswind) you will need to crab to keep your track parallel to the runway. Test your spoilers to make sure they are working; give them a full pull of the handle. I discovered mine were jammed one time due to dirt in the rigging pulleys. I simply extended my pattern to compensate.

Figure 49. Sailplane Landing Technique

The point for turning onto base leg will vary according to wind velocity, but 1,000 feet past the end of the runway is about right for calm wind conditions. During this turn you should take another good look up and down and all around for other aircraft. Your altitude should be 300 to 400 feet. Your heading on base leg may involve a crab angle to compensate for wind. The runway and landing point are in plain view from base leg on, so your glide slope judgment will govern your use of spoilers. Half spoiler deflection is ideal during base leg and final approach.

When you begin your turn from base leg to final approach you should be 200 to 250 feet high and 1,000 feet from the end of the runway.

The best look at the runway comes after you are facing it on final. The glide slope you are following may or may not coincide with the one you desire. If you are sinking below the desired glide slope, reduce spoiler. Keep monitoring the airspeed indicator. It should be held constant throughout the pattern all the way to touchdown. If your glide path is carrying you above the intended one, pull the spoiler handle farther back.

The Touchdown

As a student you should ease the spoiler handle all the way forward, beginning when you are a few feet above the ground. The touchdown is

Figure 50. Pattern Adjustments

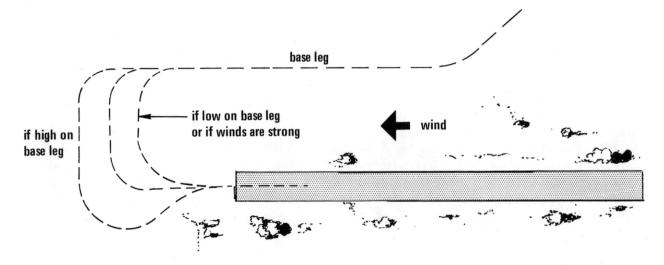

base leg

if low on base leg
or if winds are strong

wind

if high on
base leg

accomplished by flying down to the runway until the wheel is rolling on the ground, using the same airspeed which you had on final approach. After the wheel is firmly on the ground, keep the wings level and put on the brake by full spoiler application. As a more advanced sailplane pilot you will use less runway if you land by using spoilers and make a slight flare just before the wheel touches. This is not the same as the stall landing commonly used in power planes. Power plane pilots often ruin their first few glider landings because of the uncontrollable urge to flare and to hold the glider airborne until the airspeed dissipates and the ship settles to the ground.

The flare-type landing is fine for power planes, but it isn't safe for gliders. The glider has a very light wing loading, and a stall landing would present the wing to the wind at a very high angle of attack. If you then encounter a gust of headwind, your glider will be ballooned into the air perhaps often ten feet or more. As the gust subsides, you will be in stall with no altitude to recover. The subsequent crunch could damage you and/or the sailplane. The power plane's higher wing loading helps it plow through the wind gusts without ballooning. Also, the glider will fly slowly in an altitude which will let the tail wheel droop well below the main wheel. A flare or stall landing will cause the tail wheel to contact the ground first, and gliders aren't stressed to absorb landing shocks in the tail.

Additional Hints on Patterns and Landings

PATTERN ADJUSTMENTS

Spoilers provide an excellent method for adjusting the landing approach; however, they should not be counted upon to remedy every variable you might encounter. You should be prepared to alter the rectangular course of your landing pattern any time the need develops. Even though you strive to arrive abeam the runway at 600 feet, there will be times when you turn downwind and find yourself 100 or 200 feet high or low due to misjudgment, altimeter lag, lift or sink, or some combination of these.

After detecting an error, plan to fly a longer or shorter downwind leg to compensate. Don't attempt to fly a 360° turn to dissipate excess altitude. Turns of 360° require about 200 feet of altitude. They are fine outside the pattern. They are even permissible on the entry leg, but not on downwind, base, or final. The FAA has ample accident records to show the wisdom of this rule. It is much better to use spoilers and slips. You should be able to perform forward and side slips with confidence before you ever solo a glider.

It is also much better to be above normal altitude than below at any point in the pattern. It is easy to spend excess altitude by using full spoilers, slips, and extending the pattern. On a low approach you close spoilers and fly a short pattern, but you are flirting with danger when this happens.

A good glider approach is at or above the normal approach described where partial spoilers are used throughout the pattern. An approach where little or no spoiler is needed is a mistake and should not be repeated.

TOO HIGH ON FINAL

When you turn from base to final and find you are too high, don't panic. It's much better than being too low.

The slip is an excellent way to spend excess

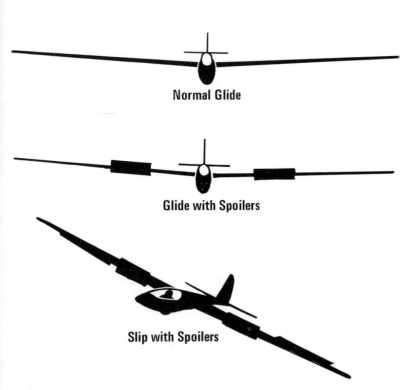

Normal Glide

Glide with Spoilers

Slip with Spoilers

Figure 51. Silhouette of Drag Area of Sailplane

altitude on final approach. It is accomplished by holding one wing down with stick pressure and applying opposite rudder pressure. For example, a slip to the left requires left stick which lowers the left wing, and right rudder which yaws the nose to the right. The plane now flies sideways and is much less efficient, so you come down faster. When used together with full spoilers, your glide slope can be reduced from 18/1 to 8/1. The final approach slip should be a forward slip and can be made with either wing down. Be sure you keep the airspeed constant, which means holding the nose fairly high during the slip to prevent an increase in speed. Both spoilers and slips are most effective when your airspeed is at or below 50 mph.

Don't touch down in a slip as you could catch a wingtip and put severe side loads on the wheel. Always stop the slip and line up with the runway when fifteen feet or more above the runway.

Strong Winds

A safe sailplane pilot will always fly a full pattern. There is a good reason for flying each leg of the pattern. The approach leg allows an opportunity to study the field for obstacles, determine wind conditions, and study the pat-

tern for traffic. The downwind leg gives the pilot a feel for the wind speed and direction. The lower your altitude, the more apparent is the wind drift. At 500 feet high on downwind leg you will perceive a strong tailwind by the rapid ground speed and will know to turn to base leg early.

When you perceive strong tailwinds or crosswinds on downwind leg, your plans for the rest of the approach should take shape immediately to account for these conditions. With a 25 mph tailwind on downwind leg you should start the turn to base as you come even with the end of the runway. Plan to land halfway down the runway. You will need a healthy crab angle of 20° or more on base, and I also recommend carrying an extra 10 mph of airspeed during the pattern when dealing with high winds. Sixty miles per hour is a reasonable speed on base and final. Use spoilers only after you are sure your glide slope will carry you to the runway.

Crosswinds

You deal with crosswinds on landing a sailplane in the same way as with a power plane. Lower the upwind wing and keep the fusilage in line with your final approach path to the runway.

With winds from the right, lower the right wing and hold left rudder. This is a crossed-control condition called a "slip," and if you have the proper bank angle to match the wind, you will slip sideways against the wind and track directly toward the runway centerline. If you're still drifting left, you need to lower the right wing still further.

Don't allow the wing to get too close to the ground. When approaching the touchdown, reduce the slip so that the main wheel touches first. Use rudder to keep from weathervaning, and full brakes and nose skid to make the landing roll as short as possible. A glider is especially vulnerable to ground looping because of the large tail surfaces.

You should not even attempt a crosswind landing with a glider when the crosswind component is above 12 or 15 mph. It would be safer to choose another landing spot directed into the wind.

Downwind Landing

The prudent pilot who is aware of wind and his altitude and distance from the airport will never be forced to make a downwind landing. If you *are* somehow forced into one, however, keep a close monitor on the airspeed during final. An illusion is created for you by the rapid ground speed on landing approach. You may think you have plenty of airspeed when it is actually falling dangerously low. Even with spoilers your glide slope will be quite flat while landing downwind, so make an effort to cross the runway threshold low. Get the wheel on the ground as soon as possible and use brakes and nose skid to decelerate. The control surfaces will lose effectiveness while you are still coasting. You may be able to avoid a ground loop if you can keep the wings level and stop as short as possible.

Runway Obstacles

Throughout the pattern you should verify that your landing area is clear. It is surprising how many things can get in the way of a landing airplane. The sailplane makes a quiet approach, so spectators, children, livestock, vehicles, etc., are even more likely to move into your way.

It is most desirable to do your flying from a gliderport which has spectator control fences, ropes, or barricades. Even so, you should not relax your vigilance.

Be prepared to take evasive action if your landing area is occupied or threatened as you approach. Land long, land short, divert to another runway or taxiway, or land off the runway, do anything rather than bore in unrelentingly because you have the right of way. There is just one thing you can't do when landing a glider, and that is to make a "go around," which means to abandon the landing and make another trip around the pattern.

Spot Landings

To pass your flight check for a glider rating you will have to demonstrate ability to set a glider down close to a predetermined landing point. Some gliderports have three white lines 100 feet apart across the runway in the landing area. During all your landings you should attempt to land on or just past the first line.

If your runway doesn't have landing lines, pick out a marker of your own and use it for a landing spot. Most of your approaches will be from the same side of the field. When you are feeling confident in your spot landings, try a few with the landing pattern flown on the opposite side of the field. You should be able to make consistent spot landings with pattern turns in either direction.

Turbulent Air Towing

Very little glider training is done when the air is severely turbulent. However, some of the best soaring conditions occur when the air is gusty and tumbling along like white water in a raging river.

The experienced sailplane pilot who wants a launch during gusty and turbulent wind conditions may have to undergo a tow, which is demanding, to say the least. Air turbulence will work continuously against both tow plane and glider to force each of them out of normal position. The tow becomes a period where you must concentrate very hard and make continuous corrections with the stick and rudder. Under severe turbulence don't try to keep the meatball perfectly centered. If you allow yourself a little latitude, remaining, for example, within a twenty-foot cone, you will work less hard and may arrive at release altitude without excessive tenseness, fatigue, and perspiration.

One important point is to have your seat belt and shoulder harness tight, and secure all loose objects in the sailplane. Be certain that your seating position will allow you full command of all the controls.

The opportunity may present itself by choice or circumstance for you to make a landing at an unfamiliar site. The site may not be an airport, either. If possible, choose a large field that is level, smooth, and clear of obstructions. These are not always available, and a compromise is sometimes called for.

Please try not to compromise to the degree of an acquaintance who once landed his LK-model sailplane safely on a widing mountain road amid the tall Douglas fir trees near Mt. Rainier. If you are out of range of your airport, you should be ever watchful for suitable landing fields. You can search for upcurrents and landing fields while above 1,000 feet. You will cover much more territory if you glide downwind. When you drop to 1,000 feet, choose the best field available and don't change your mind. Your choice should be determined by safety to yourself and ship first, and personal convenience, such as roads, houses, and telephones, second. By virtue of its slow landing speed, low center of gravity, and rugged construction, a sailplane may be safely landed on a field which could demolish a power plane.

Your glider is not indestructible, however. So please bear the following safety tips in mind when evaluating a field for landing:

1. Determine wind direction from smoke, flags, trees, or ripples on water, and pick a field with an obstruction-free 1,000 feet and parallel to the wind.
2. Harvested fields are best, cultivated fields may be very soft. Pastures may have humps, rocks, and bothersome livestock. Avoid areas downwind of hills.
3. Land parallel to furrows, uphill, and into the wind. It is better to land uphill even with a tailwind.
4. Fly a full pattern with downwind, base, and final approach. Study field during pattern and pick landing spot to avoid wires, trees, fences, and ditches.
5. Don't watch altimeter because you don't know field elevation. Monitor your airspeed instrument only, and keep all other visual attentions outside the cockpit.

6. Plan the final approach so that spoiler and/ or slip is needed. It is better to overshoot because you would have something less than flying speed during an overshoot.
7. Use brakes and nose skid to stop short.

Working Lift

After you have made some solo flights and feel confident in your pattern and landing judgment, you will undoubtedly want to try working some lift, or upcurrents of the air.

Before your flight, find out what you can about the lift conditions prevailing. Other pilots who have already been up and have come back may be able to tell you where the lift is or where it isn't. Sailplanes circling are a good updraft indicator, as are soaring birds. The tow pilot is an excellent source of tips on updrafts, but you may not be able to corner him for a discussion if his tow schedule is heavy. Usually you can get a short message to him via the ground helper, or line boy, such as "Tow me to the lift." He will then do his best to take you to an altitude and location where updrafts are most likely.

During the tow you can monitor your variometer and may discover lift areas to which you could return after release. Don't release too early. I have seen so many eager glider guiders pull their release at the first or second good bump encountered during tow only to find the updraft too small or weak to carry them aloft. This is good for the tow-plane operator's business because he will get to make a second tow when one may have done, if the glider pilot had held on until 2,000 or 3,000 feet high.

Working updrafts successfully requires a lot of practice, just as landing does. Don't be too disappointed at your failures to remain aloft during your first attempts without an instructor to help you. I can help you with an understanding of what the types of lift are, but experience is the best teacher when it comes to sustaining your glider flight.

If you could see updrafts, soaring would be easy, but air looks the same whether it is stationary or in motion. Sometimes the atmosphere will give a clue in the form of a special cloud or a tiny tornado of dust, called a "dust devil," which you can interpret as a sign of lift.

The following discussion will help you to recognize the various types of lift.

Ridge Lift

Ridge lift occurs when wind is deflected upward when it meets a hill, bluff, ridge, or mountain. It is ridge lift that gulls use to soar along bluffs. It was ridge lift that the pioneers of gliding used in the 1920's when they launched their flimsy primary gliders into the wind from a hilltop. This is also called "slope soaring."

The hill should have at least an 800- to 1,000-foot rise if it is going to be used for soaring. The less trees the better as they interfere with the windflow. You will be most likely to soar on a ridge if the wind is fifteen miles per hour or greater and striking the ridge at or close to a 90° angle.

It is best if the tow plane can tow you directly into ridge lift before you release. If you release on the downwind side, you will very likely never make it to the lift area. The sink or downdraft on the lee side of the hill will draw you down at a surprising rate.

Bush and tree foliage rippling on a ridge will help you determine the direction and speed of the wind. This sometimes works at a considerable distance. During the summer I can tell from the Skyport if the 3,000-foot-high ridge,

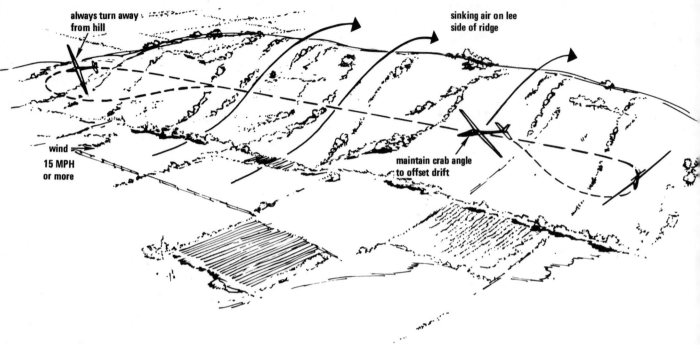

Figure 52. Ridge Lift

five miles away, is working. The upslope wind makes the alder and maple leaves turn over, and the undersides have a silvery shimmer which is visible for miles.

To work the ridge lift, simply tack back and forth on the upwind side of the hill. Your crab angle into the wind should relate to the wind velocity. The stronger the wind, the more directly you should fly against it. After you climb to a comfortable altitude, try to define the limits of the lift by flying along the slope each way and also penetrating into the wind away from the slope. Usually there will be a spot where lift is stronger, and it is there that you can reach your highest altitude. Your height potential is rarely more than 500 to 800 feet above the peak of the ridge unless you encounter an assist from another type of lift.

Always turn away from the slope when working ridge lift. A downwind turn into the hill could spell disaster. Don't fly downwind of the peak or you may not get back across it.

If the air is moist, clouds may condense on or above a ridge. Take care not to climb into these clouds if they develop.

Very stable air with high humidity may form a cap cloud on the ridge. Your height potential may be greater when ridge soaring under these conditions. Keep upwind of the lacy fingers of the cap cloud and you may be able to climb well above it.

Wave Lift

A fascinating condition for soaring exists when a ridge or mountain obstructs a certain kind of air mass. If the air mass is stable and flowing about 90° to the slope, and speed increases with altitude, then the conditions for wave development exist. Ridge lift will be on the upwind side of the hill, sink on the lee side, but just downwind of the sink will occur another lift area which may extend far above the ridge top. I have soared above 10,000 feet in the wave stimulated by a hill only 1,500 feet high.

Wave lift off the Sierras is responsible for the world sailplane altitude record of over 46,000 feet. This type of flight requires high altitude indoctrination, oxygen equipment, special clothing, and a supplementary heat source for hands and feet. However, some great experiences in wave flying are awaiting the novices who fly in an area of lower mountains.

If you attempt a tow into a wave, remember that upwind of the wave lift is sink and downwind may lurk another unpleasant experience called "rotor area." The rotor area is characterized by violently tumbling air which can be very uncomfortable to fly in.

Fly the wave lift similar to ridge lift by tacking back and forth with all turns into the wind and with a crab angle to match wind velocity.

Cloud development in the wave area will de-

Figure 53. Mt. Rainier

MT. RAINIER WAVE

Two types of lift are illustrated here. Looking to the east we find a stable north wind flowing across Mt. Rainier. An area of ridge lift is found on the windward side of the mountain. A sailplane could fly here beneath the cap cloud. However, downwind of the peak occurs a zone of stronger lift as a wave-like rhythm is established in the wind flow from passing over the peak.

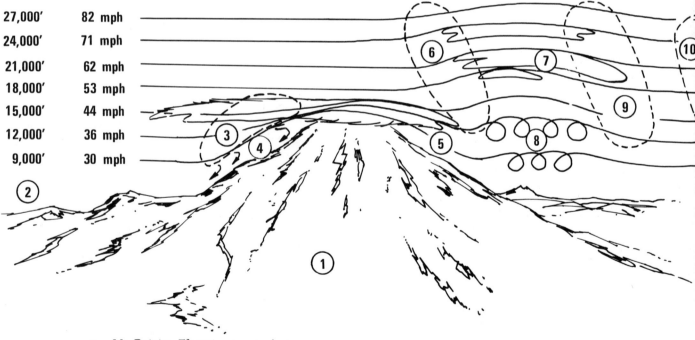

1. Mt. Rainier. Elevation 14,200 feet.
2. Stable north wind with velocity increasing with altitude.
3. Zone of rdige lift in upslope flow.
4. Sometimes strong downcurrents occur next to slope.
5. Strong downflow or sink on lee side of peak.
6. Zone of wave lift may extend to three times the altitude of the peak. Note lift zone tilts in an upwind direction.
7. Decks or layers of lenticular clouds.
8. Rotor, area of severe turbulence, may contain cumulus-like clouds.
9. Zone of sinking air on downwind side of wave.
10. Zone of secondary wave lift, usually less strong than the primary wave.

pend on the humidity and temperature in the air. Often a layer of the atmosphere will have sufficient moisture to condense into a lenticular cloud, so named because of the curved cross section of the cloud. These clouds generally remain stationary over the ground and do not necessarily define the top of the wave. Sometimes several layers or "decks" of lenticulars will occur in a wave, and the sailplane pilot may climb above all of them.

The rotor area is sometimes apparent by the wispy fragments of clouds called "fracto cumulus" that form and dissipate rapidly. When humidity is higher, this cumulus will become more dense and is then called a "roll cloud."

Thermal Lift

Thermal lift is probably more responsible for keeping sailplanes aloft than any other kind of lift. You will have a better chance of successfully finding and working thermal lift if you understand what makes it develop. Following is a quick lesson on meteorology concerning thermals.

Air is "stable" when it tries to remain stratified, or in layers. Air normally decreases in temperature at higher altitudes. The stability of an air mass is determined by how its temperature changes at various altitudes. If you measured the temperature of stable air at various altitudes, you would find a slow rate of temperature drop. Indeed, in extremely stable conditions a layer of warm air will overlie cooler air. This is called an "inversion." Unstable air always has cooler air overlying warmer air. The cooler the overlying air in relation to that below, the more unstable it is.

In unstable air the sun's radiant energy will warm an area of ground, which in turn warms the adjoining air. When this air becomes warmer and less dense, it will tend to drift upward like a bubble. It is cooling as it rises, of course, but so is the air around it. The bubble will continue to drift upward as long as it remains warmer than the surrounding air through which it is passing.

Eventually an altitude is reached where the bubble is no longer warmer than the surrounding air, and that is where the upward motion stops. The trip from ground to inversion layer may be only a few hundred feet, or it may ascend to 20,000 feet.

Thermals are sometimes topped with a cumulus cloud. The ascending bubble is cooling as it rises, and since cooler air will hold less moisture there is a good chance of the thermal reaching the condensation level before reaching the inversion layer. When this happens a cumulus cloud will develop. If the inverson layer is reached first, no cu will form. This is called a "dry thermal."

Puffy white cu's, which often pattern the spring and summer sky, are strong stimuli to the glider enthusiast because he knows that beneath each cloud lies an upcurrent which could sustain him aloft.

When the moisture begins to condense in a thermal, heat is released to the air, which gives it a further upward bouyancy. This is why lift is often found to be strongest near the base of the cumulus clouds. When flying near the base of well-developed cumulus, it is sometimes necesssary to apply full spoiler to keep from being lofted right into the cloud by the powerful upcurrents.

Under ideal thermal conditions the convection, or heat transfer from ground to air, occurs rapidly enough to form a continuous column of rising air instead of just a periodic bubble. In

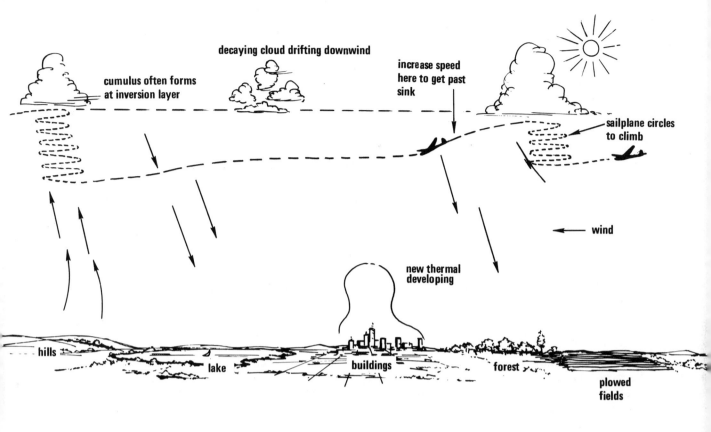

Figure 54. Thermal Soaring

dry or dusty areas the upcurrent may be strong enough to form a tiny tornado called a "dust devil." The cu's and dust devils are the only atmospheric evidence that you can see of thermals existing.

Some types of ground are more likely to spawn thermals. Plowed ground, bare sand or dirt, rocky ground, rooftops of buildings, and streets are all good thermal generators. Lakes and ponds, green fields, forests, and shadowed and wet areas are unlikely to produce thermals.

The thermals will sometimes have a core or center which is spiraling as it rises. More commonly, there will be no spiral or circular action in the thermal, and it will be simply a cylinder of ascending air which will be bent in a downwind direction.

A lot of complicated techniques on centering and climbing in a thermal have been described. I could never apply these techniques effectively, and finally developed my own.

When thermal searching, you may pass through many "bumps" which will cause the green pellet to bounce up momentarily. It is best to ignore such brief climb indication on your variometer

and continue searching until you find the green pellet up for four or five seconds. Begin a tight circle with 45° bank in either direction. Monitor the airspeed and variometer as you make the first 360° turn. Keep an eye outside, though, and you will no doubt find by the completion of the first 360° turn that you were climbing during part of the circle (green pellet up) and sinking during part (red pellet up). You should notice which segment of your circle was the lift segment. To climb you want the circular pattern of your flight to lie within the rising column of air. You should adjust your circles to move toward the lift.

You make your adjustments by altering the angle of bank. The steeper your bank, the smaller the radius of your turn. If you simply fly a steeper bank while on the sink side and a shallower bank on the lift side, you should be showing steady lift all the way around by the third circle.

Be careful to hold your airspeed as steady as possible because inadvertent pitching up of the nose will make the green pellet rise just as though you were in lift. A climb indication which

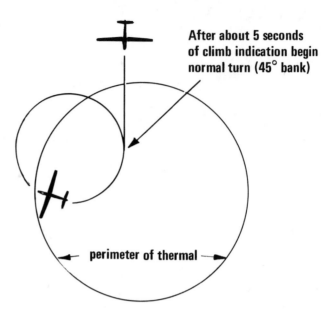

After about 5 seconds of climb indication begin normal turn (45° bank)

perimeter of thermal

FIRST CIRCLE

Figure 55. Centering a Thermal

results from pulling back on the stick is called a "stick thermal," but it will gain you altitude only by sacrificing airspeed. Proper airspeed will depend upon type of sailplane, size and strength of lift, and angle of your bank. Forty miles per hour is a comfortable speed in a 1-26 with bank angles of 45° or less. For really steep turns, you'll need forty-five miles per hour to prevent buffeting and partial stalls.

Don't expect a smooth ride when working thermal lift. The rising air invariably has turbulent areas, especially near the edge of the thermal. However, you soon grow to like the bouncing around and feel of the air nibbling at your controls. It gives a sense of aliveness to the air, which most soaring pilots find stimulating.

Commonly the beginner doesn't bank steeply enough to remain in the thermal. Forty-five degress is a good angle, and sometimes 60° is called for, especially when working small thermals at lower altitudes. The dizziness which you might encounter when first circling in thermals will pass as you gain experience.

Clouds

I have already explained that cumulus clouds often cap thermals. If the wind is blowing, the thermal source will not be vertically below the cu, but will lie somewhere upwind. The cu's often drift away from the thermal which promptly builds up a new cloud. The lift may remain good under the old cloud even without the thermal feeding it. The base of the cloud is called the "condensation level," which is where vaporized moisture condenses, or returns to tiny driplets. During condensation, heat is released to the surrounding air. This is called "heat of condensation" and this heated air may be responsible for strong updrafts near the cloud base. If you see cumulus clouds lined up for miles in a row, you are witness to the above phenomenon, which is called a "cloud street."

Flying downwind under a cloud street is a very successful way to travel cross country in a glider. Remember, though, it is not so easy to return upwind. I once cruised easily in strong lift down a cloud street to Redmond, twelve miles north of the Skyport. When I reached the end and turned for home, I found the clouds dissipating, and lift had fizzled out. I searched everywhere within range and finally settled to 800 feet high directly over the town. The city rooftops were bubbling off with an occasional tickle of lift which I worked with feverish concentration. The only landing site was a golf course which was heavily populated on this sunny Sunday afternoon. My hopes would build as the altimeter crept to 1,200 feet. Three minutes later I was back at 800 feet. I wondered how I could let those people on the golf course know I was coming. I had no horn to honk, and couldn't rev the motor. I kept the glider at minimum sink airspeed and flew with the most

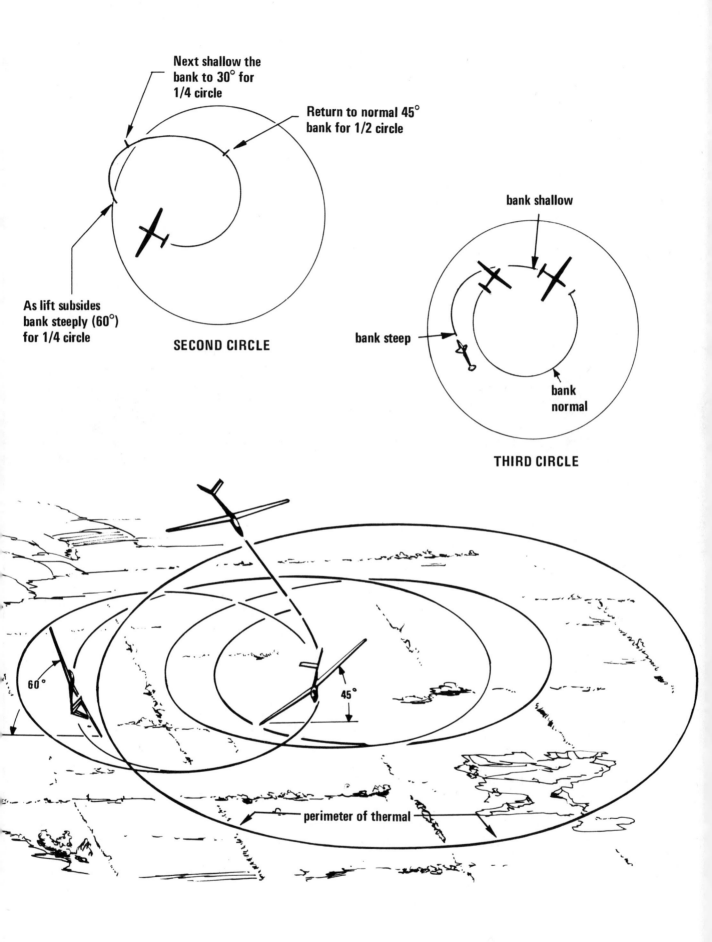

Next shallow the bank to 30° for 1/4 circle

Return to normal 45° bank for 1/2 circle

As lift subsides bank steeply (60°) for 1/4 circle

SECOND CIRCLE

bank shallow

bank steep

bank normal

THIRD CIRCLE

60°

45°

perimeter of thermal

Figure 56. Cumulus Cloud Street

perfect coordination possible with fingertips on the stick and toes tenderly touching the rudder pedals.

After dangling between 800 and 1,200 feet above the rooftops for thirty-five minutes, a gull came into view. It was circling a little east of me, climbing upward without flapping. If I ever received a message from heaven, it was surely that gull. I swooped into a circular pattern just below the gull's, and six minutes later was at 5,000 feet.

Circling birds are a good indication of up-drafts; hawks, vultures, eagles, gulls, and terns all utilize lift to carry them aloft. Don't expect to climb every thermal that a bird is working. They have a slower minimum sink rate and can turn in much smaller circles than a glider.

The direction you circle is optional. The good soaring pilot will be smooth and comfortable in either right or left circles. You should practice both ways, particularly the direction which feels most awkward or uncoordinated.

If you enter a thermal where other sailplanes are circling, you should all circle in the same direction as the first sailplane in the lift.

One other tip on direction of circles. When thermals are small and very concentrated, you may find one wing or the other bumping up as you pass by the thermal. You may turn into the lift if you push that wing down and begin a bank immediately. This technique will not work if thermals are of a larger diameter because turbulence and sink areas surround the uprising air. In this case you should turn toward the wing that drops.

Other Types of Soarable Lift

Wave, ridge, and thermal lift may be the most frequently used; however, many other atmospheric circumstances may cause air to go up and carry sailplanes with it.

CONVERGENCE OR SHEAR LIFT

When two masses of moving air come together there is often an upward surge at the meeting area. Mild convergence conditions can afford good soaring, but watch out for strong frontal situations. The cold front is an extreme example of convergence which can cause lift that is too strong. A cold air mass underrunning a warmer mass will lift it upward, and strong thermals, squalls, and thunderstorms often develop in the convergence area. This is no place for a novice pilot in a sailplane.

SEA BREEZE FRONT

This is also a type of convergence lift which is also sometimes called "shear lift." Seacoast areas often develop an onshore airflow during the day. Where this wind meets the hazy, stagnant, flat-land air mass, an upwelling occurs often defined by cumulus clouds and a conspicuous break in the haze. To work a seabreeze front, fly at minimum sink airspeed parallel with the frontal line.

OROGRAPHIC LIFT

Air which is sufficiently unstable will often continue an upward course if given any manner of boost or start from below. Besides creating ridge lift a hill can stimulate orographic lift by providing the air with an initial upward deflection. Flying technique is similar to thermal flying except that the lift area is usually large, and steep banks are not required. Chances are that orographic lift is responsible if you see a hill topped with billowing cumulous clouds on a sunless day.

It is impossible to define and predict all kinds of lift. The more you soar, the more you will realize that lift is where you find it, even though you can't always explain it. I have had many satisfying hours of soaring on days when the sky gave no hint of lift. When in doubt, take a tow anyway. You may be pleasantly surprised and unexpectedly sustain your flight.

ADVANCED SAILPLANE EXPERIENCES: CROSS-COUNTRY SOARING

You should have at least fifty hours of sailplane experience before attempting cross-country flight. You should have a good deal of experience in map reading and be able to determine your position from charts. You should have the ability to judge wind and weather conditions while aloft. Many cross-country flights require a non-airport landing, so your landing judgment must be consistently good.

A cross-country flight will usually be a one-way voyage like a balloon flight, and seldom does the pilot know where his ultimate landing will be. The return trip is usually made by automobile with the glider disassembled and riding a trailer behind. This return part of the trip is called a "retrieve," and you need at least one devoted helper to act as your retrieve crew to drive your car and trailer and meet you at the landing site. If your car and glider are both equipped with VHF radios, you can keep your crew informed of your position and they can follow below. Often the sailplane will outdistance the crew, or fly a route which has no roads, and the crew will lose radio contact with the glider. When this happens you resort to the old reliable telephone method. Atfer landing, the pilot finds a phone and calls a pre-arranged number and leaves words of his landing location. The crew calls the same number periodically, and eventually learns their destination.

Soaring Awards

The Soaring Society of America is affiliated with the Fédération Aéronautique Internationale and issues achievement badges recognized the world over. The Silver C Badge, for example, is given when the soaring pilot has completed and verified three tasks consisting of a five-hour endurance flight, a 3,281-foot altitude gain (above release point), and a 31.1-mile cross-country flight. The verification of these tasks is no simple matter of your testifying that you completed the task. Documents must be submitted, including barograph records and witness statements. It may take years to qualify for the Gold Badge and Diamond awards, but these awards represent truly worthy soaring achievements, and the holders wear them proudly.

Soaring Society of America

The principal magazine on the subject in this country is *Soaring,* published monthly by the Soaring Society of America. It carries excellent coverage of all that is new in the sport. The contest writeups are excellent, and the first-person stories of notable soaring flights are always interesting and educational. New equipment is pictured and described, sometimes even before the designs are in production. The classified section of the magazine is valuable to the person interested in buying a sailplane or kit. Besides the magazine, the SSA publishes *The American Soaring Handbook* in ten volumes, each one a comprehensive treatment of the subject and priced at $1 each. Titles are:

1. History of American Soaring
2. Training
3. Ground Launch
4. Airplane Tow
5. Meteorology
6. Cross Country and Wave Soaring
7. Instruments and Oxygen
8. Radio Rope and Wire
9. Aerodynamics
10. Maintenance and Repair

Soaring Information Kit

An information kit from SSA includes the following items:

1. Sample copy of SSA's monthly *Soaring* magazine.
2. "Soaring in America," a 16-page illustrated booklet.
3. "Soaring . . . the SSA . . . and YOU!" pamphlet.
4. List of soaring clubs in your area.
5. List of commerical soaring schools in your area.
6. List of books on soaring that are available.
7. Lists of sailplanes available, new and used.
8. List of soaring merchandise available from SSA.
9. List of SSA membership benefits.
10. SSA membership application form.

Items 3, 4, 5, 6, 8, 9, and 10 are available free of charge, or the entire kit will be sent for just $1. Inquiries to SSA for membership ($13 per year), which includes a subscription to "Soaring", or information kit, should be addressed to: Soaring Society of America, P.O. Box 66071-A, Los Angeles, California 90066.

Foreign Publications

Three fine foreign publications on the sport are available in English.

Sailplane and Gliding, $3.50 per year (6 issues), British Gliding Association, 75 Victoria St., London S.W.I.

Australian Gliding, $4.25 per year (12 issues), Gliding Federation of Australia, Box 1650M, GPO Adelaide, South Australia, Australia.

Gliding Kiwi, $3.50 per year (6 issues), New Zealand Gliding Association, Box 487, Rauranga, New Zealand.

Soaring Club Publications

Aloha Skysurfer (Hawaii Soaring Club and Honolulu Skysurfers, Inc.), c/o Thomas Winkler, Box 2776, Honolulu, Hawaii 96803.

Chicagoland Glider Council Newsletter (Chicagoland Glider Council), c/o Dale May, c/o G. May Int'l. Co., 111 S. Washington Ave., Park Ridge, Illinois 60068.

Spirals (Texas Soaring Association, Inc.), c/o G. Coder, 1514 Tulip Drive, Arlington, Texas 76010.

SSD Newsletter (Soaring Society of Dayton, Inc., Box 581, Dayton, Ohio 45419), c/o Judy Payne, 2317 Adrian Court, Dayton, Ohio 45439.

The Thermal (Southern California Soaring Association), c/o Ted Sharp, 4624 Placidia Ave., North Hollywood, California 91602.

Towline (Seattle Glider Council, Inc.), c/o Marion Barritt, 2212 77th Ave. SE, Mercer Island, Washington 98040.

Towline (Oak Brook Soaring Club), c/o Barbara White, 333 E. High St., Mundelein, Illinois 60060.

Towline (Wabash Valley Soaring Association), c/o Wallace Brown, Route 2, Lawrenceville, Illinois 62439.

West Wind (Pacific Soaring Council, Inc.), c/o Pat Page, 393 Cronin Drive, Santa Clara, California 95051.

Wind and Wings (Associated Glider Clubs of Southern California, Ltd.), c/o Mary Wemple, 1201 Archer St., San Diego, California 92109.

Zero Sink (Orange County Soaring Association, Inc.), c/o Doug Lamont, 1403 N. Towner Ave., Santa Ana, California 92706.

For a current and complete list of newsletters, write to the Soaring Society of America and ask for their item #57 (list of soaring publications and their editors).

SOARING GLOSSARY

To avoid duplication the terms appearing in the soaring glossary are only those pertaining to this sky sport. Many flight terms are also common to power plane flight and will appear in the power plane glossary.

AERO TOW—A method of starting a glider on a flight by towing it aloft with a power plane.

AUTO TOW—A method of starting a glider on a flight by towing it aloft with an automobile and a long line or cable.

BAROGRAPH—An instrument which records a graph or trace of a plane's altitude during flight.

CLOUD BASE—Cumulus clouds have flat bottoms called "cloud base."

CLOUD STREET—Cumulus clouds sometimes occur in a row called a "cloud street."

CUMULUS CLOUDS—or simply CU's, are white and puffy or billowing on top and flat and gray below. They often indicate the presence of thermal updrafts.

DIVE BRAKES—Sometimes found on high-performance gliders, dive brakes are spoilers which are so efficient that they will prevent the glider from diving faster than the plane's maximum permissible air speed.

GLIDER—A fixed-wing aircraft without a motor, used for recreational and competitive flying.

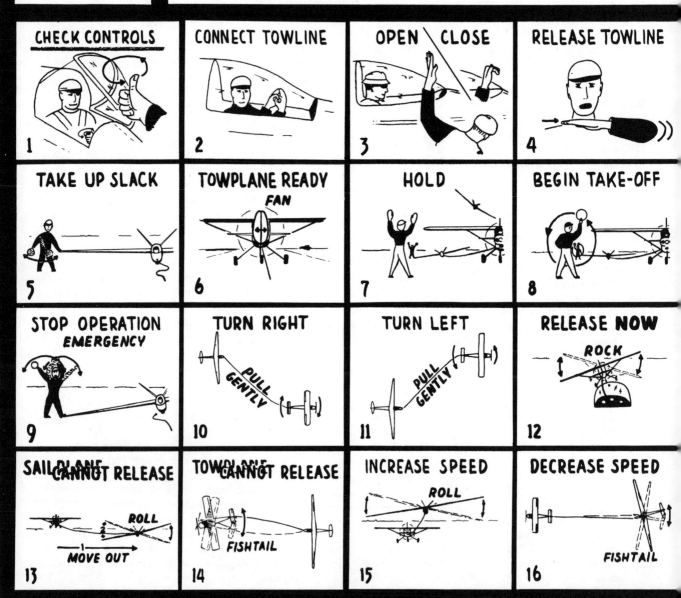

Figure 57.

GLIDE RATIO—Also called Lift/Drag Ratio, or simply L/D. This is a figure representing a glider's efficiency which depicts the plane's forward travel in ratio or relation to the vertical or descent travel.

GLIDESLOPE—The actual descending path of a glider in flight. It will be identical to the glider's glide ratio only in calm air when standard atmospheric conditions prevail.

HEAT OF CONDENSATION—When moisture begins to condense in the ascending air of a thermal, heat is released to the surrounding air. This is called "heat of condensation" and it gives the air further upward bouyancy.

HIGH TOW—During aero towing the glider is in high tow position when it is flown above the prop wash of the tow plane.

INVERSION LAYER—The altitude level where the air ceases to decrease in temperature.

LAUNCH—Any method of starting a glider on a flight. The three most common modes of launching are airplane, auto, and winch.

L/D—Lift/Drag ratio. See Glide Ratio.

LENTICULAR CLOUDS—Lens-shaped clouds, which often occur in a wave.

LIFT—Any upward moving air current usable to sustain a glider aloft. Also the force exerted on the wing which allows it to fly.

LOW TOW—During aero tow, when the glider is flown below the prop wash of the tow plane.

MAXIMUM L/D—Same as Glide Ratio.

MAXIMUM L/D AIRSPEED—This is the airspeed at which a glider achieves its best glide ratio.

MINIMUM SINK AIRSPEED—Every glider has a certain airspeed at which it will lose altitude most slowly. It is usually just above stall speed.

MINIMUM SINK RATE—This is a figure which helps to describe a glider's efficiency. It is usually given in feet per second.

RETRIEVE—When a glider lands away from its take-off point, its return trip, usually by car and trailer, is called a "retrieve."

RIDGE LIFT—The upcurrent which results when wind blows up the slope of a hill, cliff, or mountain.

ROTOR—The area of tumbling, turbulent air which lies downwind from a hill and beneath a standing wave.

SAILPLANE—Same as Glider.

SINK—A downward moving air current.

SPOILER—The movable slat which projects above and sometimes also below a wing. It is controlled from the cockpit and is used to increase the glider's rate of descent.

STABLE AIR—Usually refers to a mass of air which tends to remain stratified and resists vertical movement and thermal development.

STICK THERMAL—When a pilot applies back pressure to the control stick, a climb indication will show on the variometer. Sometimes this is misinterpreted as a thermal.

THERMAL—An upcurrent of air which results from contact with sun-warmed ground.

TOWLINE—Commonly a ¼-inch plastic or nylon line 160 feet long with a 2" diameter steel ring at each end. It is used to link the glider to the tow plane.

TOW PLANE—Usually a single-engine plane with a release hook at the tail. Used to aero tow gliders.

UNSTABLE AIR—An air mass in which vertical movement such as thermals occurs easily.

VARIOMETER—An instrument used in gliders to show very slight changes in altitude.

WAVE—Also called "mountain wave" and "standing wave." A wind phenomenon which occurs when stable air blows across a ridge or mountain and then develops consecutive upward and downward movements in wave fashion.

WINCH—A large engine-driven windlass which holds 2,000 feet or more of cable and is used to launch gliders.

ZERO SINK—When a glider is flying in air which is rising just fast enough to offset the glider's minimum descent rate so that its altitude remains constant, it is flying in zero sink.

3 BALLOON DRAFT

Flying of any type is a challenge, but probably the mode of flight which offers the greatest challenge of all is ballooning. The balloon pilot is really little more than a passenger suspended beneath a vehicle ten times as big as he is by weight, and 5,000 times as big by volume. I say he is a passenger because even by exercising good judgment in the use of all the controls at his disposal the balloon pilot still has only a marginal bit of vertical control and no horizontal control of the flight path at all.

It would seem that only an idiot would place himself aloft in a vehicle so awkward to fly and so vulnerable to damage. However, a close acquaintance with many leading balloonists revealed very stable and knowledgable people who are most enthusiastic about the pursuit of their sky sport.

Most balloonists today are men in their twenties and thirties. About half of them have experience in one or more other flying sports such as airplanes, gliders, or parachutes.

As with gliding, a balloonist may become licensed without passing an FAA medical exam and anyone over fourteen years of age can obtain a student permit for solo flight. Sixteen is the minimum age for a hot-air balloon rating which will permit carrying passengers.

Persons with physical handicaps could still qualify for balloon flying because it requires only one hand to manipulate the burner controls on a balloon.

Quite a bit of physical work is required for operating a balloon, which may account for the lack of female balloon pilots. However, many ladies fill responsible support-crew positions, and a few have piloting experience.

At this time there are few training schools operating where you can go to learn balloon flying. A list appears at the end of this chapter. You could get some valuable experience by serving on the ground crew for a balloonist, but to be captain during a free ascent you may have to take the same bold steps I did and purchase a complete ship.

The cost of balloons is about the same as airplanes: $2,000 to $3,000 for a single-place balloon, $3,000 to $4,000 for a two-man, and $4,500 to $6,000 for a four-passenger size.

This initial investment is rather staggering; however, there are some compensating circumstances that help encourage ownership. Storage of a balloon is almost as easy as a parachute. You don't need hangar space because the envelope can be packed into a bundle the size of a sailor's sea bag, and most gondolas or baskets will fit into a station wagon. Fuel costs for flying are nominal. Propane is furnished free to some balloonists by liquefied petroleum companies who are compensated by the advertising value of displaying their emblem on the balloon's propane tanks. I have never been able to promote this angle in my area, but wholesale propane is only twenty cents per gallon. A fifteen-gallon fueling is only $3, which is enough for two hours of free flight.

Maintenance is a very real cost consideration for the would-be balloonist. The burner, basket, and controls are quite trouble-free, but that gigantic nylon envelope is rather vulnerable if improperly handled. My very first flight resulted in a $185 repair bill from the manufacturer. It takes almost a half-mile of seams to assemble a balloon from the large triangular sections called "gores." I succeeded in disassembling quite a

Figure 58. Semco 93083 Dumping Balloon.
The author flying his Semco dumping balloon.
Placed second in the 1965 National Balloon
Championships at Reno, Nevada.

Figure 59. MEROPE Balloon.
Don Kirsten aloft in his blue, yellow, and white Piccard balloon. Notice the load plate/burner assembly above the basket is not rigidly mounted, but is suspended by cables between basket and balloon.

Figure 60. Instruments.
Instrumentation is extremely simple on a balloon. I carry only an altimeter and vertical speed indicator (common aircraft rate of climb indicator) mounted to the frame by rubber shock cord. This protects the gauges from jarring due to the jolts of a rough landing. A pyrometer (not shown) tells the internal temperature near the top of the balloon.

number of these seams by simply neglecting to open the rip seam before proceeding with the deflation after a flight. This was a dumping balloon, which is deflated by releasing the envelope from the gondola. A static line, or crown line, attached to the gondola on one end, and the balloon apex on the other, causes the balloon to roll over as it drifts upward. When it becomes inverted, the warm air dumps out the open mouth. With the rip seam closed the mouth was too restricted an opening, and the hot air tore through the balloon itself. This was just one of the many ways I have discovered you can convert a beautiful, colorful, round sphere of a balloon envelope into a shredded, lifeless heap on the ground.

If your balloon is not equipped with instruments, you may spend over $100 on an altimeter, a variometer, an inside and outside temperature indicator, and a watch. I recommend wearing a parachute, but this practice is not commonly observed by balloonists. The crash helmet also is a good safety precaution.

If you are going in for competition or record setting, you will need a barograph, which keeps a record of your altitude during a flight. It is basically an altimeter connected to a recording needle which scribes a trace of your altitude

Figure 61. Raven Ripping Balloon. The Raven S-40 has a circular ripping panel in the top secured at the perimeter by velcro tape. The balloon pilot can pull the panel open to deflate after landing.

during flight. Barographs cost $140 for a new one and $50 to $75 for a used one. Public liability insurance is an excellent measure of protection for the balloon pilot and costs $150 per year on a group basis through the National Aeronautics Association.

The only other costs are those associated with the support crew and vehicles used for a retrieve. A balloon flight is a one-way affair, and ground transportation is necessary for the return trip.

It is impossible to put ballooning on a cost-per-flight-hour basis; there are far too many variables. However, I can say that even though flight fuel is cheap, ballooning is still one of the more expensive of the sky sports.

AERODYNAMICS

There are two main types of hot-air balloons in use today: the dumping balloon, which takes its name from the deflation technique used; and the ripping balloon, which remains attached to the gondola, but can be deflated by opening a special ripping panel in the top of the balloon. Arguments have gone on for years about which type is superior. The fact is that both work well under no-wind landing conditions, but when you are drifting along in winds above 6 or 8 mph, both the ripping and dumping designs have serious drawbacks. It takes a minute or more for a ripping balloon to deflate itself and lie down. During this time it can drag you along with the breeze as though you were tethered to a wild rhinocerous. The dumping balloon is unloaded from the gondola more quickly by just a yank on the dump handle during the moment after a landing when there is slack in the suspension lines. However, a windy landing does not always put enough slack in the lines to allow a release. I'll never forget that minute or two I spent bouncing from boulder to boulder with a ten-knot wind along a rocky Nevada mountainside. The only safe thing to do in this type of circumstance is not to land. Keep flying until you encounter a clear area and then descend and touch down with enough vertical component to slacken the suspension lines and allow a release. If given a choice, I'd take the dumping balloon, but there are those who prefer the other.

The hot-air balloon get its lift by holding a volume of air captive, which air is less dense than the outside air by virtue of higher temperature. A normally loaded balloon will have to have its captive air heated to about 70° to

90° hotter than the outside air to achieve flight buoyancy. If it were not for heat loss through conduction, the balloon would remain aloft for a considerable length of time on one heating. Conduction, or loss of heat through the envelope to the outside air, is surprisingly rapid. To maintain level flight the burner in an average single-place balloon will have to replace lost heat at the rate of 700,000 BTU's per hour. This is roughly the rate at which a furnace burns to heat a six-story apartment house.

When you first see a deflated balloon you wonder how it could become so solid and firm with just the pressure of a little warm air inside it. Your credulity is challenged even further when you consider the ten-foot-diameter hole in the bottom over the burner. You can make a simple home demonstration model of a balloon in a few minutes which will convince you that the hot-air principle of lift really works. Take a large plastic bag such as cleaning establishments use to cover garments. Seal up any holes in it with cellophane tape. Secure the open end into a roughly round shape with a thin wire or long narrow strip of cardboard attached with tape or paper clips. Hold the open end of the bag over a lighted can of sterno or a stove burner or hot plate. As heat builds up inside the bag it will lose its flimsy shape and begin to tighten up. Within a few moments it will be tight and firm and if you let go, the bag will ascend to the ceiling and remain pinned there by the buoyancy of the warm air inside.

This is exactly how Jacques and Joseph Montgolfier experimented with smoke-filled paper bags in November of 1782. They didn't know why their balloons ascended and believed it to be a function of smoke. In spite of their primitive techniques they startled the world with many noteworthy flights including the first manned free flight in November, 1783. Later two other Frenchmen, Pilatre deRozier and the Marquis de-Arlandes, sustained a twenty-minute flight over Paris and thus stimulated the beginning of 100 years of balloon flight activity throughout the world.

The early balloon craft had little to offer in the way of navigating controls. To gain altitude the pilot would simply build a bigger fire. A descent would result within a minute of letting the fire die down.

Today's craft have many design improvements which make them safer and more durable. Flame-resistant balloon cloth, for example, prevents a stray spark from perforating the envelope. This occurrence caused many untimely descents during the paper and linen era of the Montgolfier-type balloons.

However, the real problems of balloon flight remain unchanged after almost 200 years of experimentation. About 30,000 cubic feet of air are held captive in a balloon designed to lift one person. This air has about 2,000 lbs. of mass. So immense is the power of this much weight that one or two men cannot hold a balloon still if a 6-mile-per-hour breeze begins pushing it. Even damping out the oscillations which can develop is more than a one-man job.

The balloon is balanced or at equilibrium only if allowed to move freely with the air. Any attempt to hold it still when the wind blows will precipitate accelerated cooling and unmanageable oscillations. Oscillations, or wobbling back and forth, usually occur during inflation. The envelope is held horizontal on the ground until partially inflated. If released suddenly when it becomes buoyant, it will rise not just to an overhead vertical position, it will swing pendulum-fashion far to the other side. The back-and-forth swinging will continue with slowly diminishing arcs until finally it stands calmly upright. My first experience with this type of oscillation came on the very first inflation after my balloon was delivered. Ed Thomas, my ground-crew chief, was holding down the crown line. I ran the blower and burner controls until the envelope was well inflated and straining upward on the crown line. At my signal the line was released, and wow! what a lot of excitement *that* started. The crowd standing behind me suddenly began scrambling out of the way as the balloon came alive. It swung in an arc overhead and bore down on the heads of the spectators. I was occupied keeping the burner flame directed into the balloon mouth to prevent scorching the fabric. Ed shouted, "How do you make this thing hold still?" "I don't know, try leaning in to that crown line, if you can catch it," I yelled back. On the second backswing he got a good grip on the line and dug in his heels. As the forward swing began he was snatched neatly off the ground without remotely affecting the balloon's oscillations. That was my first awareness that the balloon is bigger than we are, and knows it. The envelope weighs only about 100 pounds empty, but when inflated it becomes a 2,000-pound monster.

Oscillations of another type may easily be induced in the balloon's flight path. If you make a slow liftoff and ascend to, say, 100 feet and then shut off the burner, you will start down within a minute. The descent will accelerate and ground contact will be a little more than a gentle thump. The balloon will act like a gigantic rubber ball and will bounce right back into the air and loft perhaps fifteen feet high before starting down again. The next thump onto the ground will be less severe than the first, but the lofting cycle will be repeated until you feel like a yo-yo. The way to prevent this bouncing (or lofting, which is the proper term) is to make gentle landings with a vertical speed of only a few feet per second.

Figure 62. Raven 12005.
This photo of a Raven S-50 partially inflated will help you understand why I say balloons become unmanageable on the ground when the wind blows.

Figure 63. Semco Windy Inflation Oscillations.
The crew of this Semco balloon is struggling to control the envelope when a wind gust interferes with inflation. A 5 mph wind can make the inflation difficult.

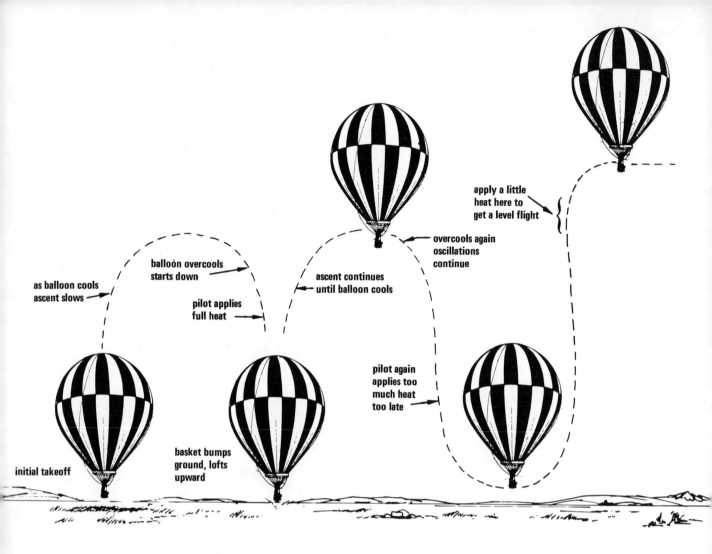

as balloon cools ascent slows →

balloon overcools starts down →

pilot applies full heat →

ascent continues ← until balloon cools

overcools again oscillations continue

apply a little heat here to get a level flight →

pilot again applies too much heat too late →

initial takeoff

basket bumps ground, lofts upward

a balloon pilot must anticipate the need for more heat by from 12 to 20 seconds

Figure 64. Altitude Overcontrolling

Following the tense episode of inflation oscillations on that first ballooning experience I gained more valuable knowledge about flight and landing oscillations. The envelope was up to flight temperature and was just about neutral buoyancy. I was in the pilot seat. My crew chief grasped the arm of the gondola chair and lifted me into the balloon with one hand to his waist level. The sensation of remaining suspended and motionless above the ground is truly unique. I considered the completely calm wind conditions and decided a short free flight would be called for after one last check on the equipment. I motioned for Ed to take my seat in the chair while I stepped back to survey the rigging and admire the shape of this weird and wonderful flying machine. Ed is a few pounds lighter than I, but I didn't perceive the importance of this until he had drifted out of reach overhead. The

burner puts out a roar like a six-inch-diameter blowtorch even when adjusted to low-pressure flight settings, so I hand-signaled for him to turn his burner down. He was only about thirty feet up, but before he could figure out the right combination for the burner controls, he had ascended to over 150 feet. Finally, with the burner shut down the envelope cooled and a gentle descent began. As a balloon descends its surface friction accelerates heat loss. By the time he was fifty feet high Ed perceived the descent rate to be getting a little too brisk, so he quickly turned up the flight burner. This had no immediate effect on the descent rate because once in motion it takes a great deal of force to alter the direction or speed of a balloon. Also there is a ten- to twenty-second lag between burner adjustments and flight responses. He winced noticeably on the landing, but it was the next event that really shook him. As the balloon lofted back into the air it wasn't just a few feet high. It didn't stop climbing at all, but proceeded upward at about 500 feet per minute. I was jumping around and shouting and waving to turn off the flame, but Ed was out of earshot and left to his own devices. With the heat off again the balloon leveled off at about 500 feet and I heaved a sigh of relief as it began to descend. Highway traffic had come to standstill as motorists watched our antics. As the balloon descent rate increased Ed attempted to anticipate the need for heat and turned up the burner to compensate for the rapidly cooling envelope. He had drifted across a road and if it hadn't been for two barbed wire fences we'd have been on hand to hold him down on that next bounce. Alas, he was out of reach and on his way up again before our group of ground assistants could catch him. It was obvious to everybody now that the situation was out of hand and we would have to catch him on the next bounce. Each oscillation was higher than the last. He was at least 1,000 feet high now and a slight wind was carrying him so that one more loft would carry him into the heavily forested slopes of Cougar Mountain. As Ed finally began a descent our rescue posse was quickly organized. We surged across the pasture toward the next anticipated landing point. As we scrambled along with eyes on the sky, mole holes and cow pies reduced our number. Still there were a dozen hands reaching for Thomas as he fell earthward. Luckily nobody was crushed by the gondola's impact and the subsequent loft carried Ed, myself, and three others upward, all clinging to the aluminum gondola framework. It was only a low bounce and the runaway balloon was finally anchored to the ground.

It seems rather incredible that we could have had such problems with a simple bag of hot air.

However, I now recognize and hope to convey to you that balloons are not toys. They are deceptively powerful, and anyone attempting to operate one should heed the need for study of flight techniques before he flies. I learned the hard way. You shouldn't have to.

Figure 65. Raven S-50 Gondola.
The gondola of a Raven S-50 multiplace balloon is made from square welded tubing. The large propane tanks clamped to the floor allow good flight duration.

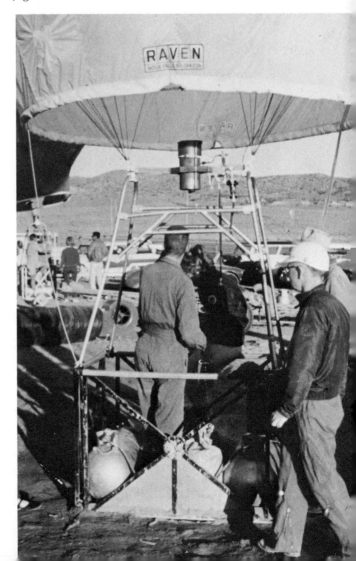

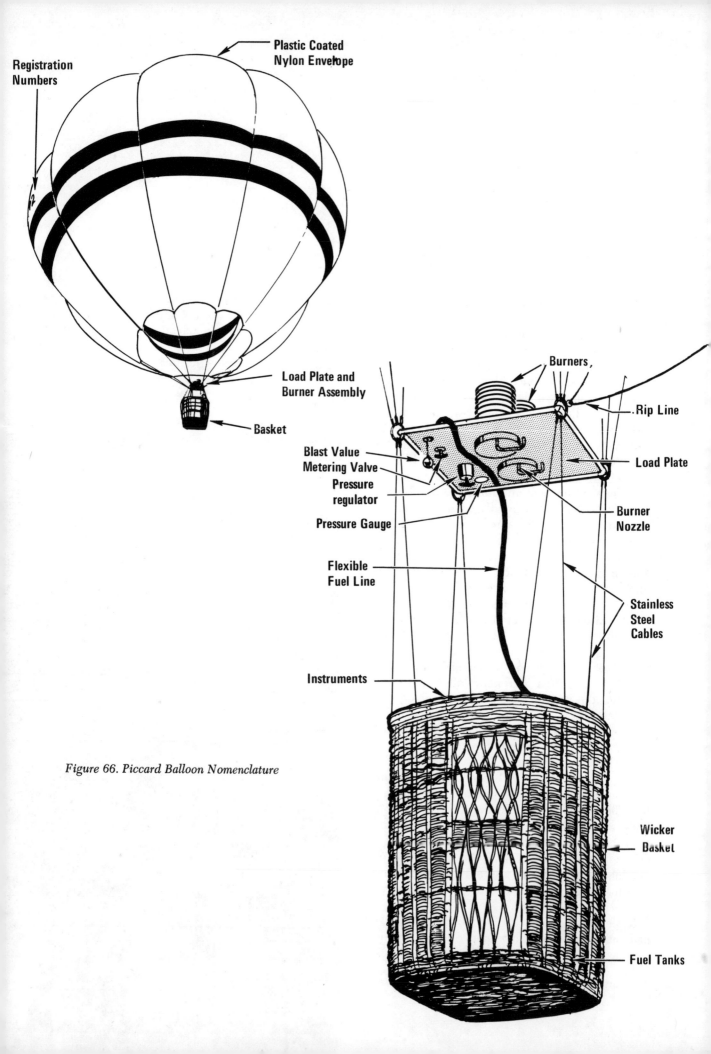

Registration
Numbers

Plastic Coated
Nylon Envelope

Load Plate and
Burner Assembly

Basket

Burners

Rip Line

Blast Value
Metering Valve
Pressure
regulator

Pressure Gauge

Load Plate

Burner
Nozzle

Flexible
Fuel Line

Stainless
Steel
Cables

Instruments

Wicker
Basket

Fuel Tanks

Figure 66. Piccard Balloon Nomenclature

BALLOON CONSTRUCTION

Both dumping and ripping balloons are constructed from ripstop nylon similar to parachute cloth, only heavier. The fabric is impregnated with plastic to make it airtight, which should be a pliable type that will allow the fabric to retain its resilience and strength. There have been some balloons made with a plastic-coated cloth which became hard and brittle with age. I have seen balloon cloth so crisp that it rattled like paper when handled. This some cloth could be ripped under the stress of flight loads in turbulent air. If you should consider a used balloon for purchase, be sure to test the fabric. If you can tear it by hand, it is not airworthy fabric.

The cloth is sewn into gores and assembled with a few miles of nylon thread. The number of gores depends upon the manufacturer's design preference and the balloon size. The Piccard two-man balloon has only eight gores which bulge into a graceful solobrigidine shape when inflated to flight pressures. The Raven Model S-50 has 32 gores, and other models have even more.

The weight of the gondola, or basket, fuel, and crew are supported by the envelope through load-carrying tapes sewn into the gore seams. On some designs such as the Semco the multiple layers of the seams bear the load, and tapes run only a few feet up from the balloon mouth.

It would be hazardous to have nylon suspension lines in the burner area. One stray tongue of flame could lick through nylon in an instant. Stainless steel cables are the rule for the suspension lines, or foot ropes, which run from the skirt, or lower edge of the balloon, to the load ring, or burner platform.

The gondola may be a wicker affair to emulate the early designs, or a modern welded and bolted assembly of aluminum tubing.

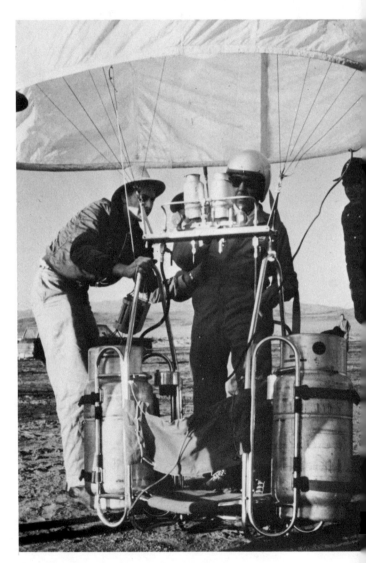

Figure 67. Raven S-40 Gondola.
The Raven S-40 single-place balloon uses twin burners and a lightweight aluminum tubing chair. The side mounted tanks hamper pilot visibility somewhat, and there is no structure to protect the pilot's legs.

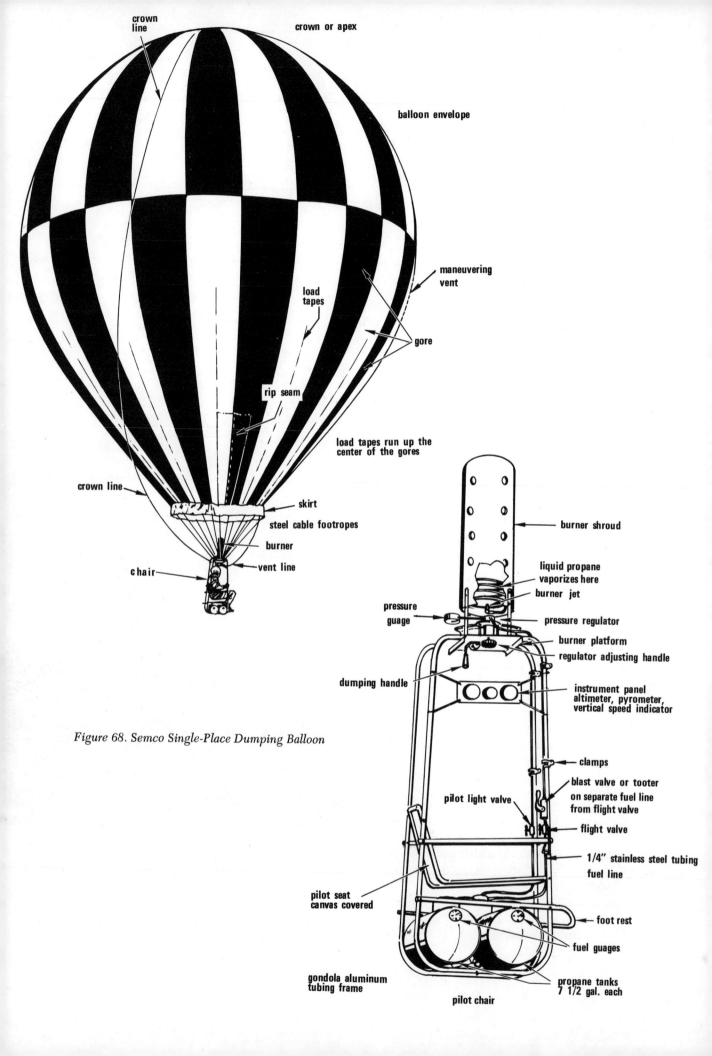

crown line

crown or apex

balloon envelope

maneuvering vent

load tapes

gore

rip seam

load tapes run up the center of the gores

crown line

skirt

steel cable footropes

burner

chair

vent line

Figure 68. Semco Single-Place Dumping Balloon

burner shroud

liquid propane vaporizes here

burner jet

pressure guage

pressure regulator

burner platform

regulator adjusting handle

dumping handle

instrument panel altimeter, pyrometer, vertical speed indicator

clamps

blast valve or tooter on separate fuel line from flight valve

pilot light valve

flight valve

1/4" stainless steel tubing fuel line

pilot seat canvas covered

foot rest

fuel guages

gondola aluminum tubing frame

propane tanks 7 1/2 gal. each

pilot chair

Two propane tanks are bolted or clamped to the gondola and may carry from seven gallons each on a single-place balloon to twenty gallons each on the larger craft. Valves on the tanks control fuel flow into tubing which passes through two main burner supply lines, each with a control valve.

One valve is on a line which also flows through a regulator, adjustable to control the pressure of gas supplied to the burner. The other valve is on a line which bypasses the regulator and feeds the propane gas directly from the tank to the burner. This is called the "blast valve," or "tooter." It is used when a large volume of heat is wanted in a hurry. There is also a small needle valve to control the burner pilot light.

The balloon envelope controls consist of a vent line, commonly called the "hoo hoo," which opens a slit and allows the escape of some hot air. The only other envelope control is the collapsing system. On ripping balloons a line runs from the gondola up to the large circular rip panel at the top of the balloon. This line is secured by velcro tape. The panel may be pulled partially or fully open by use of the rip cord. On dumping balloons there are no openings of any kind above the balloon's equator and the ripping system is simply a seam, or pair of seams, which open near the balloon mouth. They may open automatically when the balloon is dumped or may require manual ripping. The dumping lever is pulled to release the suspension lines from the load plate.

The dumping process is one of the more exciting moments in ballooning. Spectators often think the balloon has accidentally broken away as it lofts upward and then turns over when the retaining line comes tight. There is always a moment of suspense as you speculate on where the monstrous bundle of flapping fabric will

Figure 69. Balloon Dumping.
The dumping balloon looks like this after being released from the chair. With the apex secured to the chair by the crown line, the envelope inverts and the hot air dumps out the open mouth.

Figure 70. Pre-inflation, Connecting Balloon and Inspecting.

Before inflating, the balloon is rolled out on the ground, inspected, and then connected to the burner platform of the chair or gondola.

land. You try to plan for it to land in a clear area, but once my crew and I had to make a panic leap out of the way when the balloon plopped straight back down on top of the gondola.

PREPARATION

Serving some time as crewman for a balloonist is the best way to prepare for becoming a pilot yourself. Don't be fooled by the simple appearance of a balloon. Like any aircraft it has the power to destroy itself and its passengers when just slightly mishandled. After some crewing experience you will already know the following prerequisites to making a flight. You need:

1. An airworthy balloon.
2. A crew of three trusted helpers who will take their responsibilities seriously.
3. A windless or sheltered inflation site of at least an acre, with assistants or barricades to keep spectators at a safe distance.
4. Several hours of daylight to allow for the flight and retrieve.
5. A retrieve vehicle, preferably with four-wheel drive.

PREFLIGHT PREPARATIONS

Early morning is a good time to fly balloons because the air is often most calm and stable for a few hours after daybreak.

With your crew's help lay your equipment out and begin the preflight checks. It is best to move the gondola before installing the fuel tanks because it is awkwardly heavy after the tanks are clamped into place.

If you are using a ground blower to assist with inflation, check the fuel supply and give it a test run to warm the motor.

Carefully examine the gondola. The jogging and vibrations of transporting can sometimes cause bolts, screws, or plumbing fittings to loosen.

With flight burner and pilot light valves closed, turn the main tank valves on and check for propane leaks. Large leaks are easily spotted by the hissing sound and appearance of frost on the fittings at the leak. Small leaks can be detected by sniffing the fittings for that unmistakable aroma of liquefied petroleum. Open the valve and ignite the pilot light. Turn up the regulator control valve and check to see that the gauge pressure changes with regulator adjustment and that the burner is functioning properly. A balky or intermittent burner flame could mean dirt in the lines or burner jets. You will never be troubled with dirty fuel lines if you keep the hose ends capped or taped when the tanks are disconnected.

Be sure everyone is standing well clear before you test the blast valve. The roaring ten-foot blast of flame which shoots forth when you trigger the tooter can scare the wits out of an unsuspecting bystander.

If all systems check out okay, then dump the balloon from its carrying bag and unroll it from a starting position near the gondola and in a downwind direction. Never attempt a crosswind or into-the-wind inflation. When calm air conditions prevail (and they are much to be preferred), the balloon layout direction is optional.

Lay the gondola on its side facing the balloon and make all necessary connections with the balloon foot ropes. Marking the connections will help prevent attaching the balloon backwards. Spread the envelope and inspect it for flight readiness: rip seam or ripping panel secure, vent and control lines unobstructed, ground handling and static line clear of tangles.

When these preparations are complete, clear the area of spectators. While well meaning and curious, they represent a threat to your safety and their own when inflation and flight time approaches. Brief your crew on the nature of the intended flight and their duties. One person should tend the crown to hold the balloon horizontal as it inflates and to let it ascend slowly at your signal. It takes two persons to manage the balloon mouth. They should wear gloves because the steel suspension lines can become very hot if they sag into the burner flame. One of the crew should act as chief to whom you direct signals and commands as flight preparations progress. This crew chief will (1) be in charge of checking your weight as flight buoyancy develops; (2) manage the tether line, if used; (3) manage fuel tank switching if an

Figure 71. Semco Inflation (no gloves).
The Semco single-place balloon comes equipped with a special gas engine powered blower which sits on the chair during inflation. This ground crewman should be wearing gloves. Those wires can easily become hot from the burner flame.

auxiliary fuel source is used for inflation; and (4) direct the rest of the crew at your request. During inflation procedures you, as the pilot, manage the burner controls and ground blower, if used.

Light the pilot light, and when the crew is in readiness, start the ground blower.

The simplest inflation is achieved by blowing plain air into the envelope mouth until the balloon is about one-third full, then turn up the flight burner valve and be sure the burner points directly into the center of the balloon mouth. As soon as a good flow of heat and flame is di-

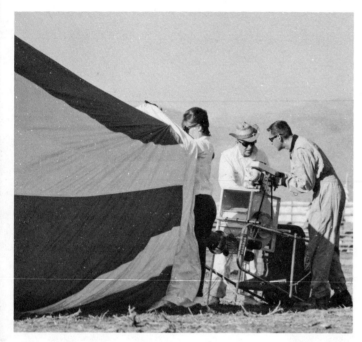

(left) Figure 72. Semco Ground Blower.
A four-man crew is best when inflating a Semco;
three at the mouth and one at the apex. Notice
how the blower rests on the reclining chair during
inflation.

(below) Figure 73. Crown Man Holding Tension.
The envelope is blown partially full of air with
the blower, then the burner is turned up to heat
the air. The crewman at the apex must hold tension
on the crown line.

Figure 74. Inflation MEROPE.

The Piccard balloon has a large mouth, and a big fan such as an airplane propeller can be used for rapid inflations. This method was used when racing the clock at the 1965 Reno National Balloon Races.

rected into the balloon the ground blower may be shut down. The velocity of the flame and superhot air from the burner causes surrounding air to be induced into the balloon and inflation continues just as though the blower were still running. It is possible to begin and complete an inflation using induced air exclusively, but the blower is a handy aid, especially for the novice balloonist.

The crown man should keep some tension or slight stretch on the balloon to prevent its crowding the crew at the gondola end. Slack in the foot ropes and sagging around the balloon mouth indicate the need of more tension at the apex.

Hold the tooter valve open for short bursts to accelerate inflation, but be very watchful for sags or billowing inward of the material which could be scorched and melted by the flame from the blast valve.

When 70° to 80° volume is reached, have the crewman gently and slowly ease up on the crown line, allowing the balloon to float upright. Tilt the gondola upright as the balloon rises to keep the burner pointed into the mouth. Board the gondola, attach the static line to the gondola, and proceed with final rigging inspection while the envelope is building up to flight tem-

perature. It is wise to take your time during inflation, but it is possible to reach flight temperature in about five minutes by keeping the tooter open continuously. Examine vent control lines and ripping lines; ascertain that the dumping mechanism is secure and safetied, burner controls are all functioning properly, fuel quantity gauges are normal, instruments normal, and altimeter set.

Beware of too many hands on your gondola. Enthusiastic spectators and crewmen are tempted to clutch tightly to your gondola and you may become buoyant without realizing it. A desirable ascent is to "weigh off" the ground with just a few pounds of buoyancy. Almost every experienced balloonist has faced the problem of being held on the ground until overheated and then, when everybody finally lets go, he booms into the air with uncontrolled speed. On one occasion, during an exhibition flight near Mill Valley, California, in 1963, the balloon was not released until it had over 200 pounds of lift. One of the spectators, an eleven-year-old boy who had been helping with ground handling lines, was snatched aloft when the line tightened into a half hitch around his wrist. The pilot's first awareness of the problem was at an altitude of 3,000 feet when the terrified boy's feeble pleas of, "Help, mister, hellpp!", finally penetrated the burner roar and crash helmet. A rapid descent was begun immediately and the passenger was landed safely.

A safe and proper lift-off is made by checking the buoyancy every twenty or thirty seconds as

Figure 75. Raven Ground Blower.

*The factory-built ground blower for the Raven
balloons has a built-in propane heater and gas
engine. This tube-type blower is not popular now
because of its awkward size and weight.*

flight temperature is approached. A nod from
pilot to crew chief will signal the weight check.
He shouts, "Hands high," and every hand should
release the gondola. The crew chief may make
a further physical check by attempting to lift
the gondola. If he can lift it with ease, the balloon is almost up to flight temperature.

Use of a tether line is highly recommended
until the pilot develops a "feel" for the heat controls and is able to maintain a constant altitude.
You may develop the ability to control altitude
after just a few minutes on the tether, or it may
require several flights. Remember the main
tendency is to overcontrol. If you keep the
tooter open until an ascent begins, you've put
too much heat into the envelope and may have
thirty to fifty pounds of buoyancy.

While manuevering near the ground, try to
set a regulator pressure which will keep you
slightly negative in weight. Regulator pressure
feeds to the flight burner and it is better to set
a pressure which will not quite sustain you in
the air. Short bursts on the blast valve will make
up the needed BTU's to keep you level or
ascending.

The exact setting in pounds of pressure varies
with balloons and is affected by temperature,
humidity, weight of the balloon cloth, size of
the propane plumbing, kind and size of burner,
etc. My balloon will maintain level flight on
twenty-two pounds pressure showing on the
regulator and twenty pounds is a good setting
for near the ground and tether flying.

The tether line should be 150 to 200 feet long
and not less than ⅜-inch in diameter. Half-inch or
⅝-inch is even easier to handle, although it becomes a bulky package when you have to coil up
these larger sizes. Don't use polyethelene or
polypropylene for a tether line. They are in-
expensive and light weight, but they are slippery
to handle and the tether line crew must be
able to grip that line. Gloves are a must for
the tether line crew. The ground crew chief may
be the best tether line handler if he weighs 160
pounds or more, but he should have at least
one more full-sized man as an assistant to help
him snub down an inadvertent surge from a
momentary wind gust or overheat.

Make several gentle climbs to the tether line
limit, then without use of blast, see how long it
takes for a descent to begin. Within two minutes
you should start down and use five-second blasts
on the tooter to keep the descent progressing
slowly. Try a longer blast when about fifty feet
high to attempt a flare before landing. After you

Figure 77. Semco Multiplace.
This is Mark Semich in one of his early design multiplace balloons with aluminum and wicker basket. Note the slack tether line, indicating no wind. The only safe way to tether-fly a balloon is during wind free conditions.

Figure 76. Tether line Handling.
When tether flying, the tetherman should wear gloves and handle the line securely, as illustrated.

have proficiency in altitude control and can maintain any height you choose within the tether line limits, you may proceed without the tether. Be sure you have plenty of unobstructed elbow room before flying free of the tether. A football field would be all right for tether flying, but too small for a nontether hop even in calm winds. Ballooning takes lots of space. A square mile of unobstructed pastureland or grain fields would be enough for beginning low-altitude free flights. A medium-size county is nice to roam around in if there is a little breeze blowing and you contemplate making a two-hour flight. Don't take off cross-country if your retrieve crew isn't in readiness. Preparations for retrieves will be discussed later.

THE LANDING

There are several important things to remember about landing. I like to set up in level flight about fifty feet high and run through a mental checklist before proceeding with a landing.

1. All heat valves, including pilot light, should be off.
2. Open manual rip seam (dumping balloons with rip seam near skirt).
3. Release safety pin on dump level (dumping balloon only).
4. Check rigging of ripcord and vent lines (balloons with crown-type ripping panel).
5. Drop guide rope, if used.
6. Plan landing point.
7. Remember to duck (balloons such as Piccard with nonrigid basket suspension).

EXPLANATION OF ABOVE:

1. Sometimes landings are rather hair-raising experiences whereby you bounce and drag through boulders, brush, or other obstacles. If all flame is not extinguished prior to landing, there is a chance that a valve could become opened and the burner come alive at a bad time.
2. For a successful dump, the ripseam must be open to allow the escape of heated air when the envelope inverts. Failure to open the ripseam will likely result in a damaged envelope during the dumping.
3. Dump levers are safetied in various ways. Timing the lever pull must be at the very precise instant after touchdown when there is slack in the foot ropes. Release safety in anticipation of the lever pull.
4. The only way to collapse a ripping balloon is to pull the crown open with the ripping cord. Be sure this cord is in the clear and ready to function. If you have tied vent control line to gondola, be sure to release it before landing in a dumping balloon.
5. A tether line is sometimes carried aboard the gondola or left dangling during free flight. A ground crew, if present, might utilize the tether to help control your landing.
6. You may want to drift along for some distance until reaching a more favorable landing point.
7. On Piccard and some other designs the gondola hangs by cables from the load plate or burner platform overhead. On a landing the burner platform will settle right into your lap and if the landing is a hard one, the unwary pilot could get beamed.

When you are certain all is in readiness, valve off some heat with the vent. With burner shut down a descent will develop within a few seconds as the envelope cools. Upon impact pull the rip cord and hold it open, as escaping air through the crown and internal pressures will try to close the rip panel again. On dumping balloons simply pull the lever at the moment of impact when slack develops in the footropes. If the first ground contact is quite hard, wait until the second bounce before dumping.

Dumping a balloon which is still fairly hot or close to flight temperature can lead to an uncomfortable bounce. As the released ascending envelope reaches the end of the retaining line, it may snatch the pilot and gondola back into the air a few feet. A more gentle dumping is achieved by making a soft landing and simply sitting there on the ground until the envelope cools and softens up, showing sags in the fabric in the lower areas of the envelope. Now you can dump by stepping out of the gondola (keep a firm grip) and raising it about two feet manually. Thrust your full weight back aboard, bearing it firmly down to the ground again. Grasp the dump level and pull sharply when the suspension cables are loose. There will be slack cables for only a second or less, so you must time the pull accurately or repeat the whole process.

Getting the empty balloon back into the carrying bag can be quite a job, especially if you don't have help. Pull on the crown and fold the widest parts together until the envelope is lying in a long ribbon about four feet wide. Start rolling at the crown as though rolling up a sleeping bag. Keep a tight roll, and if possible, have an assistant lie across the envelope just ahead of the roll. He rolls over and over, pressing the trapped air ahead of him as you follow immediately behind him with the envelope roll. It's the last third that gets awkward because the cloth is slippery and the roll tries to squirt out sideways from the inside. You must be careful to keep it tight and balanced. Once into the carrying bag the envelope becomes more manageable again.

NAVIGATION

At the beginning of this chapter I mentioned that the balloonist has no horizontal control of his flight path. I would like to qualify this because some flights are made to prechosen destinations by predicting wind flow. Often the wind will flow from different directions at various altitudes. The normal characteristic is for a wind to change both in direction and velocity with altitude. The direction change will be clockwise and the velocity will increase with altitude.

A southwest ground wind will become westerly about 3,000 feet above the surface. A northeast ground wind will normally go through a 45° direction change and become a due east wind at 3,000 feet. By choosing his flight level carefully the balloonist may alter his course within this narrow angle of wind shift by changing his flight altitude.

The clockwise shift with altitude is not a firm rule, however. I have seen counterclockwise shifts and 180° shifts. There is one undeniable certainty about wind and weather. It will keep you guessing, especially in coastal and mountainous areas.

When to Fly Balloons

Plains and arid areas usually enjoy periods of early morning calm. Providing there are no fronts passing you can expect summer months to offer calm airs and ideal ballooning conditions for the first four hours after daybreak. Until you are thoroughly familiar with your balloon I would recommend flying it only under ideal weather conditions. If sunshine is causing thermals to develop which stimulate periodic ground winds, you would be wise to land and deflate at the first opportunity. A balloon is too fragile to subject to the stresses of thermals.

Figure 78. Bill Berry in Basket.

Bill Berry is studying his barograph as he ascends in the basket of his Raven S-50. The basket and burner assembly are not of a standard design. Note the hole in the balloon skirt to the left of the pilot. A moment's inattention during inflation can easily cause such a scorch.

Coastal areas usually have an onshore flow of wind in the daytime and an offshore breeze at night. Here again the early morning hours are often becalmed, and a safe, enjoyable flight may be made before breakfast.

INSTRUMENTATION

As a minimum instrument package I suggest an altimeter and variometer. The variometer may be an aircraft-type vertical-speed indicator with a zero to 2,000 feet per minute scale. Other sensitive variometers of the type used in sailplanes are also satisfactory. A Pyrometer, or inside temperature gauge, will help prevent overheating the envelope. If you should inadvertently push your internal temperature past the redline of 250°, you may bake and permanently weaken the fabric.

Ballast is seldom used in hot-air ballooning because adequate vertical control is possible with the burner controls and vent.

The rate of fuel consumption depends a great deal upon the type of flight you are making. If much vertical maneuvering is done, the fuel consumption goes up considerably. Rate of heat loss through the envelope relates to movement of air across the envelope. When climbing or descending your heat loss may be twice as rapid as during level flight. Descents are espe-

cially costly in fuel consumption. The balloon is the only flight conveyance I know of which uses more fuel during descent than it does in climb or level flight. This fact I learned the hard way at the 1965 National Balloon Races. My tanks were full at takeoff and fifteen gallons, I thought, would suffice for a two- to three-hour flight. I made a rapid ascent to 16,500 feet and noticed after only forty minutes that the gauges were reading in the area of ¼ tank. The rapid climb and cruising at high altitude in cool air had caused a surprisingly fast rate of fuel consumption. I began the letdown and was puzzled by the fact that it required almost constant full blast with the tooter to keep the descent rate from developing greater than 700 feet per minute, which I considered a safe maximum letdown speed. At 10,000 feet the burner spurted out its last BTU of propane and I settled back in my chair comforting myself with the thought which one of the more experienced balloonists had told me. He said, "One thing you don't need to worry about is a flame-out. These big balloons act like a parachute and will let you down like a feather." After a few moments of watching the gauges and fidgeting in the seat, I thought, "This is a pretty heavy feather I'm riding. That gauge says 1,200 feet per minute." When the needle crept down to 1,400 feet per minute I became downright nervous and my eyes shifted back and forth between the gauges and the envelope which was compressing in on the sides and becoming more streamlined as the descent rate built up. I toyed with my parachute ripcord handle, looked down between my knees at the rocky, uninviting slopes of the Nevada mountains, and back at the gauges. "1,550 feet per minute. My gosh, that's almost 20 miles per hour. I could get hurt landing at that speed. This is ridiculous. I couldn't really be in trouble, and yet. . . ."

I snugged up my parachute leg straps and studied the balloon envelope again. "Maybe if I open the ripseams the balloon will blossom out." As I yanked the two balloon ripcords the ripseams spread open all right, but the descent rate kept going up. At 1,800 feet per minute I still had over 3,000 feet to fall and tried to convince myself to jump and use that parachute. I have made hundreds of jumps for the fun of it, but this was different. I couldn't seem to force myself to bail out. The vertical speed was pegged now on 2,000 feet and the stresses on the envelope were terrific. Any second I expected to hear it rip wide open. Finally I had the answer, "Jump now and ask questions afterward." So I jumped.

As I stablized in freefall and made an unproductive tug on the ripcord I thought, "Oh my gosh! what have I done now? The ripcord's stuck." Repeated attempts with both hands finally got the desired results: a pilot chute in the air. Then, wham! I had almost forgotten that emergency chutes have a brisk opening shock. The landing was also brisk, but between boulders, and I sustained only a bruised shin. I lay on the ground awhile with my head on the bundle of nylon, looking up at my beautiful balloon which was now relieved of my weight and gently drifting earthward.

As my fright over the narrow escape subsided I puzzled over the high rate of fuel consumption. I could understand that flying high in cool, thin air could account for rapid burnoff during the cruise, but why should I have exhausted the tanks from ¼ full to empty in less than eight minutes? Everything else that flies becomes quite economical with fuel when coasting downhill.

As the balloon thumped into the sage brush a quarter of a mile away, an inkling of the answer began to penetrate my clouded consciousness. The hole in the bottom of that balloon is ten feet in diameter. That is a third of the balloon's diameter. When descending, there is nothing to shield that open balloon mouth from gulping in cool air as fast as the burner can heat it. Of course, the physics of it are really quite simple. The faster the descent, the more rapid the cooling, and the greater amount of fuel needed to maintain a given descent rate. As I made my way through the sage brush to the balloon I made a mental note that the next time I went high in a balloon, I intended to keep the descent rate slow, such as 500 feet per minute or less.

As for the parachute-like descent, I had been told about, I was convinced it was thought up by somebody who had never tried it, and I expected to have a few words with him at the earliest opportunity.

The rule to remember about fuel consumption is simply that you gain the most endurance by flying along at a constant flight level. Climbs and descents can double or triple your rate of burn off.

Hazard landings, such as rocks, water, or trees, are to be avoided if at all possible. If you don't have enough fuel to sustain your flight past the hazard, then you'll have to deal with the emergency. Water landings shouldn't be too serious if you have a retrieve boat waiting for your ditching. Butane tanks when empty provide good bouyancy, and after landing, just cling to your craft until help arrives. Boulders can be circumnavigated in light or zero winds. In gusty airs you must take your chances with a steep approach and be sure to rip or dump on that first bounce. No point dragging out your agonies by thumping from one boulder to the next. I've tried that too, and it wasn't fun.

Trees will surely cause damage to your envelope if you are forced down among them. In light air you may be able to cruise along 100 feet up and then descend steeply into a clear or sparse area. Don't wait until your fuel is completely exhausted before making a landing.

If you are riding with an 8 mph wind or better and are forced to land in tall trees, I would prefer to climb away and bail out. Parachute landings in trees are quite safe, but careening through the branches anchored to a billowing balloon could unsettle and unseat you.

Remember, there are no seat belts in a balloon gondola.

RETRIEVES

A balloon flight is a one-way aerial voyage. There are records of a few balloon flights where the pilot took advantage of wind shifts and made an airborne return to near his starting point. However, this would be a rare exception to the normal routine whereby the balloonist relies upon the retrieve crew to pick up him and his equipment at the landing site.

The retrieve crew should be at least a party of two, and they should be equipped with three main items: (1) a four-wheel drive vehicle for back country travel; (2) a good set of charts and maps for tracking the balloonist's progress, and (3) an unchallengeable sense of responsibility. This third point cannot be overstressed because the balloonist cannot carry sufficient survival equipment for a prolonged outing. He is very dependent upon his helpers reaching him promptly.

If winds aloft are over 10 mph, it is likely that the balloon will outdistance the retrieve crew, especially if they are traveling over rough terrain. In this situation there is no substitute for good VHF radio communications. The Regency Standby I is a good solution for under $400 per pair, but the best range would be obtained with Bayside portables which cost about $1,500 per pair. Some good "Citizen Band" tranceivers are now available for under $150 per pair.

The balloon pilot should carry aeronautical charts which would allow him to maintain an accurate fix on his position which he could radio to his crew. He should also attempt to land in an accessible area.

If you are looking for a method of flight to pioneer in, ballooning may fill the bill. People have been pioneering it for 200 years, and the research and experimenting will undoubtedly continue as long as people are motivated to pursue this unusual, spectacular, and expensive flight medium.

BALLOON ORGANIZATIONS

The Balloon Federation of America, a division of the National Aeronautic Association, offers membership and an interesting periodical publication for $10 per year. Mail membership request to: Secretary, Balloon Federation of America, Menlo Oaks Balloon Field, Menlo Park, California 94025.

BALLOON MANUFACTURERS

Daedalus School of Free Ballooning
894 Ringwood Ave.
Menlo Park, California 94025

Don Piccard Balloons
P.O. Box 1902
Newport Beach, California 92660

Raven Industries, Balloon Division
P.O. Box 1007
Sioux Falls, South Dakota 57101
Attn: Mr. John Kittelson

Semco Balloons
2002 North 11th St.
Coeur D'Alene, Idaho 83814

Tracy Barnes Balloons
Chester, South Carolina

BALLOON SCHOOLS

Daedalus School of Free Ballooning
894 Ringwood Ave.
Menlo Park, California 94025

Minnesota Balloon School
Matt H. Wiederkehr, Mgr.
1604 Euclid St.
St. Paul, Minnesota 55106

The Aerostats
Box 342
East Hartford, Connecticut 06108

BALLOON GLOSSARY

APEX—The upper pole, or top center point, of the balloon.

APEX LINE—Same as crown line.

BALLAST—Sandbags used and carried in gas balloons to help regulate flight altitude. Rarely used on hot-air balloons.

BASKET—The main carrying framework suspended beneath the balloon. Classically built from wicker, but the modern trend is aluminum tubing. Contains fuel supply, burner controls, and balloonists.

BLAST VALVE—Same as tooter.

BURNER—The coil of tubing and nozzle which ejects propane, which is the primary heat source for obtaining buoyancy.

BURNER PLATFORM—The burner is mounted on a frame, or platform, which attaches beneath the balloon by footropes. The basket or gondola is suspended below it. On gas balloons this component is simply a large wooden or metal ring called the Load Ring. Also called Load Plate.

CROWN—Same as apex.

CROWN LINE—A line attached to the top center of the balloon to assist in inflation and ground handling. On dumping balloons this line attaches to the gondola frame or burner platform during flight and acts as a static line to invert the balloon during dumping.

DRAG LINE—In gas ballooning a long hemp rope was sometimes dangled from the basket to help regulate altitude during low-level flights. Seldom used in hot-air ballooning.

DUMPING BALLOON—A balloon design whereby deflation is achieved quickly by releasing the balloon at the bottom while holding the crown securely. The balloon inverts, spilling the air out the upward-facing mouth and rip seams.

FLIGHT VALVE—The valve which controls propane flow through the regulator to the burner. Also called Metering Valve.

ENVELOPE—The large fabric balloon sphere, usually sewn together from gores of plastic-coated nylon.

FOOTROPES—Flexible steel cables which support the gondola beneath the balloon. They connect to the load tapes at the balloon mouth.

GONDOLA—Same as basket or chair.

GROUND BLOWER—A gasoline-powered fan or squirrel cage-type blower which is used for starting balloon inflation on the ground. Some use a propane burner to heat the air as it is blown into the balloon.

HANDS HIGH—A command from the balloon pilot used during preflight heating to determine if flight buoyancy has been reached. The crew responds by all hands releasing their holds on the basket.

HOO HOO—A slit in the side of the balloon called the "maneuvering vent" is controlled by a line dangling within the pilot's reach. This line is popularly called the hoo hoo.

JOY VALVE—Same as Tooter.

LOAD PLATE—See Burner Platform.

LOAD RING—See Burner Platform.

LOAD TAPES—Nylon tapes are sewn to the balloon from the crown down to the mouth where they are connected to the footsteps. These tapes distribute the load of the basket and pilot evenly up to the crown of the balloon.

LOFT—When a balloon is landed, if the impact is too great, it will bounce back into the air. This is called "lofting."

METERING VALVE—same as Flight Valve.

PYROMETER—A devise for measuring the temperature of the trapped air in the upper section of the balloon envelope. This temperature is reflected on a gauge in the basket and may be compared with an outside air temperature gauge to determine temperature differential.

RIPCORD—The line at the basket which controls the rip panel.

RIPPING BALLOON—A balloon design which deflates by ripping open a large hole in the crown, called the "ripping panel."

RIPSEAM—Dumping balloons have seams near the mouth which are opened before deflation by pulling a ripcord.

SKIRT—The lower edge of the balloon envelope sometimes has an extension, or skirt, with round portholes. The purpose was to help direct burner heat upward and minimize effects of wind gusts.

SUSPENSION LINES—Same as Footropes.

TEMPERATURE DIFFERENTIAL—The difference in temperature between the captive air inside the balloon and the outside air. Average for flight is 70° to 90°.

TEMPERATURE REDLINE—The maximum safe temperature for air inside the envelope. About 300° F. for a nylon envelope.

TETHER LINE—During training and for captive balloon flights when no wind is blowing, the balloon gondola may be kept anchored to the ground by a crewman holding a tether line. 200 feet is the maximum practical length for a tether line.

THERMAL AEROSTAT—Hot-air balloon.

TOOTER—The flight burner control which bypasses the regulator and sends full tank pressure through the burner. Used when heat is needed quickly. Also called Blast Valve and Joy Valve.

VARIOMETER—An instrument for measuring the balloon's relative movement upward or downward through the air. Best used in conjunction with an altimeter.

VENT—A slit in the side of the envelope may be pulled open by a control line called the "hoo hoo" to spill off some hot air.

WEIGH OFF—A gentle lift off the ground with just a few pounds of positive buoyancy. This is the desired type ascent as opposed to the "blast off" wherein the envelope is overheated and the pilot climbs several thousand feet before gaining control.

4 GYROCRAFT

If you have a yen to be a pilot and owner of a plane but can't finance the undertaking, consider these facts about gyrocopters.

They are simple to construct and can be built complete with power plant for less than $1,000. You don't have to take a flying course to get a pilot license. A person who follows the recommended training steps can teach himself to fly and obtain a private pilot license. The glider models require no pilot license at all and can be equipped to operate on either land or water. Gyrocopters are small, compact, and can be stored easily in a garage or basement.

A complete gyrocopter weighs only 240 pounds and can be transported in a pickup or on a boat trailer. One man can prepare his machine from trailer to flight readiness in less than half an hour with a couple of wrenches. Operating costs for the glider models amount to nothing more than gas for the tow vehicle. The powered model can be flown for $3 to $5 per hour. The pure fun of piloting one of these versatile and fully maneuverable vehicles is indescribably stimulating and exciting.

These facts are partly responsible for the rapid growth in interest in gyrocopters. "Whirly Bugs" are whirring into the air at airports all over the country.

The craft consists of a pair of ten-foot rotor blades which rotate about a center pivot called a "spindle bolt." Suspended from the bolt is the rotor mast upon which is mounted a seat for the pilot, a five-foot axle for the two outboard wheels, and a keel tube with steerable front wheel on the front and a rudder and auxiliary tail wheel on the rear. An aircraft airframe could hardly be designed for greater simplicity of construction. The frame is made from two-inch square aluminum tubing, and joints are made by drilling and bolting the tubes together.

The rotor is made of ⅛-inch plywood skins glued together around a flat, tapered steel spar. The leading edge is solid beechwood which is planed and sanded into an airfoil shape after gluing.

The novice would spend perhaps a month of spare time effort to build a pair of rotor blades. My second pair took me about two weeks, working four hours a day. A good craftsman can crank out a finished pair, sanded, painted, and balanced in a week.

The Bensen factory offers a beautiful pair of aluminum rotor blades ready to mount and fly for $325. These are internally balanced and trimmed so they need no nose weight or trim tab. They do not change weight or trim with variations in temperature or humidity, and have an infinite useful life.

The gyrocopter is a true autogyro. This means that the rotor is free-wheeling. It gets its rotational power by airflow and not by engine drive, as with the helicopter.

Since the autogyro rotor is not connected to the engine, construction is much simplified. The transmission, tail rotor, gearing, and blade controls required in a helicopter are not needed in a gyrocopter.

Forward thrust is commonly provided by a seventy-two horsepower, two-cycle McCulloch engine driving a forty-eight-inch pusher propeller. This engine was used years ago to power the target drone aircraft and is still available surplus for as low as $50. A factory-new ninety horsepower McCulloch engine ready to install can be purchased from the Bensen factory for $995. If a surplus engine is used modifications are necessary for the carburetor, bearings, and ignition. The McCulloch engine uses no muffler, so earplugs are recommended when operating it. Also, it has single ignition, meaning one spark

Figure 79. Gyrocopter in Flight

plug per cylinder. All other aircraft engines which meet the FAA airworthiness standards have two complete independent ignition systems. To be reliable, the McCulloch single ignition engine must be properly maintained. Besides normal preflight and postflight inspections the engine must have its magneto, spark plugs, and harness checked over every twenty-five hours. A mag shop will charge about $20 for servicing the magneto, which includes recharging the magnets.

The gyrocopter can carry only the pilot; however, a two-passenger seat can be built on the glider model and flown on tether behind a vehicle. This two-place gyroglider is used by Bensen dealers and clubs for teaching beginners the fundamentals of controlling an autogyro.

The powered gyrocopter must be flown solo, although family and group participation is often involved with the construction and crewing matters.

The most popular design is the Bensen Model B8M, which may be built from plans or in kit form from the Bensen factory in Raleigh, North Carolina. The gyrocopter does not carry a Standard Airworthiness Certificate and is licensed under the "Experimental" category. This means you must build the major portion of it yourself to get the FAA license to fly it.

It is legal to fly a Bensen constructed and licensed by another person, but beware of the possibility of getting a pig in a poke. You may be buying a pack of problems. I would consider buying a used Bensen only after having it thoroughly inspected by a Bensen dealer, or someone who really knows the equipment.

This rotor craft is the only type of flying machine which I can recommend as a means for you to teach yourself to fly. Planes, gliders, helicopters, even parachutes, require the training and supervision of instructors.

The gyrocopter will take off in 300 feet and fly with full maneuverability at 42 miles per hour. Landings can be made with a very short roll after some practice. In fact a slight headwind will allow a full flare landing with no forward roll at all.

Remember, this craft is not a helicopter. It will not take off vertically or hover. At least 1,000 feet of clear level ground is required to practice takeoffs, and 2,000 feet or more is preferred. An experienced gyrocopter pilot can navigate in and out of a 500-foot airstrip or road, but as a novice you should have plenty of runway. Probably the best gyrocopter training field in the country is the huge, flat, dry lake bed at El Mirage, California.

This is not a craft for taking long cross-country flights. The six-gallon fuel supply limits the duration to less than two hours, and the longest nonstop flight on Bensen's records at this time is an hour and 21 minutes.

A longer flight of 406 miles was made in December, 1966, by two gyrocopters piloted by Ken Brock and Chuck Layne with several refueling stops and one overnight rest. They flew their ships in formation from El Mirage to Las Vegas and back to El Mirage during their two-day cross-country. The trip was made in short hops of thirty to fifty miles with stops on roads for refueling by the ground crew traveling the highway below the whirlybirds.

Most owners use their ships for weekend recreational flying in the local area around an airport. I would like to be able to say that it is a great machine to use for commuting from home to work, but this is not yet so. It is true only when you have a landing strip at both ends.

The ease of building and low cost of the Bensen are not the only attractive features about gyrocopters. The flight characteristics offer some real interest and excitement even for an old pro. You sit in the open where the wind can tickle up your sleeves, and you can fly slowly enough to enjoy the scenery.

Your maximum economy speed is 40 to 45 mph, which is about the stall speed of a conventional plane. You have no threat of stalling because even at zero forward speed the rotor will keep spinning and let you down at something less than crashing speed. Maneuverability must be seen or flown to be appreciated. Extremely tight turns can be made without overstressing the ship, and very short landings can be made even without a headwind. Top speed capability is about 85 mph, but 60 is more comfortable for cruising.

You don't need to pass a medical exam to fly the gyroglider models. You will need an FAA medical certificate and student license for soloing in the gyrocopter, and sixteen is the minimum age.

To get the student license an applicant must demonstrate capable ground handling and three takeoffs and landings during towed flight. The FAA has dropped its parental consent requirement for a student license. If you already have a private pilot license you can fly a gyrocopter without any additional paperwork. Don't try to do it, though, until you have been properly checked out.

The student license will allow you to fly the gyrocopter solo, but it must be renewed every two years. The FAA will issue you a private license good for life after you have forty hours of solo experience and have passed a written and flight exam.

Both men and women can excel in this sky sport, and many youngsters have developed flying skills at any early age in Bensens. The glider model has been piloted by preteenagers, and men in their sixties and seventies have been licensed to fly the gyrocopters.

One of the founding fathers of rotorcraft flight was Igor Sikorsky, who experimented with one-passenger rotor craft until he had a successful design. He began his experiments in 1909, and the progeny of his rotorcraft are in use today as military and civilian helicopters. Sikorsky says, "I have never been in the air in a machine that was as pleasant to fly as the light helicopter with completely open cockpit . . . it was like a dream. . . . I succeeded to teach myself to fly by first taxiing on the ground and making a considerable number of short straight-line hops, and finally making my first circle in the air."

If you think you would like a sample of the same unique flying pleasure that stimulated Igor Sikorsky, then proceed with the assembly of this craft made available to you by Igor Bensen.

COSTS

You can begin your Bensen project for as little as $2 for a set of drawings and specifications, or $30 for the plans for the complete powered rig. You may save money by hunting up your own raw materials, although I can guarantee you will put a lot of time into the searching and purchasing. For example, you can't buy aircraft bolts or square aluminum tubing at the corner hardware store.

Be careful about substituting an available

Figure 80. Gyroglider

Figure 81. Bensen Kit Components

part for the recommended one. This might be a great temptation, but remember, your safety is at stake. A gyro pilot was fatally injured when he broke free of the seat when his craft hit the ground during low-altitude maneuvers. Investigation revealed he had substituted a seat made from parts of a light aluminum lawn chair. This seat looked just fine in outward appearance, but was not strong enough to hold the pilot securely in a hard landing.

Bensen kits are available in raw materials, semi-finished, or factory-built components. Remember, though, you can't order all prefinished components and just assemble them over the weekend. You could do this only if you intend to fly the gyroglider on tether without ever making a free flight. To qualify for free flight you must build over fifty percent of the craft yourself, the FAA says. The airframe is the recommended homebuilt portion of the craft since it requires only a hacksaw, vise, file, electric drill, pencil, hammer, and wrenches to construct.

Space does not permit the listing of all kits available from Bensen, but following is a schedule of the most popular plans and kits:

PLANS

Gyroglider 3-view drawings, photos, specifications	$	2.00
Gyrocopter 3-view drawings, photos, specifications		3.00
Gyroglider construction plans & flight manual		15.00
Hydroglider construction plans & flight manual		22.50
Gyrocopter construction plans & flight manual		30.00
Hydrocopter construction plans & flight manual		35.00

KITS

Gyroglider complete materials kit	425.00
Hydroglider complete materials kit, except plywood for pontoons	369.00
Gyrocopter complete materials kit, less engine	995.00
Gyrocopter deluxe kit with metal rotor offset gimbal rotor head and all critical components prefinished at factory, less engine	1,495.00
Gyrocopter complete materials kit including rebuilt surplus McCulloch engine	1,610.00
Joystick control kit (for fixed-wing pilots)	60.00
Training trailer kit	99.50
Offset gimbal control head	249.00
Gimbal head and prerotator	569.00

A complete catalog and illustrated brochure will be sent to you free if you send a request to: Bensen Aircraft Corporation, P.O. Box 2746, Dept. BR-10, Raleigh, North Carolina 27602.

Other than the expense of the Bensen kits your only additional outlay will be for apparel, transportation, and insurance.

Helmet, goggles, and coveralls can be had for under $20 through Sears or Montgomery Ward, or you can use a deluxe fiberglass helmet and double-zippered jump coveralls if you have a spare $50 and want the best attire available. You might remember that your flight performance isn't affected by the price of your garb. As long as your clothes, goggles, and helmet stay secure during flight, they are suitable.

Some people think the helmet is just a device to support a bubble face shield. It really is an indispensable piece of flying equipment, and you should never even run up your rotor without having your head protected by a good helmet. Like seat belts, you never know when you're going to need it.

Goggles, too, are a must. Your eyes need protection, not just from the wind blast, but from flying dust or insects. The only serious mid-air collision I have had was one in which I was spared injury by virtue of my plastic goggles. I was only going about 80 mph, but that was fast enough to make evasive maneuvers impossible. The collision occurred just ahead of my right eye. A fat, hard-shelled Texas beetle exploded himself against my goggles and actually cracked them.

If you want orange flight coveralls, they can be purchased used from most surplus stores, or new from: Flight Equipment Mfg. Co., Cleveland Overall Co., 1768 E. 25th St., Cleveland 14, Ohio.

If you drive a pickup, a board ramp with winch works nicely to assist in loading and unloading. Boat trailers can easily be modified to carry a gyrocraft.

Most owners who fly regularly compute their operating costs to be in the neighborhood of $3 per hour. No other type of flying can compete with this cost figure.

Remember, you can do your own maintenance on the Bensen. You don't have to hire FAA licensed mechanics at $6 or more per hour to inspect and maintain your craft.

CONSTRUCTION

I recommend building the Model B8 gyroglider first. The complete kit costs only $425 and can be constructed in a few weeks. You can fly this glider model in a variety of ways.

When the wind is 20 to 30 mph you can tether the nose hook of the glider to a sturdy post or stake with a fifty-foot nylon or polyethylene line and float off the ground like a kite. Or in calm air you can tether to a vehicle and tow aloft.

The gyroglider makes an excellent training vehicle, especially if you make the training trailer with castoring wheels.

The airframe and rotor of the B8 are identical to the B8M powered gyrocopter. After you have constructed and flown the glider version you can install the power plant.

The airframe is all-aluminum, assembled with steel bolts. There is no welding or riveting required to build the basic frame and rotor. A few parts in the rotor head require a drill press and metal lathe. These can be easily done at a local machine shop, or you can purchase your kit with the rotor head parts already machined from Bensen.

The average home shop will have enough tools to construct the balance of the craft. You may have to buy or borrow some six-inch C clamps to build the rotor. Twenty clamps are needed to pressure the glue joints properly when assembling the ten-foot rotor blades. Don't try to make do with fewer clamps.

The Bensen factory offers a kit called the "critical components kit," which includes all the structural parts which require special treatment for construction such as welding or machining. Included in the kit are the seat bent from aluminum tubing, rotor head, aluminum rotor blades, and motor mount and joystick frame, both welded from chrome-steel tubing.

If you build your ship around this kit you will find construction of the rest of the airframe very simple.

The construction plans and manuals provided by Bensen are quite complete. I have nothing to add to their instructions except the advice to work carefully. Drill, glue, and bolt each part as though your life depended on a perfect job because it will, if you fly the machine.

If you expect to license your gyro for free flight either as a glider or gyrocopter, you should contact an FAA inspector at your nearest General Aviation District Office before you start building. He will make periodic examinations of your craft during construction and issue your license after his inspection of the completed craft.

After construction you should also have your work inspected by a Bensen dealer or experienced Bensen owner. He will be glad to look over your ship to be certain it has been properly put together.

At least one eager Bensen builder was caught by a more knowledgeable pilot, trying to get his rotor up to speed when it was mounted upside down on the teeter bolt. While the factory claims a rotor will work upside down, nevertheless it works much better right side up.

Beware of advice from well-meaning friends and bystanders. Whirly bugs have grown past the "blind leading the blind" era when technical data was not readily available to the builders.

FAA inspectors and fixed wing experts, too, have been guilty of misleading the homebuilder. On at least one occasion an "expert" advised the homebuilder to eliminate the flexibility designed into the teeter hinge. He tightened the teeter bolt so that the hinge became rigid. As a result the machine rolled over to the left on the takeoff.

Consider the Bensen manual as your bible and consult for technical advice *only* the Bensen dealers or persons with fifty hours or more of logged gyrocopter time. If you have technical questions not covered by the Bensen manual or this text, then a letter to the factory will bring you prompt answers either directly or in the magazine published by the Popular Rotorcraft Association.

Don't take liberties with the design and try to incorporate your own improvements or innovations. I am convinced that there is only one way to build your first gyrocraft. That is exactly according to the Bensen plans. This doesn't mean that improvements are impossible. Plenty of fine modified Bensens are flying about the country, but few, if any, of them were built as a first effort.

Be particularly sure that you don't add extra weight to the gyrocopter. Every pound will noticeably reduce flight performance. A streamlined fiberglass body is a tempting attraction to incorporate, but the added fifteen or twenty pounds of weight will really reduce the climb rate and maneuverability.

PRINCIPLES OF FLIGHT

The rotor is a long, limber wing, twenty feet in diameter, seven inches wide, and with a lift-producing airfoil section. As the wing pivots about its hub or axis, lift is generated in an amount proportional to rotating speed. Most of the lift develops from the outer third of the rotor. This is the area that bites through the air at the greatest speed.

When at rest the rotors flex and allow the tips to sag below the hub. When rotation begins the blades lose their sag and the rotor mass builds up centrifugal forces; at the same time the rotor blades begin to strain upward from the lift forces. At flight speed, lift forces and centrifugal forces balance at a slightly upward angle of about 3° above the horizontal.

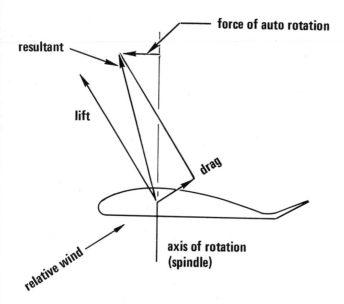

force of auto rotation

resultant

lift

drag

relative wind

axis of rotation
(spindle)

Figure 82. Aerodynamics of Autorotation.

As the rotor of an autogyro moves forward through the air, the relative wind meets the airfoil on an upward angle from the front. Drag acts on the airfoil in a direction parallel to the wind line. The resultant force (balance between lift and drag) will lie in an upward direction ahead of the axis of rotation. Thus a portion of the lift is acting to accelerate the rotor forward.

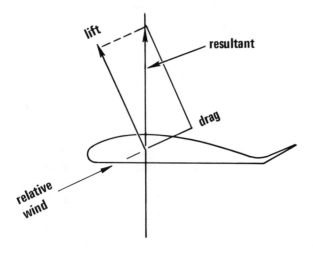

lift

resultant

drag

relative wind

Figure 83. RPM Is Self-Governing.

As the rotor accelerates faster and faster the relative wind will meet the airfoil at a reduced angle causing the resultant to move closer and closer to the axis. When the resultant overlies the axis, rotor speed stabilizes. Thus the rotor RPM is self-governing and tends to remain constant.

This upward angle is called the "coning angle" and it varies slightly with the gross weight of the machine. An upward angle of 3° is built into the wood blades at the hub to approximate the coning angle in flight. The metal blades do not have a built-in coning angle, but they have a long hub which flexes upward 3° in flight.

Airflow through an autogyro rotor is always upward. This is different from a helicopter. Its engine-driven rotor, which draws air from above, accelerates it downward through the rotor disk.

The circular plane in which the rotor turns is called the "rotor disk." For autorotation to occur, the rotor disk must be inclined upward on the leading edge. This upward tilt or "angle of attack" can be varied with the control stick. The pilot thus can control the autorotational forces on his rotor by manipulating the control stick. Refer to the diagram for a description of how the airflow causes autorotation.

Thus the rotor RPM is self-governing and tends to remain constant.

A high angle of attack of the rotor is used to apply maximum autorotational forces on the blades. It is used for takeoff and slow flight of 20 to 30 mph.

During cruising flight of 40 mph and above, the disk has a shallow angle of attack of about 10° and the rotor has considerably less drag.

To obtain good climbing performance the rotor disk should be flying in the area of a 10° angle of attack. If you are in slow flight with a high disk angle and attempt to climb with full power of the engine, results will be disappointing because the engine power is all being used up in rotor drag. To climb in a gyrocopter you must first accelerate in level flight to 40 or 45 mph.

Rotor tilt about 10° during cruising flight

Figure 84. Rotor Tilt 10°

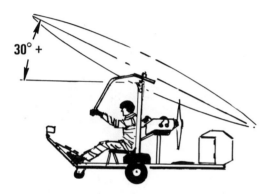

Maximum rotor tilt is used only for maximum acceleration of rotor and for slow flight

Figure 85. Maximum Rotor Tilt

As the rotor disk is subjected to forward speed you can easily understand that the advancing blade is moving through the air at a faster rate than the retreating blade. This differential speed gives rise to unbalanced lifting forces. The advancing blade has greater lift than the retreating blade. If the rotor were rigidly attached to the spindle the extra lift on the right side of the rotor disk would cause the craft to roll to the left during flight.

A simple solution was found to deal with unbalanced rotor lift. I don't know who first tried it, but some enterprising inventor took a rotor with blades rigidly bolted to the hub and mounted them to the axle or spindle with a loose bolt which allowed the rotor to teeter back and forth freely on the spindle. This allowed excess lift from the advancing blade to be spent in lifting the blade, which simultaneously lowered the retreating blade. In effect the retreating blade absorbed the excess lift from its opposing blade.

Flight control is achieved by the control stick which is attached to the lower end of the spindle, which is the rotor's center pivot or axle. The stick acts as an extension of the spindle so that as you grasp the stick, you are in effect holding onto the rotor's axle. The spindle floats on a bearing just above the control stick attaching point, and the rotor hub mounts to the spindle just above the bearing. If you move the stick you change the axis about which the rotor is turning. The rotor disk thus is caused

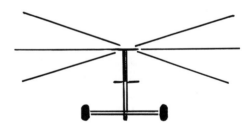

Figure 86. Rotor Teeter

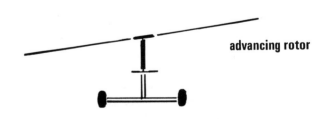

advancing rotor

Figure 87. Cruise Flight View from Rear

stick back to level rotor disk

stick forward to tilt disk back

Figure 88. Overhead Stick Flight Control

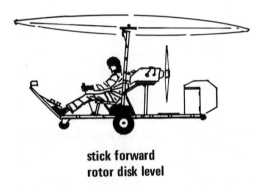

**stick forward
rotor disk level**

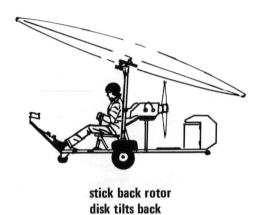

**stick back rotor
disk tilts back**

Figure 89. Joystick Flight Control

to incline either fore and aft or to the side by manipulating the control stick.

The gyrocopter stick has to be moved by hand to accomplish maneuvers. Remember you are flying the rotor and not the airframe. The airframe follows in response to the imbalance created when you tilt the rotor disk. Forces needed to move the control stick are very light, and even during top speed of 80 mph very little pressure is needed to accomplish maneuvers.

Besides the control stick the glider has a tow hook release cord, a steerable nose wheel with brake, and rudder pedals which work independently of the nose wheel steering. However, the controllable rudder is not required on the gyroglider. Its main purpose is to assist with yaw control during takeoffs and landings with the gyrocopter. The copter model also has a twist grip throttle on the control handle.

Vibrations and Flutter

Because it is long, narrow, and limber, the rotor is subject to aerodynamic forces which could easily cause it to flutter. To undersand why, drop a postcard or narrow strip of stiff paper from shoulder height. Air pressure acts to lift the leading edge of the card, while the center of gravity pulls downward on the midpoint. The resultant tumbling flight path is called "fluttering." If one edge of the card is weighted with a paper clip or two, the CG is shifted forward of the center of pressure and the card will make a stable descent like an arrow without fluttering.

Any wing or control surface must be properly balanced with a forward center of gravity to prevent fluttering oscillations when subjected to forward air speed.

The gyrocopter rotor has two design features

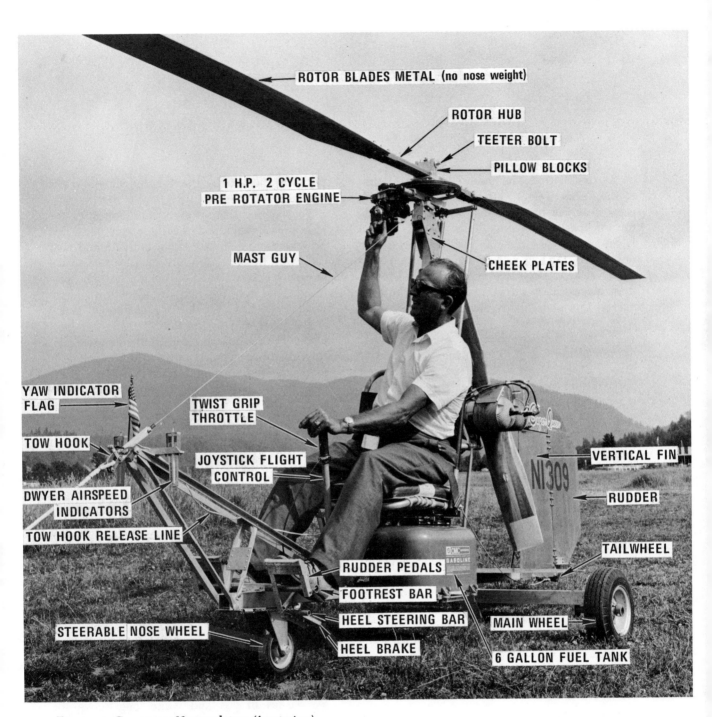

Figure 90. Gyrocopter Nomenclature (front view)

to prevent flutter. The most important feature is the "nose weight" attached to the leading edge near the tip. This moves the blade's CG toward the leading edge. The second feature is an airfoil designed to give no upward or downward pitching forces when subjected to strong airflow. The "zero moment" airfoil found most successful on gyrocopters has a flat bottom, curved top, and sweeps upward at the trailing edge.

The best balance point for a rotor is one-quarter of the way back from the leading edge. This is called "quarter chord" balancing. When unbalanced, the CG is aft of the twenty-five percent point. A slightly underbalanced blade will still operate, but will be oversensitive to control. Flutter will develop if the underbalance goes much over twenty-five percent from the leading edge. Slight "over" balance is better than "under" in that flight characteristics tend toward increased stability. The overbalanced rotor is less affected by wind gusts, requires larger control movements, and may seem "sluggish" to the pilot.

An excessively overbalanced rotor will go into a "weave," which is instability of the rotor disk. A weaving rotor disk dips and pitches randomly. It may go violently out of track and not respond to controls because the tip area is warping itself and not responding to commands from the hub.

Rotor Balance

Proper balance and trim are critical to good rotor performance. It is amazing how many different things affect the rotor performance. Vibrations must be kept to a minimum for the machine to fly safely.

The out-of-balance rotor will transmit a once-per-revolution shake through the hub into the frame.

To check balance with blades bolted to the hub and mounted on the mast you must first be sheltered completely from drafts. Stand near the rotor tip and sight it against some visual reference. Now place a penny on the nose weight and note the rate and amount of downward deflection. If the blade doesn't swing down, there may be friction in the teeter bolt. Shake the control stick and try the penny again. Now rotate the blades until the second blade is in exactly the same position as the first and repeat the procedure with a penny on the nose-weight. If that blade goes down at the same rate and distance, spanwise balance is close enough and will not be a source of vibration.

Out of Track

Other conditions also produce a once-per-revolution vibration. If the blades do not follow exactly in the same plane as they rotate but each assumes a separate plane of rotation, they are "out of track." The once-per-revolution shake in the mast from "out-of-track" rotor blades may be confused with rotor imbalance. This is why balancing must be done first. To test for an out-of-track condition, paint the extreme tip of one blade white and the other red. Tape will work as well. Set up in a good wind of 10 to 15 mph and observe the tips by looking tangent to the blade disk. If they are out of track, you will see flashes of red and white, one above the other. The blade which has slightly more pitch will have the higher orbit. It can be made to rotate in a lower orbit and match the lower blade by bending the trim tab down. It is best, however, to make small adjustments to both tabs, one up and the other down, rather than making all trim tab adjustment to just one blade. Blades should track within one-half inch. Two inches of tip separation at flight RPM is the maximum allowable.

Out of Pattern

One other condition that can cause the once-per-revolution shake is when the blades are not exactly 180° apart. To check, make a mark at the quarter chord point on top of each blade tip. Lift both tips and sight from one to the other. Your line of sight should pass within one-eighth inch of the hub center. This is the maximum allowable error, and more than one-fourth inch out of pattern would be unsafe for flying.

Stiff Teeter Hinge

The teeter hinge should operate freely, or a twice-per-revolution stick shake might result. Friction in the hinge could come from an over-tightened teeter bolt, or dirt which could stiffen the hinge and cause abrasions on the metal surfaces. This "galling" could even occur during flight under certain dusty conditions. Be certain the teeter bolt is clean and lubricated during assembly.

Another small vibration occurs in rotors, which is complicated to describe and cannot be eliminated. It relates to the varying drag forces on each rotor blade as it makes a full circle. When in flight at 40 mph forward speed, a given point on the rotor at about mid-span would be moving at roughly 200 mph as the rotor passes over the tail. As this point comes abeam the craft on the right or advancing side, its airspeed will be 240 mph. When dead ahead it will drop again to 200, then to 160 on the retreating side, and back to 200 again in the aft position. As a result of this changing airspeed each blade goes through a cyclic variation in drag and lift forces and the consequent two-per-revolution vibration cannot be avoided. There must be some manner of compensating for this vibration, however, or it would surely cause fatigue to develop somewhere in the structure. The Bensen method is to use a flexible mast of heat-treated aluminum alloy, which flexes fore and aft slightly without developing metal fatigue.

Some home builders think the mast as designed is too flimsy, and they are tempted to beef it up with lateral supports. This is a serious mistake because the mast must be free to flex slightly.

Resonant Vibrations

The vibrations discussed so far have all been "forced" vibrations. That is, they develop from an imbalance of forces such as unequal weight in a revolving body. There is another kind of vibration called "resonant vibration" which can cause problems in the rotor craft. A resonant vibrator is any object or device which has mass and begins to vibrate when acted upon by an outside force and tries to return to its original position of rest. A piano string, a tuning fork, a flag pole, a rubber ball, are all resonant vibrators. The rotorcraft is an assortment of resonant vibrators. The mast, axle, tail fin, rotor blades, keel tube, and control stick all qualify under the definition. Since the rotor is the device that sustains the craft in flight, it is the main concern when considering resonant vibrations. The point you should realize about this type of vibration is that it can develop in response to an external rythmic force.

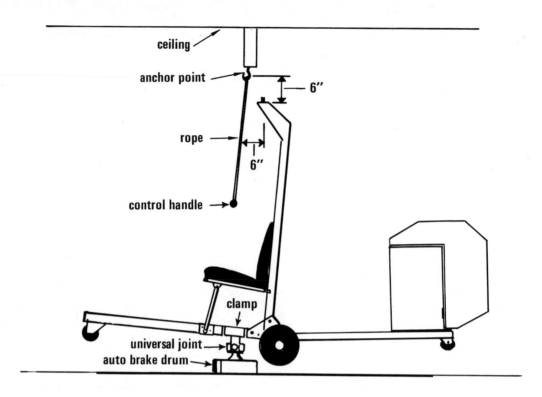

Figure 91. "On the Point" Trainer

A basketball will continue its up-and-down path between the player's hand and the floor as long as the hand applies a slight downward push at the top of each cycle. A very small rhythmic external force may induce a resonant vibration of such magnitude that a machine can destroy itself.

As the rotor turns, very slight imbalances causing one-per-revolution or two-per-revolution vibrations can serve as that small energy to trigger the buildup of violent resonant vibrations in the blade. Bensen blades are designed free of this bugaboo and will perform properly as long as they are constructed according to the plans. If you tamper or experiment with the blade design, or use your own innovations, no matter how innocent they may appear, you may be laying the groundwork for a vibration to develop that will, as one home designer expressed it, "almost shake the teeth out of my mouth."

HOW TO FLY A GYROGLIDER

If you are a beginner you can start your flight training while the rotor is still under construction. You should go through the steps of training "on the point" (see below) before proceeding with towed flights on a tether line.

The experienced pilot with fixed wing or helicopter experience is usually unwilling to take the time for these preflight training maneuvers, which may stretch over several weekends. The only short course I can recommend for pilots is to take dual training in a two-place gyroglider.

Bensen dealers offer dual training for nominal fees. About six half-hour sessions are normally required. Even before making any dual flights, read the next section on the gyroglider on the point and in towed flight.

To fly, the gyroglider must be held in balance by the pilot manipulating the control stick. This is not difficult because the gyrocraft is inherently stable. Like a fixed wing craft the gyroglider tries to maintain its equilibrium and remain stable. Indeed there is proof of the inherent stability of the gyro, especially when it is equipped with the offset gimbal head (an optional extra). Takeoff, climb, turns, descent, and landing are performed with no pilot. It takes a smooth helmsman to jockey the boat, but the gyrocraft has come through several of these pilotless flight demonstrations without damage.

Flying "On the Point"

The pilot should be adept at control movements which will keep the craft under his command at all times. The easiest way for a beginner to get the feel of balancing the craft with the control stick is to "fly it on the point." This is a simple indoor training device which has been used for years at the Bensen factory to develop proper control reflexes.

An automobile universal joint is welded or bolted to an auto brake drum on one end, and clamped to the keel tube of the gyro on the other end. The attaching point is under the center of gravity which is approximately one foot ahead of the keel mast joint. The brake drum rests on the floor and props the ship about three inches off the ground. Leave the rotor off when practicing indoors in the point trainer.

A solid anchoring point must be prepared above the craft to mount your "control handle." A tripod, an overhead beam, or a projection nailed to the ceiling will do. The important thing is to locate this anchor point six inches above and six inches in front of the teeter bolt position when the frame is leveled.

A rope or cable is attached to the overhead anchor point and the handlebars of your control stick are attached to the rope so that they are exactly in the flight position above the seat.

When you are strapped into the seat the craft will be listing to one side and resting on two wheels. The balance practice should be done in three stages. First master the lateral ground control of balance by leaving the nose wheel on the ground and attempt to keep the main wheels up. Apply steady down pressure on the handgrips and use whatever side deflection is necessary to remain balanced. Sit erect and centered in the seat, lean against the backrest, and don't proceed to stage two until you can maintain the axle horizontal for at least two minutes.

Next learn the longitudinal control by keeping both nose and tail wheel off the ground.

Either main wheel may be left down. Push forward on the handgrips until the nose wheel lifts and then return the control to neutral. Keep a light and steady down pressure on the handgrips and correct for balance with fore and aft hand movements.

When you can balance consistently for two minutes, you are ready for the third stage. Now practice keeping all four wheels off the ground until you can remain on the point for five minutes. When you begin to be confident and can remain balanced without having to concentrate, have a helper deliberately tilt the frame and allow you to make recovery control movements.

The beginner should put in several hours of this type of balancing. The pilot who chooses a joystick control for his craft cannot practice on the indoor rig. However, he can utilize the next practice procedure.

On the Point Practice with Rotor

The next stage of control coordination practice is done outdoors and should be practiced by both beginners and experienced pilots. Set up the gyro on the point with the same universal mount just described. Mount the rotor on the rotor head. You need at least 12 mph of wind to give your rotor enough speed. If the wind is blowing over 15 mph, you must anchor the nose hook to a ground stake or post with a ten-foot length of 1,000-pound rope. Use a sturdy lashup because you could build up loads as high as 250 pounds on the anchor line. Hold the rotor disk level with your left hand. Sit in the seat with seat belt attached. Turn to face directly into the wind with craft pulled back to the end of the anchor line. Make sure all bystanders understand that they must remain well clear of your

Figure 92. Jane Woo

craft when the rotor is turning. Hold the control stick neutral with the left hand and start the rotor turning by reaching overhead with the right hand and grasping the smooth part of the blade's trailing edge just outboard of the hub. Do not pull downward on the rotor when starting or stopping it, or else the rotor tip might catch the anchor or towline.

It takes twelve to twenty forward thrusts to get the rotor turning 30 rpm's, which is enough for the wind to take over and begin autorotation. Keep your feet on the ground and tilt rotor back (forward stick) slowly and gradually as the rotor picks up speed. Do not push the stick forward too quickly because a wind gust can cause the forward blade to flap upward forcing the teeter stops to rub on the rotor head cover plate. This will cause unnecessary wear and will slow down rotation.

When the rotor is turning nicely in autorotation, you can proceed to practice balancing on the point. Learn to balance laterally first as with the indoor practice. When that is mastered,

leave one main wheel down while keeping front and rear wheels up. Finally practice holding all wheels off the ground. A 20 mph wind will yield higher rotor speeds of 250 rpm's or more and will give a little quicker response to control stick movements.

If you are using a joystick, your stick movements will be opposite to that of the overhead stick. Pull the joystick back to tilt the rotor disk back. Push the joystick forward to level the rotor disk. It is easy to remember. The joystick, by virtue of its linkage, makes the rotor axis tilt in the same direction as the joystick.

On-the-point practice is so important that you *must* do it for several hours if you expect to make a single successful flight. The only shortcut to the above practice would be dual training in a two-place gyro, or converting your gyro to a training trailer. This costs about $100 for the necessary materials. The axle is replaced with a longer seven-foot axle with castering (free-swiveling) wheels, and a rigid boom is bolted in place of the nose wheel. The eight-foot boom attaches to the car by a ball hitch. The wheels are connected by a tie rod, and spring loaded to steer straight.

The training trailer is also called a "boom trainer" and has proven itself to be an excellent training aid. It is especially nice for a club where several people need flying experience in a safely controlled situation.

When towing behind a vehicle in the training trailer you actually become airborne when the rotor reaches flight rpm's. Altitude is restricted to two or three feet, and an off-center landing will not upset the craft because the wheels will caster whenever you land in a crab position.

The tow-car driver can slow the car in case the pilot trainee should get an oscillation started from overcontrolling. The trailer will respond not only in altitude, but it will drift when the rotor is tilted sideways. This gives the trainee an opportunity to learn the art of "anticipating" in the use of the control stick.

The frame upon which you ride swings beneath the rotor like a pendulum, and to prevent overcontrolling you must apply corrective stick movements ahead of the lagging response. This

Figure 93. Training Trailer. Also called "Boom Trainer."

is called "anticipating," and must be developed to a reflex-like skill.

Training Boom Practice Flights

Try to pick a windless day for your first training trailer or boom flights. 1,000 feet of runway will do, but the more the better. After assembling the craft and attaching to the tow car hitch, make a final preflight inspection.

At this time you should have a meeting with the tow driver and safety rider to discuss the following details of the tow practice. Hand signals are the primary communication link between pilot and tow driver. The pilot can signal by gesturing with his right hand as follows: (1) Up-and-down motion with fist clenched, thumb extended upward means, "Let's go," or "More speed"; (2) same movement, thumb down means, "Less speed"; (3) horizontal stroke of index finger across your neck means, "Stop now, but not abruptly."

The tow driver should maintain a constant airspeed by reference to the windmeter, not the speedometer. Mount a windmeter on the hood of the tow car along with a small flag or piece of yarn. This gives the driver a wind speed and direction reference. A simple mount can be made from a broom handle tied to the front bumper and grill. The driver should always use brakes and throttle gently. An automatic transmission is best for smooth shifting.

The safety rider should be in the rear seat facing aft to watch the pilot and to relay signals to the driver. An experienced driver can use a rear-view mirror in lieu of a safety rider. Don't carry any other passengers in the tow car, as they might distract the driver.

Wear your hard helmet and goggles during boom training. The first few runs should be at 15 mph. This speed will be enough to give a rotor speed of 200 to 250 rpm. You won't lift off, but will get a good feel of rotor response to the control stick. Also you can check the tow driver's ability to hold a constant speed.

Next, call for 20 mph and make a few runs. At this speed the rotor goes into its second stage of rpm range. This is the range where it accelerates easily and makes a whistling sound, which is music to the ears of the enthusiast because it occurs only moments before takeoff when the rotor is approaching flight rpm. When the wheels lift off the ground, you should "dump the lift" immediately by leveling the rotor disk (pull stick back). Then ease stick forward again until you lift off and again land immediately. If 20 mph doesn't give you clean takeoffs with the stick full forward, then up the towspeed to 25 mph. Keep your altitude below one-foot and stay on the centerline behind the tow car. Take a breathing spell after fifteen or twenty minutes of practice.

Next, increase tow speed to 30 mph and make at least ten full-length runs. After you have achieved good judgment in takeoffs and landings, practice maintaining a constant altitude of two to three feet high. Stay on the centerline behind the tow car until you can hold your altitude accurately. Don't let your gaze become fixed on the tow car during tows. It is better to watch the horizon with periodic glances at your airspeed and the ground.

When approaching the end of a run, drop to one-foot high and signal thumbs down. The driver should lift his foot from the throttle and you will settle to a smooth landing as your speed drops below 20 mph. This is the same landing technique used later when towing on a tether line at higher speeds.

Next you can practice lateral control move-

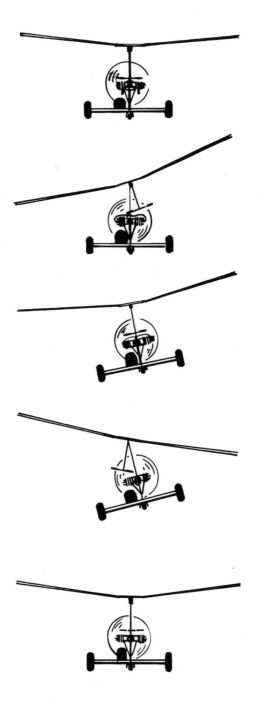

1. Straight and level flight

2. Move stick right to initiate left bank and drift. Airframe remains level monentarily

3. Airframe gradually tilts in response to out of balance forces in control head. Craft will continue a steady turn.

4. To stop the bank, move stick left as to begin a right turn. Airframe lags behind control movement.

5. Anticipate recovery by centering stick before airframe reaches vertical attitude.

Figure 94. Gyrocraft Turns

Figure 95. Kiting

ments by tilting the rotor disk to the side and
drifting off centerline. You will not notice the
pendulum effect of the craft when you make
lateral control movements. Remember, the airframe is hanging from the rotor by a universal
pivot. There is a time lag between the control
stick motion and the tilt of the airframe. Also
the frame will probably overshoot your intended motion just as a free-swinging pendulum
will overshoot when you push it. You will soon
learn to deal with this pendulum effect by anticipating the lag in control response. For example, if you want to drift left you tilt the rotor
disk left with a little right stick. Hold the stick
right for only a moment, and then return it to
neutral. The airframe tilt will occur a second or
so later. The craft will now drift left. Level the
rotor disk by a momentary jab to the left with
the stick. The airframe will take a second or
more to respond.

To return to centerline behind the tow car
you must again make two corrections. Drift

right, and then level the rotor disk. This is accomplished by first tilting the rotor disk right
with left stick. Use only a momentary stick dis-
placement and return it immediately to neutral.
After the right drift begins, start your recovery
to level the rotor disk as you approach the
centerline. Again a momentary right stick and
then neutral.

A jab does the job. The gyrocraft is unique
among aircraft because you use only momentary
control deflections. Lateral control movements
boil down to a series of jabs to the side with
the stick in neutral for all the intervening time
between jabs. If you find your jab *didn't* do the
job, make another, and perhaps another. Several
short jabs are better than one, for one long jab
might trigger a recovery jab which is also too
long, and before you know it, you're in a pendulum "pilot-induced oscillation." If this happens,
your tow driver should decelerate immediately.
You could stop the oscillations by properly
timing the control stick movements, but if your

reflexes were properly timed, you wouldn't be oscillating in the first place. The best recovery for oscillations is to land immediately. It's like a flat spin recovery when sky divers are learning freefall technique and lose lateral control. Many times I have been asked, "How do you break a flat spin?" "You pull your ripcord," I say. If you had enough control of your reflexes to break a spin by counter control movements, you wouldn't be spinning in the first place.

Normal airspeed during trailer operations should not exceed 35 mph. The pendulum swinging effect of the airframe will not be apparent in a fore and aft direction because the gyro's nose is anchored to the tow car. Your first free flights in a gyrocopter will make you aware of the similar longitudinal swinging tendency. Anticipation and short jabbing control movements are the rule for dealing with the pendulum action.

As a beginner you will want to accumulate at least two hours of boom flying experience before proceeding to towline flying. Don't try to check out in one day. Six half-hour periods on three or more days is much better. Don't overdo the practice during this stage of training or subsequent ones. The excitement of gyro flying may draw more on your physical and emotional stamina than you realize. It is wise to terminate practice before you get too tired and start making mistakes.

FIRST SOLO

If terrain and weather permit, your first truly airborne experience can be kiting in the wind on a twenty-foot line. Wind speed should be 25 to 30 mph and not over 35 mph. Set up facing the wind with the twenty-foot tether line anchored to a really solid stake in the ground.

The stake should hold as much load as the towline breaking strength, which should be 1,000 pounds. Accelerate the rotor with the technique described for flying on the point. Just before the rotor reaches flight rpm the gyro will rock back on its tail wheel. Now, a little forward stick will lift you off the ground. Quickly reduce the rotor tilt to hold you just above the ground. You don't want to balloon up to the tether line limit until you have felt out the rotor at lower altitudes. When you have relaxed and become confident, work your way up to fifteen feet. Practice a gentle drift slightly off center line and back until you can control altitude and drift accurately.

After about four fifteen-minute periods of kiting you should be ready for tether towing behind a car. If you don't find an opportunity to kite at all, you can proceed directly from boom flying to tow flying, but take it easy. Don't rush your progress because this teach-yourself process *has* to be slow in order to be safe.

Towing Training

A thirty-foot towline is best for a beginning. This keeps you close enough to the tow vehicle for verbal communication. Make several runs without the rotor at speeds of 10, 15, and 20 mph. Don't exceed 20 mph without the rotor because the short wheel base and quick steering make steering very touchy and you could lose control. After the rotor is installed and spinning rapidly, you will be able to tow faster than 20 because the spinning rotor has a braking effect like a drag chute, which stabilizes the gyro during taxi runs.

The steering bar and brake are both operated with your heels, and believe me, it takes a lot of practice to become smooth with that nose

Figure 96. Auto Towing Gyroglider

wheel steering. During this taxi practice, learn to release your tow hitch by grasping the line where it ties to the seat frame and giving it a quick pull. You should develop this releasing technique until you can do it without looking.

Be critical in your selection of a tow driver, for he is in a very responsible position. Don't fly if the driver is likely to horse around or do anything other than follow prearranged tow duties and follow your commands. Many gyro glider flights have come to grief because the tow driver either didn't understand his job or chose to ignore his responsibility in favor of some smart trick like weaving or overspeeding.

Be sure to conduct a driver's briefing before you proceed with towing with the rotor installed. It would be best to have the driver read this entire chapter on towed gyrocopter flight, but the very minimum reading for him should be the following section.

What the Tow Driver Should Know

1. Driver should read the chapter on towed flight in the book or in the Bensen Flight Manual.
2. Check car for (a) proper gas, oil and running condition; (b) rear-view mirror; (c) sturdy tow hitch anchored to car frame (don't tie to bumper); (d) airspeed meter and flag mounted in driver's view; (e) safety rider facing rearward to watch gyro.
3. Inspect towline for knots, frays, metal thimble in loop at glider hitch, or tie a two-inch metal ring to towline to engage gyro tow hook. 1,000 pounds breaking strength is proper size. Quarter-inch polyethylene or nylon will do, or ⅜-inch manila.
4. Tow against the wind. Use the airspeed indicator for speed reference, not the speedometer. Don't exceed 30 mph unless gyro is airborne. Don't slow below 35 mph while gyro is over two feet above the ground.
5. Examine the terrain to be used for towing. It should be clear of obstructions, ruts, rocks, puddles, and soft spots.
6. Carry a set of hand tools in case you need to do some work in the field.
7. Understand pilot hand signals from gyro seat. Safety rider should understand these signals, too.
8. Don't carry passengers other than the safety rider in the tow vehicle.
9. Gyro pilot should drop into landing position (one foot high) while there is still plenty of towing space left.

10. Do not apply brakes or make turns abruptly. Keep slack out of the towline.
11. Hold a constant tow speed as directed by pilot. Don't speed up just because he is airborne.

Before you start towing, be sure your towline is secure to the tow car and doesn't contact any sharp edges that could cut it. One lad who neglected this advice had serious problems when the bumper cut the towline after he was airborne. It came recoiling back and was hooked by a rotor blade. Before the pilot could do anything he was pinned to the seat as the line wound around him. Just before the coils reached his throat the rotor was jammed to a stop by a loop of towline around the hub. It is best to tie to a smooth surface such as the neck of a sturdy trailer hitch.

If the tow vehicle doesn't have a windmeter, you can give the tow driver an approximate speed to follow on the speedometer as follows: Take the average wind speed and apply it to the desired tow speed. If you wish to tow at 15 mph airspeed and the wind as shown on the gyro windmeter seems to be about 5 mph, the speedometer tow speed would be 10 mph.

Be sure to back your gyro till the towline is tight before hand propping the rotor. Be sure you are towing against the wind. Don't try it if you have over a 20° crosswind, or if the wind is above 15 mph.

Make your first runs at 15 mph or below. Because this will keep the rotor in the low speed range you need a little practice in handling the stick while steering with the nose wheel.

If all goes well after a half dozen runs, call for 20 mph. Be sure you have proper first stage rpm at 15 mph. If you try 20 mph too soon, the rotor may refuse to accelerate and may flap uncontrollably on the teeter hinge. The gyro will rock onto its tailwheel just before lifting off. When this happens, pull the stick back to "dump the lift" and rock the craft back on its nose wheel. Then push the stick forward again to rock back onto the tail. This teeter-totter action will help you develop a feel for the craft's attitude. Make several runs this way, rocking fore and aft on the main wheels.

While running on the main wheels, the gyro may creep off to the side a little if your main wheels are a little out of alignment. Don't try to compensate for this with the stick. Keep the stick vertical because it won't pull you back in line. You could leap sideways upon becoming airborne if you held a lateral tilt in the stick.

Now call for 25 mph and proceed with a straight-ahead lift-off. Stay on the centerline and keep your feet off the steering bar when you land. You could cause a swerve on landing by cocking the nose wheel. Neutralize the stick as soon as you're airborne and land again right away. You should spend only a few seconds in the air at a time during this leap frog practice. Maintain the main wheels level at all times. If you drift more than five feet to either side of centerline, land promptly.

As you gain confidence, remain at a two- or three-foot altitude for progressively longer periods. Try to hold a precise altitude of, say, two feet, no higher and no lower. This is a most important period in your training program because it develops your judgment and timing during low altitude and landing maneuvers. Resist the urge to climb above three feet until you can make ten full runs with precision control of altitude.

Don't maneuver off centerline because the rigid wheels won't forgive a landing in a crab. A fixed wing pilot, training in a gyrocraft, must be particularly diligent in remaining with each step of the training routine before proceeding to the next. Gyrocrafts have a unique way of lulling the trainee into thinking that he has mastered complete control. Then suddenly a wind gust or slight overcontrol will cause the pilot to tense up and make a jerky or impulsive response.

After there is no doubt about your ability to control altitude and direction at low altitude you may climb a little higher on each succeeding flight. Use a tow speed of 35 mph and don't climb above twenty feet with a thirty-foot towline. Gentle S turns should be practiced to further develop your coordination. You should also practice varying your altitude smoothly from five to fifteen feet and back.

Don't dive abruptly when reducing altitude. If you do, the towline may go slack and then come tight with a snap. This could start a towline buffet, or rhythmic oscillation. If this happens, land as soon as possible and start over. If you find the towline buffet occurs again, change the towline length or change to a different size towline.

After four to six towing sessions of twenty minutes each you can increase tow speeds in 5 mph increments with 60 mph as top speed. Do some maneuvering exercises at each new speed. You will notice that you will float longer and farther before touchdown when landing from higher speeds.

Always use the same technique for landing. While there is still adequate runway ahead, drop to one-foot high directly behind the tow vehicle and signal thumbs down. The tow driver will decelerate. You hold your one-foot high position by smoothly tilting the rotor disk back until finally your speed is so slow that the rotor cannot keep you in the air. Your tailwheel should touch down first, then the main wheels.

When you have good control on the thirty-foot towline, you can proceed to tow with a fifty-foot, and then a seventy-five-foot, towline.

Before you can release from the towline and practice free flight, descents, and landings, you will have to pass a proficiency test for an FAA inspector. Pilots already licensed will not be required to have the above FAA check, but they should be able to perform the exercises before proceeding to make free flights. Also, they will have to obtain the aircraft license for the glider from the **FAA.**

Free Flights in Gyroglider

With a thirty-foot towline, tow directly into the wind at 40 mph with only two feet of altitude. Pull the tow release and use rudder to maintain directional control. Don't touch the nose wheel steering bar during the landing. Hold two feet of altitude as long as the rotor can keep you aloft. Be sure the tail wheel touches the ground first upon landing.

After several free landings of this nature, repeat the exercise using 50 mph as the tow speed. Make at least five of these, and then repeat five more at 60 mph. You should now be ready for a higher release altitude. Using a seventy-five-foot towline and 45 mph tow speed, climb to thirty feet and start down. You may need full back stick to start the glide. Pull release as the rope begins to slacken. Watch your airspeed indicator and maintain 45 mph. Your nosedown attitude will be quite steep (about a 30° angle to the ground) with no wind blowing. Begin the flare out when above five feet high and land tail first, as before.

This is the final practice stage before you will be ready to convert to a self-powered gyrocopter. Make many free flight landings, starting from varying altitudes. Do not climb higher than half the towline length. Also, be careful

Figure 97. Banded Rotors

not to tow at excessively high speeds when you are in high tow position with the towline at a 45° upward angle. 45 mph is adequate for a good climb. Greater tow speeds at a high rope angle would put undue stress on the gyro's rotor.

Always remember, to start a glide, slacken the towline before pulling the tow release. A release under full tension would give you a wild swing backward and put you in a mid-air flare. Rotor speed would fall off and it would take considerable altitude to reestablish your proper glide angle and speed. You will have no problems with the release if you always release on a slack line and tilt the rotor full forward immediately after release to establish a 45 mph glide.

You can make tow releases up to 150 feet high without any prior arrangements with the FAA, unless you are close to an active airport. For release altitudes between 160 and 500 feet you must notify the nearest FAA General Aviation District Office in writing the day before your flight, giving your name, flight location, and time. For release altitudes above 500 feet or for any free flights within 5 miles of an active airport, you must apply for a certificate of waiver on FAA Form 663. This is valid for one year and will help alert other pilots of your operations. It is for your safety, too, because that towline is very hard to see and you wouldn't want some light plane to fly into it.

A free descent in the gyroglider is exhilarating, but brief. Your rate of descent depends

Figure 98. Gyrocopter Nomenclature (rear view)

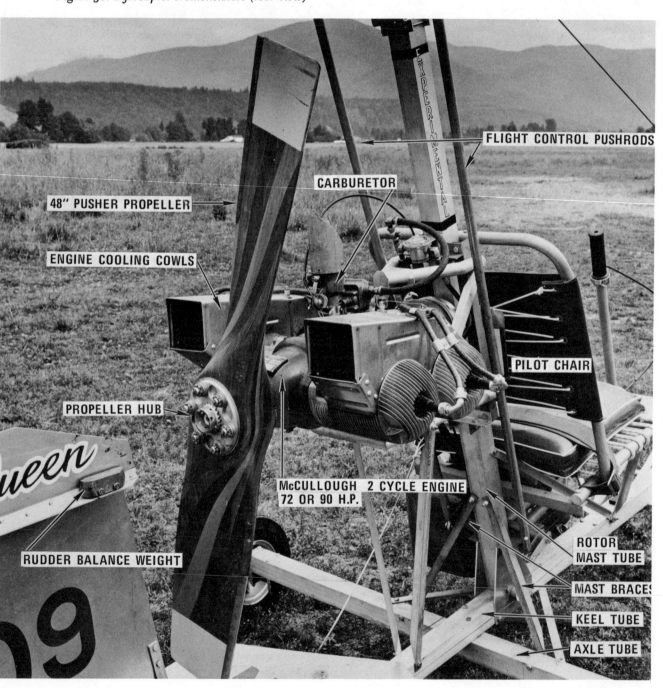

FLIGHT CONTROL PUSHRODS

CARBURETOR

48" PUSHER PROPELLER

ENGINE COOLING COWLS

PILOT CHAIR

PROPELLER HUB

McCULLOUGH 2 CYCLE ENGINE
72 OR 90 H.P.

RUDDER BALANCE WEIGHT

ROTOR
MAST TUBE

MAST BRACES

KEEL TUBE

AXLE TUBE

Figure 99. Hang Test

upon pilot weight, but 500 feet per minute is about normal. You would need to have a 500-foot release altitude to make a one-minute flight. This rate of descent is considerably slower than in a parachute, but it still rules out the possibility of working an updraft and remaining aloft. The glide ratio is about five to one, so you could glide half a mile in calm air from 500 feet high.

The visibility from a gyro is unsurpassed, but they are hard for other aircraft to see while in the air. You can do two things to improve your visibility: (1) Paint the rotor blades with fourteen-inch alternate bands of a dark and a bright color, such as yellow or dayglow orange, and black or dark blue; (2) Wear full-length orange coveralls and paint your helmet dayglow orange.

Converting to Powered Model

To convert your Model B-8 gyroglider into a B-8-M gyrocopter you must install a McCulloch Model 4318 engine, engine mount, cowlings, and accessory package consisting of fuel tank, carburetor, throttle control, magneto ground switch, and propeller unit.

Time and budget will be your guide when choosing the engine to install. The factory-new 4318-G engine develops ninety horsepower and comes ready to install from Bensen with all accessories for $1495. The 4318 A seventy-two horsepower surplus engine is still available for

as little as $50, but an extensive list of modifications are necessary before it is suitable for flight. You can look forward to at least a $500 expense to the power unit even when using the surplus engine.

Many Bensens are flying with custom installations of different engines such as the 1600 cc Volkswagen engine converted for aircraft use. You must be a really knowledgeable mechanic to undertake using an engine such as this because the engine mount, propeller, and all accessories will have to be completely fabricated.

The engine installation weight moves the center of gravity aft about five inches, so the gyro must be rebalanced by installing short "cheek plates" on the rotor head in place of the long ones on the gyroglider. This will correct for the new weight distribution. However, you should still make a "hang test."

Suspend the gyro from the teeter bolt and sit in the seat with the stick held neutral. The mast should measure 2° from vertical, nose down. The maximum allowable variation is zero to 3° nose down. Add nose or tail weights as necessary to correct the balance. Bounce hard on the seat while it is suspended to check the structure strength. A drop test from eight inches high is also recommended as a strength test.

The ship should weigh 240 pounds empty, but up to 300 pounds is permissible. Follow the *Bensen Operating Manual* for engine starting and operating techniques.

You can make your engine checks and learn the starting routine by tieing the tail wheel bracket to a tree or sturdy post. Hand-starting a propeller is quite safe if you always treat the propeller with due respect. Refer to my instructions in the power plane chapter.

Be sure to wear earplugs when running the engine. Spectators should be kept clear of your operating area when working with the engine. You can use a crew of one trained helper to act as a prop man, but no one else should be allowed under the rotor. Keep a sharp eye peeled for aggressive onlookers when the engine is running because you don't hear them approach. You can't hear anything when a McCulloch is fired up. There really is no substitute for a fence or rope barricade for keeping spectators at a safe distance.

Measure the full power engine thrust with a spring scale tied into the anchor line. It should read approximately half of the expected gross weight. To avoid overheating, don't run the engine at full throttle over two minutes.

Also, while the engine is running, examine the entire craft for looseness or vibration of any parts. The vertical fin is often prone to shake with a resonant vibration. Test the fin with all power settings and various rudder deflections. Don't be too easily convinced that the fin is stable. Try striking it to induce a vibration. It should stabilize immediately.

Be sure the tail wheel is off the ground during these checks. You may need to stiffen the fin with additional side straps.

Preflight Inspection and Maintenance Tips

If you have previous aircraft experience you will know that a preflight inspection must be performed religiously before each flight. As a beginner you should develop the habit of going over your craft carefully before each flight and especially the first flight of the day.

Begin at the gyro's nose and work your way clockwise about the craft. Any discrepancy you find that might affect the flight performance should be remedied before the flight. Be especially thorough in your examination of the craft after transporting it by truck or trailer.

Following is an itemized checklist to assist with your inspection:

1. Tow hitch free to swivel, cotter pins on pivot bolts. Release line secure. Tow hitch frame secure and all bolts tight.
2. Flag and airspeed indicator secure and working properly.
3. Footrest tight. Wheel castor pivot adjusted. Brake working, steering springs and chains just snug and safetied.
4. Check tire pressure by standing on the foot bar.
5. Seat attachments to frame secure. Check for bent or cracked angle braces under and behind seat. Safety belt and shoulder harness secure.
6. Rotor head. All bolts tight in mast to rotor attachment. Rotation stopper bolt tight and freshly greased in the slot. Head plate greased and not bent. Teeter hinge clean and freshly greased. Adjust to pivot freely, but without play. Test for teeter bolt play in spindle (hold control stick, see if hub will wobble about pitch axis). If loose, rotor will give you tracking problems. Worn hole in spindle can be reamed to next larger size hole, and old teeter bolt replaced with larger size. Galling marks between spindle and pillow blocks should be filed smooth. Check that spindle turns

freely. Grease main rotor bearing every twenty-five hours. Cotter pins in place in all bolts. Control stick attachment, or joy-stick linkage, secure.

7. Hub bolts tight and safetied. Keep scratches and nicks filled and refinished. Nose weights and trim tabs secure. You can help prevent nicks from flying pebbles or water spray by keeping a two-inch wide strip of plastic tape on leading edge of rotor blade. Don't store gyro for long periods with rotor installed. Overnight is all right, but between weekends remove rotor and keep blades flat.

8. Main wheel tires properly inflated. Axle nuts adjusted properly. Grease main wheel bearings every fifty hours or as needed. Rudder cables not binding or frayed. Clevis pins have cotter pins.

9. Tail surfaces secure, no cracks in struts or hinges. Rudder movement to full control limit, tail wheel free, axle bolt tight.

10. Engine and propeller. Examine propeller blades for nicks. Check hub bolts for tight-ness. A loose prop can fly apart. Prop hub should have clear plastic or varnish finish. Strain marks, if they occur near hub, will show through finish. Check cyclinder cowlings and brackets. Carburetor mount-ing bolts and air scoop tight. Throttle control smooth and full travel without slack motion. Ignition harness secure to plugs and magneto, no chafing. Magneto ground wire secure and working (an open circuit in this wire will cause magneto to be "hot" at all times). Fuel pump and lines secure, no chafing. Gas tank pres-surized. Loosen cap and listen for hiss, indicating no air leaks present in the tank. Check exhaust ports for carbon deposits.

Must be cleaned every twenty-five hours or as needed. Remove, clean, and test spark plugs every twenty-five hours. Recom-mended gap is .018 inch, but some owners get better results with .011 inch. Remove magneto and have it checked over by magneto shop every twenty-five hours.

If you find bent parts, a bent angle brace, or airframe tube, you must replace it. Don't straighten it. Future strain on the part will cause it to fatigue and break at the weak place.

When your McCulloch engine is installed and test run you still have a little training to do be-cause a few things are different about powered gyro flight. You have an additional control. The throttle is a twist-grip type as on a motorcycle. You need at least two days of operating the gyro on the ground and at low altitude to be-come familiar with it before venturing too far upward.

The gyrocopter has a new weight, which is about 150 pounds more than you are used to. You need to get the feel of the ship in the air at this new higher weight, and also it is neces-sary to give the rotor another thorough check out. The higher weight will cause the rotor to turn faster at any given airspeed, and towed flights with engine shut off are best for making sure the rotor is smooth at all airspeeds.

Put in about two hours, or twenty runs, in towed flight with engine shut down. Make several low-altitude straight-ahead runs under ten feet high. Use various airspeeds up to 65 mph to be sure there are no rotor vibrations present. The rotor may have to be retracked, sped up, or slowed down, to get away from vibrations if they develop. After you are thoroughly relaxed at the controls, you may proceed with powered taxiing.

I have already mentioned that you should wear a helmet any time the rotor is turning. You should also wear ear plugs any time the engine is running. An unmuffled aircraft engine puts out a lot of racket, and sustained exposure to this noise not only damages your ears, but it also is tiring and interferes with proper learning of motor responses.

Powered Taxi Practice

Either leave the rotor off, or secure it to stay stationary. An airport is best, but a playfield will do, if clear of spectators. About an hour of taxi practice spread over four fifteen-minute sessions should give you the needed ground handling skills. Practice straight-line taxi runs up to 15 mph, no faster. Practice turns until you can hold a smooth, constant radius turn.

Learn to stop quickly by depressing the brake bar with both heels. Be sure to practice turns in both directions. A figure eight is also a good taxi practice pattern. Braking should be done before starting a curve. Always close the throttle before using the brake. When your turns are smooth, you should concentrate on straight runs. Paving with a centerline is excellent for practicing straight runs.

Next, install the rotor and restart the engine. If you use a prop man, he should not spin the rotor. This should be done only by the pilot from the seat. Never start the rotor turning until the prop man is clear of the rotor area. It is best to taxi well clear of everybody before starting the rotor.

For taxi runs with the rotor you should have 1,500 feet or more. Use 15 mph again and hold control stick full forward for best autorotation. You will have to add a little throttle to com-pensate for rotor drag as the rotor picks up speed. After a few runs, try shifting your feet to the rudder pedals after stabilizing your speed at 15 mph. This allows the nose wheel to castor freely, but you still have directional control with the rudders. Practice gently turning back and forth across the centerline using rudder pedals only. At the end of a run, reduce throttle and shift your feet back to the steering bar and brake.

It is very important to have good coordination and reflexes during the ground maneuvers and taxi runs. Don't proceed with the higher speed taxi runs until you have precision control at the 15 mph ground speeds.

The next step is to make many straight-ahead runs at 20 mph with the main wheels only on the ground. You will find that at 20 mph you have sufficient rotor lift to rock back on the tail wheel, but when you do, the rotor drag increases and you will have to apply an additional burst of throttle to maintain 20 mph. Use rudder for directional control. Constant right rudder is needed to compensate for propeller torque. At flight speeds the rudder trim tab will balance the torque force, but in slow flight or fast taxi runs, you will have to use right-foot pressure on the pedal.

Don't leave the tail wheel dragging, but maintain a balance on the main gear by manipulating the control stick. Keep the stick vertical, meaning no lateral control movements. Pilots have a tendency to tilt the stick sideways during ground runs. This is taboo because it could lead to an awkward sideways takeoff.

If you have done all the above taxi exercises in one day, I suggest calling it quits. This practice is quite fatiguing whether you realize it or not. Save the first flights for a fresh day.

First Flights

The first flight should be preceded by several taxi runs at 20 mph with tail wheel close but not touching the ground. Leapfrogging, or short straight-line hops, are the rule for your first ten or more flights. Start a run as you would a straight-line high-speed taxi run, except accelerate to 30 mph with about half throttle. Maintain this speed with throttle adjustments until the main wheels lift off the ground. Reduce throttle smoothly to about one-third open and try to touch the ground with tail wheel first. This will require a little forward stick just before landing.

Be very sure your throttle changes are smooth because abrupt throttle manipulations cause fore and aft pitching of the airframe.

After ten or twelve short hops at one to two feet high, make some longer runs until you are able to fly the full length of the runway at 40 mph at one to two feet high. You will notice on the longer hops that as the gyro accelerates past 30 mph you will have to reduce throttle gently to keep from gaining too much altitude. The rotor develops its minimum amount of drag in flight at 45 mph. Your lowest throttle or power setting for level flight will be at 45 mph. Any speed above or below 45 mph will require more power. This is a very important fact to remember about your gyro. Another important fact to remember is that the throttle is your primary altitude control. The stick controls turns, banks, and dives and the throttle controls altitude.

The rudder controls yaws and is used very little in flight. Its main purpose is to control torque and keep the gyro lined up with the runway on takeoff and landing.

The flag mounted above the tow release hook is used as a yaw reference. When the flag is pointing directly at you, you know the craft is not drifting sideways. Use the flag also to check your rudder trim. During some of your 45 mph straight-ahead runs, take your feet off the rudders and watch the flag. If it shows a yaw, correct by adjusting the rudder trim.

To make smooth landings at the end of a run don't chop the throttle from ten feet high. Instead fly the gyro down to one to two feet high and then smoothly reduce power to one-third throttle. As speed dissipates gradually apply forward stick until your tail finally touches the ground at a little under 10 mph. If you're flying with a 7 to 10 mph headwind, you may have a zero ground speed at touchdown. Be sure to level the rotor disk immediately after touchdown to prevent rotor lift from pulling you backward after landing.

Be sure you have no more than one or two feet of altitude when you begin the flareout. If your speed gets below 20 mph, you will make a landing no matter how much power you apply. Even at full throttle the gyro won't maintain altitude at 18 mph. Rotor drag is simply too high at these slow air speeds.

Fifty runs are not too many to spend on the runway at altitudes below ten feet. This is where you develop the coordination and judgment that will allow you to make safe and accurate landings every time.

It is curious, but true, that most of the difficulties at this level of training happen to pilots with fixed wing experience. Many pilots have an overpowering urge to gain altitude right after they take off, for they don't feel comfortable until they have a few hundred feet of altitude. The tendency to climb after takeoff leads to a second problem: overflying the end of the run-

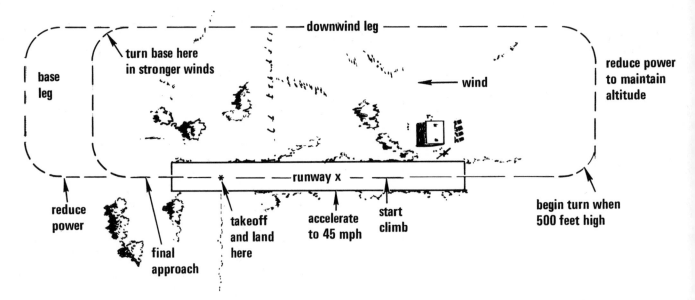

Figure 100. Gyrocopter Pattern

way instead of reducing throttle and landing with some runway to spare. If a pilot does over-fly the runway, he has little choice but to make a full pattern around the field. Many persons have had a bad experience as result of going too high too soon during early training flights when they should have been leapfrogging along the deck, building knowledge and judgment. So spend a minimum of two hours on low-altitude straight-ahead flights before venturing into a turn.

One other common mistake of experienced pilots is to "chop," or quickly close the throttle, when ready to make a landing. This is definitely not for gyros. Reduce throttle only *slightly* to adjust the glide angle, and always make throttle changes smoothly and gradually.

Now make a few straight-ahead, low-altitude runs with higher air speeds on each successive run until you have reached 70 mph. Reduce power and decelerate for landing while you have ample runway ahead. The gyro will float or remain airborne for a considerable distance from these higher air speeds. Use progressively less power on landing flareouts until you can make a smooth landing with engine idling.

Next make a series of low flights at 45 mph and make some gentle left and right turns. You will notice that rudder is not needed to make a coordinated turn. The rudder and vertical fin area act automatically to keep your gyro's keel lined up with the flight path.

Before proceeding with steeper turns during thirty-foot-high runs, consider for a moment the

loss of lift that occurs during turns. To turn you must tilt the rotor disk. A tilted disk has less of its area working to keep you aloft. It takes some additional engine power to offset the lift loss during turns. The steeper the turn, the more power you must add just prior to starting the turn in order to maintain your altitude and speed.

Don't let your speed fall below 40 mph during turn practice. You might not have enough reserve engine power available to make turns at low air speed. This would result in loss of altitude and perhaps an inadvertent landing, or worse.

Don't, under any circumstance, turn more than 45° off the wind line when the wind is blowing over 5 mph. Turning away from an upwind heading is called a "downwind turn," and it can be very hazardous if performed at low altitude. As a rule of thumb for any aircraft, powered, glider, or gyro, have at least 300 feet of altitude before you make a downwind turn.

During your low-altitude turn practice, plan your final turn so that you can land upwind. Crosswind landings aren't for the birds. You'll never see a bird landing crosswind or down-wind. They know what they are doing, and we are well advised to emulate them in this matter.

After you feel relaxed and confident and have spent hours at the low-level runs, proceed with a full traffic pattern. Take off, level off to gain 45 mph, and instead of throttling back, keep the power on and hold your air speed at 45 to 50. Your gyro will climb smoothly aloft and in less

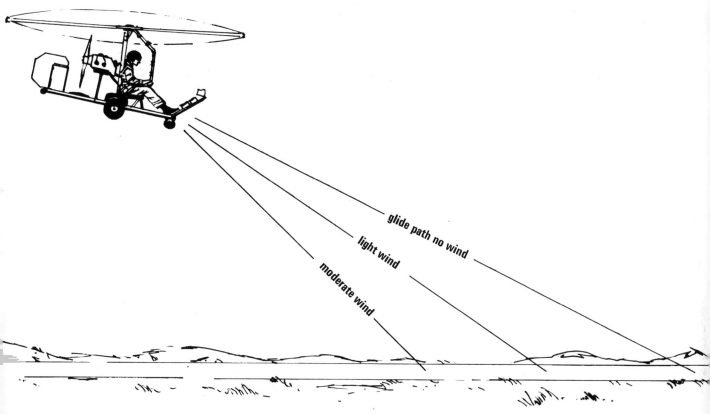

Figure 101. Effect of Wind on Glideslope

than one minute you will be 500 feet high and ready to make a pattern turn. Conform to the field pattern requirements, which usually means left turns in the pattern. Watch your speed during turns and don't let it fall below 40 mph. Your downwind leg should be at a constant altitude of about 500 feet, so you will need to reduce power to keep altitude and speed constant.

It is best to carry a little extra speed on base leg and final approach, so start descending on base leg, but don't make any drastic throttle reduction until you are established on final approach. Now use throttle to adjust your glide slope for a landing at your chosen spot. With the engine reduced to an idle your glide slope will be about four to one, or 20° to the ground. If you have a head wind, it will be even steeper. This is quite a steep approach angle compared to airplanes, but less steep than for helicopters.

If you are shooting landings during gusty winds of 15 mph or more, I suggest not making a full flare landing. Instead, fly the main wheels right onto the runway, dump the rotor, and use the brake to decelerate.

Zero Power Landing Approaches

Zero power landing approaches are excellent practice and should be rehearsed diligently after you have made a few good standard patterns. A zero power approach simulates a forced landing, which would occur if your engine failed in flight. Make several patterns without reducing power until you turn onto final approach 500 feet high and 1000 feet out. If you have a head wind, the base to final turn should be closer to the runway, perhaps only 500 feet away. Smoothly reduce power to idle and keep air speed at 45 mph to 50 mph. During the glide your line of sight over the tow hitch will intersect the ground a little short of the actual landing point. If you have headwinds, your line of sight will be ahead of your landing point.

During your first twenty-five hours aloft, keep within gliding range of a good landing site. Avoid flying over residential and business districts, forest, and lakes. Keep practicing simulated forced landings periodically as long as you keep flying. You don't always have to make a touchdown on these practice approaches. Descend just low enough so that you can see whether or not your judgment has been good.

Overconfidence

You will reach a point in your piloting ability where you start to feel you are the master of the machine. You will know its limits of maneuverability and may begin to push the machine to these full limits. This is a condition called "overconfidence," and it seems to be a fairly natural result of your existence for weeks and months in a condition whereby the machine mastered you. Now that you have an emotional feeling of control of your craft, the tendency is to use and push this control a little too far.

Be humble. This is my advice to keep you alive through the super-confident stage that many pilots blossom into. If you can't be humble and treat the craft with due respect, you will undoubtedly have a frightening experience which will force some humility upon you. The only trouble with waiting for this humbling experience is that sometimes you don't walk away from it.

When you find yourself hastening through the preflight check, cutting corners here and there, flying in marginal wind and weather conditions, wanting to show off by swooping low and fast past your friends, then it is time to sit down and have a serious talk with yourself. Remember the old saying I just made up, "There are no old, bold pilots."

Proceed with the preparations and performance of *every* flight in a thorough and unhurried way. Always keep a safety margin in altitude and speed. Don't push the performance of your craft to its limits. And above all, don't try to demonstrate your prowess as a pilot by showing off.

Over 100 aircraft accidents per year, most of them fatal, result from pilots' "buzz jobs."

Negative G Flight and Zero G

The rotor is spinning under a balanced condition between centrifugal force and lift which maintains the 4° coning angle during flight. If you make a sudden noseover following a climb, the rotor will decelerate rapidly because there will be less air flowing through it to keep up the autorotation. However, there is an even more serious consequence to this noseover maneuver. If done abruptly, you go through a moment of no gravity. You will recognize this no gravity or "zero G" state as a feeling of weightlessness on the seat. If you follow this zero G condition when the rotor is losing rpm's with a medium or high load maneuver, such as a pullup or a sharp turn, you may be disappointed and find the rotor not responding.

If your original noseover maneuver is abrupt enough to cause negative loads on the rotor, you're in real trouble. Under negative loads the rotor will bend downward, inverting the coning angle. The rotor could collide with the propeller or tail fin. It takes a fairly violent maneuver to cause this to happen, but there are several cases on record and fatal accidents resulted.

The most common cause of negative G conditions have resulted from an inexperienced gyro pilot flying too high and starting a porpoise, or longitudinal oscillation. After three or four cycles of the porpoise, the noseover at the top puts negative loads on the rotor.

You'll have nothing to fear from zero G or negative G if you follow the recommended training steps and avoid maneuvers which make you feel light in the seat. One gyro pilot I know says he always pretends to be flying without a seat belt. This keeps him super-cautious during maneuvers. I have never flown a gyroglider or copter on poats, but I have learned a lot from people who have hydrogliders and hydrocopters. Hydrogyros combine all the enjoyment and thrill of gyro flying with speed boating and water skiing. If you have access to a lake, by all means give due consideration to building a float model Bensen.

The hydroglider materials kit is $369, and you will have to buy about $50 worth of wood and plywood for the floats. The float design was made especially simple for amateur home building, and no special tools are required. You will need a flat, twelve-foot-long work bench, and the rotor blade bench can be easily modified for float building.

If built according to plans, the floats will be suitable for use on either the glider or copter model. They have adequate buoyancy for use on the two-place glider.

It is best to use either the twenty-one-foot factory metal rotor, or a thirty-four-inch hub on the wood rotor. This gives a twenty-two-inch overall rotor length, and the increased lift helps make up for the extra weight which the floats add to the gyro. The metal rotor has the added advantage of remaining balanced and tracked. The wood rotor will require frequent retrimming due to fluctuations in moisture content.

Figure 102. Hydrocopter and Hydroglider

After construction a test must be made before the floats are permanently mounted to the airframe. You must determine if the craft floats at the right attitude in the water. With the floats temporarily clamped to the airframe, check the angle of the rotor mast when rigged for flight; that is, rotor installed and pilot on the seat. The mast should tilt 10° rearward from the vertical. Less tilt would give you slow rotor starts, more

10°

temporary clamp
airframe to floats

clamp

Figure 103. Mast Angle Float Test

than 10° would allow the rotor to hit the water. Adjust the mast angle to 10° by shifting the floats fore or aft and mark the final position. The mounting brackets can then be drilled and the floats bolted to the airframe.

You must next make a "hang test" as with the wheel model to be certain the gyro is in proper flight balance. Suspend the craft from the teeter bolt and check the mast for a 2° nose-down attitude. Zero to 4° is within limits.

Alter the cheek plate size at the ratio of 1″ per degree to make any major change in the balance. Minor corrections can be made with lead weights on the nose, or aft end of the floats. A gyro simply will not fly safely if it is not properly balanced, so don't overlook the hang test.

For hydrogyro testing and towed flights, use a lake which allows you at least half a mile of unobstructed water. You should have a tow boat with at least 40 horsepower.

If you are a beginner your flight training should follow the same steps outlined for the wheel model. First learn proper control movement by "on the point" practice. Next, make towed runs on the water without liftoff. Then make many low-altitude leapfrog runs into the

wind. Gradually increase the duration of flight and altitude as your coordination develops.

The water will present a certain amount of suction to the floats when planing. A 25 mph tow speed will provide a cushion of extra lift needed to get the floats unstuck from the water.

After you are proficient in handling the gyro in towed flight, begin taxi runs under engine power. At low power the hydrocopter will taxi nicely at 6 to 8 mph. As you increase speed the floats will begin to plow a bigger wake until finally at 15 mph they begin to plane, or skim along on the surface. This planing is called "riding on the step," and further acceleration is easy because there is much less resistance since only the bottom of the floats are contacting the water. Spend plenty of time practicing water handling. Allow ample room when making turns while on the step.

If you are already checked out in gyros and are converting to a hydrocopter, here are a few further tips to help you along.

Be sure your craft has water rudders linked to the flight rudder. Check frequently for water in the floats. A couple of quarts in the aft compartments could throw the center of gravity dangerously far aft.

Water, especially salt water, will attack the metal of your craft and cause rust and corrosion. All unplated steel parts should be primed with zinc chromate. This includes the motor mount, inside and outside. Keep the engine generously sprayed with motor oil diluted with gasoline. Liquid silicone marketed as a lubricant through automotive supply stores also makes a great waterproofer. Hose the entire craft off with fresh water after saltwater operations.

When taxiing at about 10 mph, spray splashes into the propeller causing pits and damage to the leading edge near the tips. You can do two things to remedy this: (1) Keep 3M polyurethane tape # Y-9265, or black plastic electrical tape, applied to the leading edge of the prop. One application will last for six or eight takeoffs. (2) Avoid operating in the 10 mph taxi speed range. Always go from idling forward to 15 mph on the step with full power to minimize the time spent splashing spray on the prop.

A friend of mine discovered a tricky little technique to make left turns at slow speeds. He found that if your rotor is turning slowly you can convert some of its inertia into turning force on the craft. Simply brake the rotor with your left hand near the hub, holding onto each blade as long as possible.

It is best to have a wind of about 8 mph for practicing takeoffs and landings. The floats will unstick more readily from a water surface which is rippled by the wind. Also, you can't judge your altitude accurately over glassy, calm water.

If you are faced with glassy water on your only available flight day, break up the surface in your flight area with some high-speed taxi runs and step turns. It will also help your altitude judgment if you can operate near and parallel to shore.

Final Safety Reminders

1. Only two people should be near the gyro when you are ready to start: the pilot and the prop man.
2. Beware of the propeller and rotor when turning.
3. Use the proper verbal exchanges during starting, such as "switch and brake on," "switch off."
4. Pilot should taxi clear of all persons including prop man before starting rotor. Stop rotor before taxiing near persons. Never leave pilot seat while rotor is turning.
5. Slow flight (below 40 mph) requires high power. You can't maneuver or climb effectively in slow flight. If you have an obstacle to clear, dive first to 45 mph, then begin climbing.
6. Avoid negative load on rotor. Don't do any sharp noseovers or other abrupt maneuvers.
7. Don't fly with low fuel supply.
8. Avoid loading a slow turning rotor.
9. Don't make low altitude downwind turns. Have plenty of altitude and speed before starting a downwind turn.
10. Higher altitude and warmer temperatures reduce the engine power and rotor and prop efficiencies. Compared to sea level performance at 69° F your takeoff run will double and your rate of climb will decrease by half when flying at a 3000-foot elevation at 95° F.

The Popular Rotorcraft Association

This is a nonprofit club with a 1969 membership of over 10,000 persons with a common interest in gyrocraft. Membership is currently $9.00 per year, which includes a subscription to its excellent magazine called *Popular Rotorcraft Flying*. Membership can be obtained by writing to Popular Rotorcraft Association, P.O. Box 2772, Raleigh, North Carolina, 27602.

DEALERS AND TRAINERS

For more information, contact any of the following Bensen dealers:

1. Roy Clifford, 2621 Raskob St., Flint 4, Michigan
2. Ray Nebert, 1233 East First St., Port Angeles, Washington
3. Louis Darvassy, R.D. 2, Box 120, Oil City, Pennsylvania
4. J. Teerisuo, S. Kanerva Oy, Veneenteijantie 12, Helsinki, Finland
5. Joe McMillan, Arthur, Nebraska
6. Robert L. Evans, 1010 Parkway Dr., N. W., Salem, Oregon
7. Alf Crowe, P.O. Box 57, Bulls, New Zealand
8. Walter Foy, 1800 E. 22nd St., Muncie, Indiana
9. Campbell Aircraft, Ltd., Everland Road, Hungerford, Berks, England
10. T. W. Lewis, P.O. Drawer 1326, Marshall, Texas
11. Bob Fisher, R.R. 2, Stirling, Ontario, Canada
12. Derdall Gyrocopters, Inc., Box 13, Outlook, Saskatchewan, Canada
13. Eugene Neimi, Jr., 107 Winter St., Leominster, Mass.
14. Ray Hite, R.R. 2, Box 30, Baltimore, Ohio
15. Virginia Gyro Aircraft Sales, P.O. Box 281, Yorktown, Virginia
16. Eastern Bensen Gyrocopter Sales, Inc., 50 S. Main St., Providence, Rhode Island
17. Western Bensen Copter Sales, 4080 Horton St., Emeryville, California
18. Jackson Gyrocopter Sales, Box 158, Sedona, Arizona
19. Ken Brock Gyrocopters, 3087 Ball Road, Anaheim, California
20. North Alabama Gyrocopter Sales, 508 Andrew Jackson Way, Huntsville, Ala.

GYROCRAFT GLOSSARY

ADVANCING BLADE—The rotor blade which is moving in the same direction as the aircraft's flight path.

AUTOGYRO—A flying machine which uses a free-wheeling rotor blade instead of wings. The rotor gets rotational power by airflow and not by engine drive, as with a helicopter.

AUTOROTATION—Upward windflow past a rotor generates forces which cause the rotor to spin about its axis.

C.G.—Center of gravity.

CONING ANGLE—When the rotor is spinning, centrifugal forces on the blade combine with lifting forces and resolve into an upward angle from the hub of about 4° during flight.

DOWNWIND TURN—When flying against the wind any turn which results in the aircraft heading within 90° of the direction the wind is blowing is a downwind turn. They are hazardous at low altitudes.

FLUTTER—The tendency for an improperly balanced airfoil to oscillate up and down when subjected to airflow.

GYROCOPTER—Trade name for the Bensen design autogyro when it is self-powered.

GYROGLIDER—Bensen's trade name for the non-powered autogyro.

HANG TEST—Before flight the gyrocraft must be hung from the rotor spindle to be certain the center of gravity is in proper relationship to the rotor axis.

HUMP SPEED—When the rotor is "over the hump" it is above that certain speed where it readily accelerates faster. Hump speed is approximately 50–70 rpm.

HYDROCOPTER—Gyrocopter mounted on floats.

HYDROGLIDER—Gyroglider mounted on floats.

JOYSTICK—An optional control stick for gyrocraft which is positioned between the pilot's legs.

KITING—A method of flying the gyroglider by tethering the nose to an anchor point and kiting aloft in winds of 20 mph or more.

NEGATIVE GRAVITY—Certain flight maneuvers, such as a quick noseover after a climb, can put "negative G" forces on the gyrocraft which are exactly opposite the normal gravity forces. Extremely hazardous.

NOSEWEIGHTS—Steel brackets filled with lead and bolted to the leading edge of each rotor blade to give them proper quarter chord balancing.

OFFSET GIMBAL CONTROL HEAD—An optional rotor head and control system which allows improved flight stability.

OVERBALANCE—An overbalanced rotor has the balance point, or C.G., ahead of the quarter chord point. Overbalance can cause rotor disk weave.

OVERHEAD STICK—Also called "azimuth stick." It is a flight control stick connected directly to the rotor spindle.

QUARTER CHORD BALANCING—To avoid fluttering tendencies in the rotor blade, the chordwise balance point, or center of gravity, should be 25 percent aft of the leading edge.

RETREATING BLADE—The rotor blade which is moving in a direction opposite to the aircraft's flight path.

ROTOR—The long, narrow wing which pivots about a hub and is the primary lifting source for rotorcraft.

ROTOR DISK—The rotor revolves in a dish-like plane called the "rotor disk." It is actually a very flat inverted cone (see Coning Angle).

ROTOR HEAD—The parts of the rotor axle such as the spindle, bearing, bearing support, cover plate, and cheek plates combine to form the rotor head.

ROTOR HUB—The rotor blades are rigidly bolted to a central aluminum block called the "hub." The pillow blocks which support the teeter bolt are mounted on the hub.

SAFETIED—Securing a nut on a bolt so that vibration cannot loosen it. Fiber locknuts, cotter pins, and stainless steel safety wire are the three most common methods used on aircraft.

SPAR—The main structural member in the rotor blade. It is designed to withstand tensional loads of approximately 7,000 pounds during flight.

SPINDLE—A special steel bolt which serves as the rotor axle.

TEETER BOLT—The rotor is attached to the spindle with a bolt called the "teeter bolt."

TEETER HINGE—The teeter bolt passes through a hole in the spindle and allows the blade to teeter up and down. This is the teeter hinge.

TIP SPEED—Velocity in mph of the rotor blade tips.

TRACKING—Adjusting the trim tabs to make the blades travel in the same plane of rotation.

TRIM TABS—Bendable metal tabs attached to the trailing edge of the rotor blades. They are used to make the blades track in the same plane.

UNDERBALANCE—Where the chordwise C.G. of the rotor blade lies aft of the quarter chord point. Underbalance can cause blade flutter.

WEAVE—When the blade tips change pitch randomly due to lack of torsional rigidity and/or overbalanced blades. The rotor disk becomes erratically irregular.

WINDLINE—An imaginary line along the ground which coincides with wind direction.

ZERO G—A flight condition of weightlessness which occurs between normal gravity and negative gravity.

5 POWER PLANE

Today there are 620,000 licensed pilots in the United States. Over 120,000 civilian planes are registered with FAA and only two percent of these are commercial airliners. The rest belong to the flying public. Many are used as a practical solution to transportation needs. Others are used for sport or the recreation interest of home-builders and antiquers. Consider the following facets of learning to fly and perhaps you, too, will soon join the privileged ranks of sky people.

  Earth people are those who always have to look at a cloud from the bottom;
  Sky people get to see and explore the top sides of them;
  Earth people are restricted to the slow, ponderous, and often hazardous travel on congested roads and highways;
  Sky people can cruise along smoothly and rapidly in the cool, clean, uncrowded sky;
  Earth people are those who have to live with the polluted airs when a brown haze of smog blankets the ground;
  Sky people can climb aloft into the upper airs and enjoy nature's clean and perfect vastness still abounding in sky country.

It is easy to become a pilot. Almost every airport in the country has one or more flight training operation.

Once you have your pilot license you are legally permitted to carry passengers. This lets you include your friends and family in your flying fun.

Many hundreds of businesses utilize a small plane to relieve transportation bottlenecks for their executives and salesmen.

Women are catching the flying bug, too. One out of seven student pilots is a female. Many are housewives and mothers who have discovered that flying is as easy as driving a car, and much more stimulating and enjoyable.

If you are under twenty-five and are a college man, your chances are good of making a career out of flying. The airlines are expanding and so is their need for new pilots. A career pilot has one of the most satisfying and financially rewarding jobs available.

WHO CAN FLY

Any boy or girl, sixteen or over, can apply to the FAA for a student license. Seventeen is the minimum age for a private license. There are no regulations governing maximum age. The student license is like a learner's permit for driving, except you will be allowed to fly solo under a student's license if your instructor has certified that you are ready to fly solo. You must also obtain a medical certificate which is renewable every two years by taking a physical exam from an aviation medical examiner. It is an easy physical if you have normal health, and eyesight correctable to 20/30. If you are color blind, you may have a medical restriction on your flying privileges.

COST OF FLIGHT LESSONS

If you live near a Cessna or Piper dealer you can take advantage of the coupon offer and get a first flight lesson for only $5. Almost any school will introduce you to flying with half-hour dual instruction for $8.

If your first flight lights the fuse on your

enthusiasm, ask some pertinent questions about full training courses. You will find that most flight schools offer a package plan for a private pilot license. The normal fee for this course is $600, although rates will vary some with different schools. You might begin your training by taking a solo course which most schools offer for about $150, which will include eight to ten hours of dual instruction (not enough to learn to fly well) from a certified instructor. You can usually take lessons on a per-hour basis and make payments as you fly. However, there is a big advantage to signing a contract for a full private course. Many schools will give time payment privileges such as $50 per month when you are taking a full course. This way your pocketbook will not throw off your training schedule. It is imperative to take your lessons as close together as possible. Three or more per week will enable you to learn faster.

When choosing a flight school it is wise to ask a few pilots who have learned at the schools. Their recommendations might indicate that the school advertising "FAA Approved" does not mean they have the best training and rates.

You might have a buddy who is a pilot and can introduce you to flying, but his guidance or instruction can't be recorded in your log book unless he is a certified instructor. I flew for a whole summer as copilot for my brother in his Ryan PT-22, but I still had to take dual instruction from a certified instructor before I could solo.

You will have a much easier time passing the FAA written exam if you take a ground school course to learn the basics of meteorology, aerodynamics, navigation, and use of the flight computer. This course may be included in your flight school, or it may be taken extra.

You will be eligible for the private license written and practical exams after forty hours of flight time, provided twenty of these hours were solo and ten of the twenty were cross-country flights.

If you take three hours of training per week you will be ready for your "ticket" in about three months. Unfavorable weather can often set back the schedule, so a more realistic time figure would be five months. Many students spend up to a year flying occasionally on their student permit.

Besides a student permit the pilot trainee should have one further piece of paperwork from the government. The Federal Communications Commission will issue you a radio operator's permit for $2. No exam is required, and an application form will be sent on request from the Federal Communications Commission, Gettysburg, Pennsylvania, 17325.

COST OF OWNERSHIP

Many pilot trainees have reduced the cost of flying by purchasing a light plane and using a private instructor. A good Cub or Champ can be purchased for about $1,500, and makes an excellent trainer. This procedure works best only if you intend to do a lot of flying (100 hours per year, or more), or if you can share the plane with a couple of partners to help reduce your fixed costs.

In most cases it is cheaper to rent than to own your own plane as the following financial resume shows. Bear in mind that you can rent a two-place plane for solo flight for about $10 per hour.

Figure 104. Flybaby in Flight

COST TO OWN A $1,500 PLANE AND FLY 50 HOURS PER YEAR

Interest on Investment	$105.00
Tiedown Storage at $10 per month	120.00
Hull Insurance	150.00
Liability Insurance	60.00
Maintenance and Overhaul @ $2.00 per hour	100.00
Gas and Oil 50 hours @ $2.30 per hour	115.00
	$740.00=$14.80 per hour

If you flew 100 hours per year the hourly cost would drop to about $9 per hour because the gas and oil are the only additional cost items. If you are a family man and could utilize a four-place plane for 300 hours of flight per year, the Cessna Skyhawk is a very attractive buy at about $8,000 to $12,000, depending upon condition and age. Operating cost based on 300 hours of flight per year would be as follows:

Gas, Oil, Periodic Maintenance	$5.40 per hr
Insurance, Depreciation, Storage, and Reserve for Overhaul	5.20 per hr
	$10.60 per hr

Remember, you travel an average of 130 miles for each flight hour in a Cessna Skyhawk, so 300 hours will take you 39,000 miles for a cost of about eight cents per mile. You could drive for about the same cost, but it would take you three times as long.

The main rewards of owning your own plane relate to time saved and the pleasures of flight.

Homebuilts

If you are gifted in the mechanical arts you may choose to build your own plane. There are hundreds of designs to choose from, and many are quite simple and practical to build. Pete Bowers' "Flybaby" design has been duplicated in home workshops all over the country. It is a single-place, open cockpit, wood and fabric plane with wings that fold for easy hauling and storage. Mr. Bowers sells the plans for $15 per set, and the materials for the primary structure, including

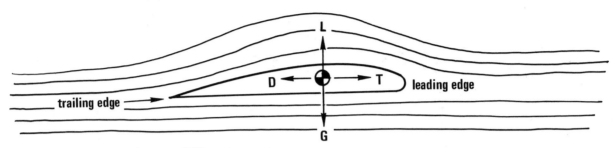

Figure 105. Lift Cross Section of Wing

wheels, brakes, and instruments, will come to about $800. Engine prices vary greatly, but the recommended 65 hp Continental will average $600 in serviceable used condition.

A list of homebuilt plans and sources appears at the end of this chapter.

PRINCIPLES OF FLIGHT

If you are a person who just accepts the fact that airplanes fly, without understanding the reason, then I want to remedy this situation right now. The physical laws which make a plane remain aloft are really very simple in spite of the fact that it took man so long to put the laws to work in the form of a man-carrying plane.

All objects on the earth are subject to atmospheric pressure which acts equally on all sides of the object. If an object is moved the air around the object is moved and changes occur in the balance of air pressures on the object. An airplane wing has a shape which best takes advantage of the principle of differential air pressure.

A look at the cross section of a wing will reveal a flat bottom, rounded leading edge, "cambered" or curved top, with the thickest part one-third of the way back, and a thin, sharp trailing edge. As air flows past the wing it divides at the leading edge. The air which flows past the flat undersurface is relatively undisturbed. The air which travels past the curved upper surface has a longer route to travel. The air accelerates, causing the molecules of the air to be further apart. This reduces the air pressure on the top

surface of the wing. The wing attempts to move upward into the area of lower pressure. The upward force is called "lift."

The force "lift" acts on the wing in a direction at right angles to the wind direction and is represented in the diagram as the arrow labeled L.

There are three other forces besides lift which act on a wing during flight.

Air causes a certain amount of resistance to the passage of the wing. This resistance is called "drag," and is labeled D in the diagram. It acts in a direction parallel to wind direction.

The airplane's weight is represented by force arrow G for gravity and is always shown vertically downward. A power plane's engine gives forward momentum or thrust, labeled T. Thrust acts forward and approximately parallel to the wing's undersurface. These four forces are in balance when a wing is in level flight at a constant airspeed. In other words, lift equals gravity, and thrust equals drag.

Angle of Attack

The balance of these forces is very delicate, especially the lift and drag forces. The angle at which the wind meets the wing has a strong effect on the lift generated. Change the wind's angle just a few degrees and the lift and drag change drastically. The angle between the wind and the wing is called the "angle of attack." It is "positive" when the wind meets the wing from forward and below. The greater the angle of attack, the greater the lift force that is produced. This is why a plane points its nose up to climb, to give the wings a greater angle of

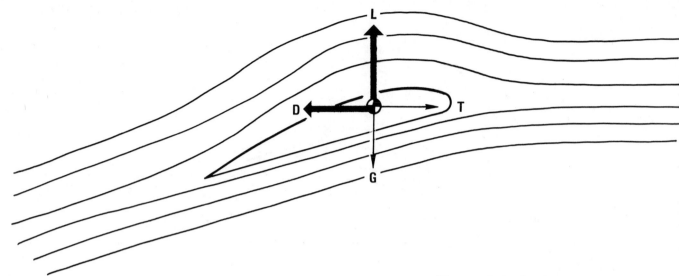

Figure 106. Angle of Attack

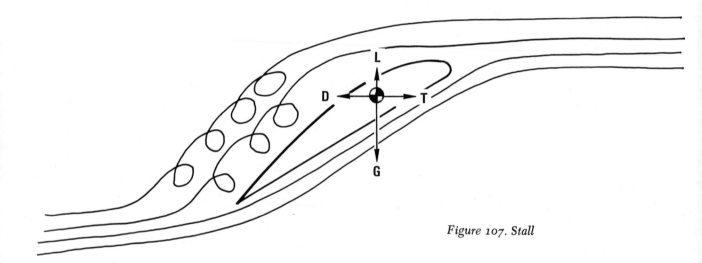

Figure 107. Stall

attack. When the wind meets the wing from ahead and above, the angle of attack is negative, and lift is reduced. This occurs in dives and glides.

Remember that the greater the angle of attack, the greater are the lift and drag forces produced. There is a limit, however. Too great an angle of attack will prevent the air from flowing smoothly over the top of the wing. Instead it will tumble and swirl about, resulting in almost a total loss of lift. This type of breakdown in the smooth airflow is called a "stall," and it can occur at any speed if the angle of attack is great enough.

The wings of most planes are designed so that a stall will not occur across the entire span at once. The outboard or tip areas of the wing are warped downward on the leading edge. This design feature is called "wash out," and it allows the wing tips to fly with a smaller angle of attack than the rest of the wing. Thus if a stall occurs on the inboard area of the wing, all controllability will not be lost because the wing tips and ailerons will still be functional.

Even after he had developed a wing of an efficient lifting design, man still had to experiment with designs until he had one which properly accounted for four different variables. These variables are airspeed, attitude, balance, and maneuverability.

Airspeed

A wing of proportions designed to lift a man will not develop sufficient lift until airflow is up-

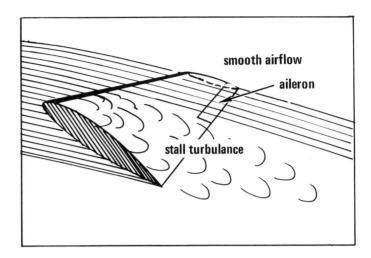

Figure 108. Wingtip Washout

wards of 30 mph. Soaring birds and model airplanes can achieve flight at only 10 or 15 mph because their weight in proportion to wing area is much less. The ratio between weight and area is called "wing loading." The lighter the wing loading the slower will be a plane's stalling speed. "Kiwi," my pet seagull, weighs three pounds and has 2.2 square feet of wing area. His super-light wing loading of 1.36 pounds per square foot will allow him to soar without flapping at only 12 mph. Sailplanes have a loading of about four to six pounds per square foot. Airplanes will range from six pounds for a Cub to sixty pounds for a modern passenger jet.

The delicate matter of maintaining the wing at a proper attitude or angle of attack to the airflow is achieved by tail surfaces or empenage. The vertical fin and horizontal stabilizer act like the feather fletching on an arrow. The aft portions of the tail surfaces are hinged to allow them to move. The movable portion of the vertical fin is called the "rudder," and the elevator forms the aft section of the horizontal stabilizer. The tail surfaces are anchored to the fuselage about 10 feet or more behind the center of the wing. The fuselage acts to tie the flight surfaces together, and also to form a compartment to carry the pilot.

Figure 109. Power Plane Nomenclature

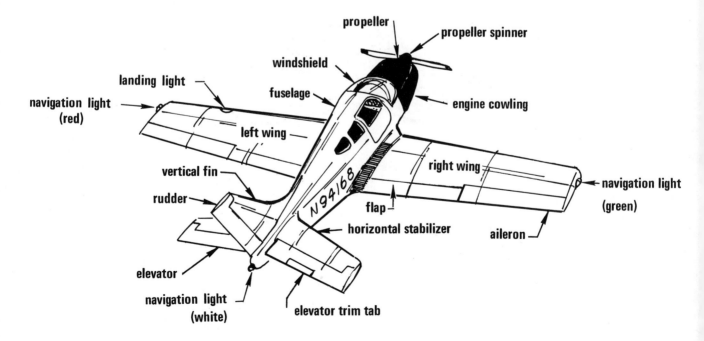

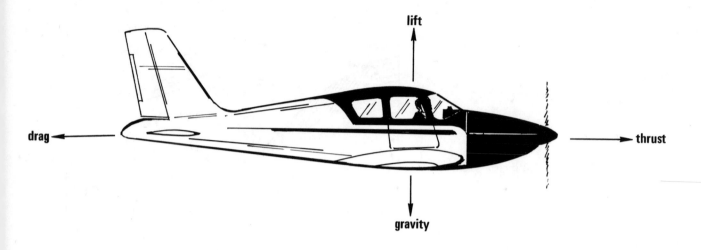

Figure 110. Forces Acting on a Plane in Flight

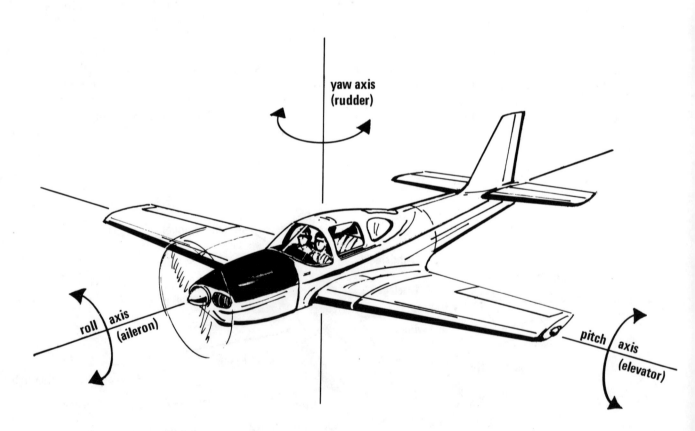

Figure 111. Airplane Maneuverability

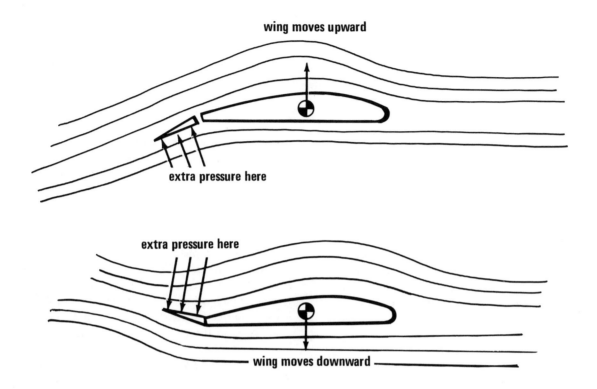

wing moves upward

extra pressure here

extra pressure here

wing moves downward

Figure 112. Deflected Control Surface

Balance

In order to fly, a plane's center of gravity must be within a few inches of the center of lift. The wings, fuselage, and tail form a structure which is hopelessly tail heavy until an engine of proper weight is placed in exactly the right position ahead of the wing. In sailplanes the pilot's seat is placed ahead of the wing so that his weight will bring the plane into balance.

Maneuverability

A plane has three different imaginary axes about which it may rotate:

1. The axis which runs along the length of the fuselage from nose to tail is the longitudinal or roll axis. Ailerons on the wings control this movement.
2. The axis which is vertically through the

center of the plane at the wing is called the "yaw axis" and movement about it is controlled by the rudder.
3. The other axis runs spanwise from tip to tip of the wing. This is the horizontal, or pitch, axis. The elevator controls the plane's pitch.

The rudder, elevator, and ailerons are the hinged portions of the plane's wings and tail the pilot can manipulate from the cabin. They all work on the principle of differential air pressure. They cause a pressure force to develop in a direction which is opposite to the direction of deflection.

When an aileron moves downward the wing tries to rise because lift is increased by the downward aileron deflection. An upward deflection of the elevator causes a downward force on the tail, raising the plane's nose. A rudder deflected to the right will cause the tail to move left and the nose to move right.

The elevator and ailerons are linked by cables and pulleys to the control stick or yoke in front of the pilot. All fixed wing planes respond to the control stick in the same manner. Whether you are flying a Piper Cub or a Boeing Passenger Jet, when you pull back on the stick, the elevator bends upward. Forward stick lowers the nose, and right stick or wheel movement lowers the right wing, and vise versa.

Other Parts of the Airplane

FLAPS

Many modern light planes have an additional hinged portion of the wing's trailing edge between the fuselage and the aileron. These are called "flaps," and they move downward on both wings simultaneously. Wing lift and drag are both increased when the flap is lowered. Flap positions of 10° and 20° downward deflection are used to shorten the distance required for takeoff and the high-drag 30° and 40° positions allow a steeper glide slope when attempting to land within a minimum distance.

LANDING GEAR

The landing gear supports the plane during parking and all ground maneuvering. The tricycle gear has come of age as the most popular design because it simplifies ground steering and landings. Visibility is also improved with this type of gear because the plane is in a horizontal position while on the ground. Tail wheel-type planes are still preferred by many oldtimers.

Individual brakes on the main wheels are operated by depressing the tops of the left or right rudder pedals. A few planes have heel pedals to apply the brakes.

POWER PLANT AND PROPELLER

An air-cooled piston engine provides the power for turning the propeller. A prop is a pair of very strong solid wood or metal wings with a hub between, which bolts to the engine's crankshaft. Most American aircraft engines rotate counterclockwise, so the propeller blades have a right-hand wing design.

When spinning at 2,500 rpm's by engine power a six-foot diameter propeller can transmit over 100 horsepower into thrust or forward acting lift from the blades. This seems like a lot of power to develop by fanning the air with such a small blade or wing. It is the speed that makes this possible. That little propeller turning 2,500 rpm's is whizzing through the air at over 500 mph near the tip.

A propeller may have its blades rigidly attached to the hub with a built-in angle of attack, or pitch. This is called a "fixed pitch prop," and is commonly used on light aircraft with 150 horsepower or less.

Variable pitch propellers have the blades flexibly mounted to the hub and the pitch is regulated hydraulically by oil pressure from the engine. They allow the pilot to select the most efficient blade pitch for his type of flight whether it be cruise, climb, or takeoff.

Using a propeller to transmit engine power gives rise to a force called "torque," which causes the plane to veer or yaw to the left. It is most noticeable at low speeds and high-power settings, such as during takeoff, climb, and slow flight. This torque effect is commonly thought of as a simple result of the airplane's tendency to roll in a direction opposite to the rotation of the propeller.

Actually the biggest cause of left yaw is the propeller slipstream spiraling backward and striking the left side of the vertical fin and rudder. A third cause is from the unequal thrust produced by the propeller during climb or nose-high flight. The right-hand, or downward-turning, blade develops more thrust because it meets the air at a higher angle of attack than the left blade. Torque effect is controlled by pressure on the right rudder.

Cockpit Controls

STICK AND RUDDER

The primary flight controls are the stick and rudder pedals. The stick may be a single vertical handle between the pilot's legs, or a control wheel similar to a car's, except with a fore and aft movement to control the elevators. Rotating the control wheel or displacing the stick sideways will deflect the ailerons. The rudder pedals deflect the rudder and also turn the tailwheel or nosewheel to assist with ground maneuvers. The individual main wheel brakes are also useful for steering on the ground.

THROTTLE

The throttle controls engine power output by regulating the amount of air and fuel vapor which flows through the carburetor. The throttle is never called an accelerator as on a car, and it is never connected to a foot pedal. A fore and aft moving knob is the rule for plane throttles mounted to the left of the pilot or sticking out from the lower center of the instrument panel.

FUEL MIXTURE CONTROL

A small fore and aft moving knob adjusts the amount of fuel delivered to the air passing through the carburetor. It is usually labeled simply "mixture," with a "rich" and "lean" position. When flying at higher altitudes in less dense air, an engine's fuel mixture becomes out of balance, or overly rich. The mixture control is used to rebalance the mixture by restricting the gas flow.

CARBURETOR HEAT

A small knob commonly placed near the mixture knob controls a valve which lets the air to the carburetor come from a new warm air source such as through a shroud around a hot exhaust pipe. When flying in cool humid air, ice can build up in the carburetor throat and restrict engine power. By placing the "carb heat" knob in "hot" position, the warm air will melt an ice accumulation and prevent more from forming. A pilot should use carb heat anytime the throttle is set at a low or idle power setting because this is when ice is most likely to develop.

TRIM TAB

As already mentioned, the balance of a plane is very delicate and critical. The center of lift and center of gravity must coincide exactly or the pilot will find himself doing the ship in balance by stick pressures. The center of lift will shift fore and aft slightly with different angles of attack and airspeeds. The CG is easily

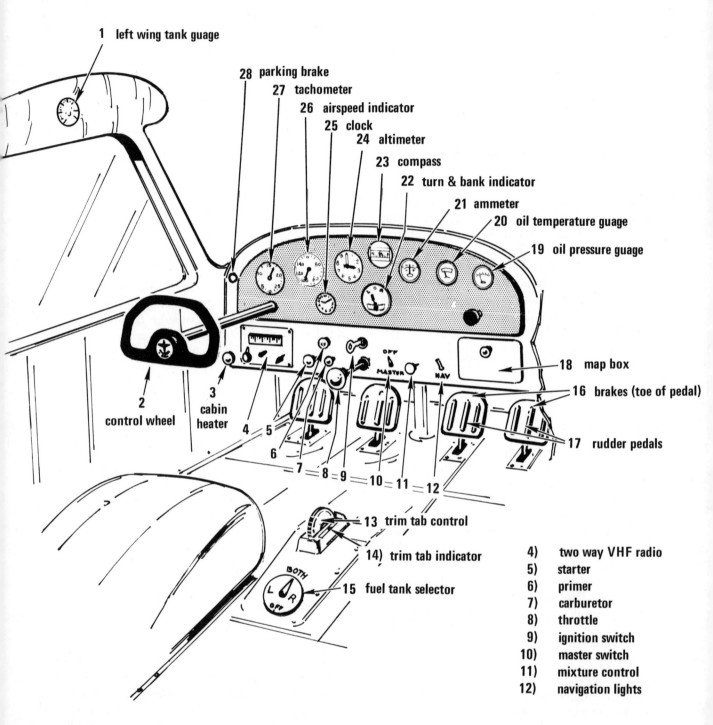

1 left wing tank guage

28 parking brake
27 tachometer
26 airspeed indicator
25 clock
24 altimeter
23 compass
22 turn & bank indicator
21 ammeter
20 oil temperature guage
19 oil pressure guage

18 map box

16 brakes (toe of pedal)

17 rudder pedals

2 control wheel
3 cabin heater

4 5
6
7 8 9 10 11 12

13 trim tab control
14) trim tab indicator
15 fuel tank selector

4) two way VHF radio
5) starter
6) primer
7) carburetor
8) throttle
9) ignition switch
10) master switch
11) mixture control
12) navigation lights

Figure 113. Controls and Instruments

influenced by the weight and placement of passengers and baggage. During flight the pilot can
account for minor out-of-balance conditions by
adjusting the trim. A knob or wheel near the
pilot seat controls the position of a small hinged
control surface on the elevator.

FLAP

A lever next to the pilot seat has a selection of
notched positions for adjusting the flap positions.
Some new Cessnas have electrically controlled
flaps, adjusted by a toggle switch.

CABIN HEAT

Most light planes have an efficient heater
which ducts fresh outside air past a hot exhaust
pipe. A separate panel knob controls the air
valve to admit heat to the cabin.

IGNITION OR MAGNETO SWITCH

An automobile uses a battery-and-coil-type
ignition system. The airplane uses the magneto
to generate the high voltage electricity for
ignition. Two magnetos connected to separate
spark plugs on each cylinder give the aircraft
engine two independent systems for extra safety.
A single ground wire called the "P lead" goes to
the ignition switch from each magneto. The
switch has four positions. The "left" position
grounds the circuit on the right magneto so that
the engine runs on the left magneto. "Right"
position grounds the left magneto. "Both" opens
the circuit for both magnetos, which is the
normal operating position. "Off" position grounds
both magnetos. The magneto ignition is independent of any other electrical system in the
plane.

If the plane is equipped with a twelve-volt
battery, the following additional items are likely
to be found in the cockpit.

A master switch energizes the electrical system.

STARTER

A knob or push button controls the starter.

LIGHTS

Navigation lights on the tail and wingtips, and
landing lights in the wing's leading edge are
useful for night flying. One or more cockpit
lights are also provided.

RADIO

Airplanes which land or take off from fields
with an FAA operated control tower are required to have a radio for communication with
the tower. The aircraft radio is useful for airport communications, and many provide a navigational feature which helps the pilot to spot
his plane in relation to various radio "OMNI"
stations.

CIGARETTE LIGHTER

Many planes are equipped with one, and it is
legally permissible to smoke aboard a plane.
However, it is a mistake to smoke, period, but
especially around an airplane. Flammable materials and fumes could easily be ignited in or
around airplanes, and our airport policy is "No
Smoking Aboard or Within 50 Feet of Any
Aircraft."

An interesting example of the evils of smoking
in a fabric-covered plane occurred to a glider
pilot who dropped a lighted cigarette as he was

making a landing approach. The fuselage fabric ignited below the pilot seat, and he scrambled from the flaming cockpit even before the ship had stopped its landing roll. It took less than five minutes for the ship to become a mere smoking framework. You can imagine the results of a fire in flight at a higher altitude.

FUEL SELECTOR VALVE

Many light planes have more than one gas tank in the wings, and a selector valve allows you to choose "left, right, both, or off."

PRIMER

A primer is a small manual gas pump, commonly mounted on the instrument panel. It delivers fuel through tiny steel lines to the intake manifold near the cylinders. The primer is useful before the first flight of the day and during cold-weather starting.

PARKING BRAKE

A parking brake is present only on some planes. It usually operates by pulling a knob after depressing the brake pedal.

Gauges and Instruments

Airplane instruments and gauges fall into three categories. Flight instruments tell you what the plane is doing during flight and maneuvers. Altimeter, airspeed, vertical speed, and turn-and-bank indicator are the basic flight instruments. A second group of gauges helps you to keep track of the engine operation. Manifold pressure, RPM or tachometer gauge, oil temperature, oil pressure, ammeter, and fuel gauges fall into this category.

The navigational instruments make up the third group. Compass, directional gyro (gyro compass), and omni range indicator are the most common. Many of these gauges are self-explanatory, but I will elaborate on some because of their unique nature.

ALTIMETER

The altimeter measures air pressure just like a barometer. It has a face like a clock, except it is numbered zero to ten. A reading is taken in feet of altitude above sea level by two needles. The long one reads hundreds and the short needle indicates thousands of feet.

Since it is sensitive to air-pressure changes, the altimeter must be set to the proper barometric pressure in your flight area by means of the adjusting knob and barometric scale which shows in a small window on the face. If all pilots keep their altimeters properly set, then everybody has the same standard or base altitude, which is sea level. An easy way to set your altimeter for proper barometric pressure is to adjust the knob before each flight so that the hands read your airport elevation.

AIRSPEED INDICATOR

The plane's speed through the air is measured by a system of tubes caled the "pitot" (pee' tow) static system connected to a gauge called the "airspeed indicator." One end of the pitot tube usually extends a few inches out from the leading edge of one wing. During flight, air is driven into the tube by the plane's forward speed. This is called "ram" air, and the resulting pressure within the tube expands a diaphragm which is geared to an indicating hand in the gauge. The static tube equalizes the static pressure within the system so that no adjustments are necessary when the barometric pressure changes.

TACHOMETER

The "tach" is operated by a flexible cable connected to the engine and indicates crankshaft or propeller rpm's. It is your primary instrument for setting engine power on planes with fixed pitch propellers. On planes with variable pitch propellers the manifold pressure gauge is used in conjunction with the tachometer for making power settings.

NEEDLE AND BALL GAUGE, ALSO CALLED TURN AND BANK INDICATOR

This is a combination of two instruments. The turn indicator is a vertical needle geared to a gyroscope. During turns the needle deflects to the right or left an amount corresponding to the speed of the turn.

The ball or slip indicator is the really novel and intriguing instrument. It is simply a one-half-inch diameter curved glass tube filled with kerosene and containing an agate or steel ball. When the tube is mounted horizontally, the ball seeks the center of the tube unless centrifugal force disturbs its position. During a properly coordinated flight maneuver, centrifugal force will exactly offset gravity, and the ball will remain centered. Any time the aircraft slips or skids sideways the ball will be displaced from center. This instrument is very useful for beginners and students who need to verify frequently that they are holding proper rudder pressures.

COMPASS

The airplane compass is a magnet attached to a face ring labeled with numbers from 0° to 360°. The ring is mounted on a bearing and is free-swinging. The magnet aligns itself with the magnetic north pole, and the compass case and airplane rotate around it. Because of the design and balance of the magnet and ring, the compass is accurate only when flying straight and level. Banks, turns, turbulence, acceleration, or deceleration all cause errors in the compass reading. This is why a compass is usually used together with a directional gyro which contains a gyroscope and will give accurate heading information during almost any flight conditions.

PREFLIGHT INSPECTION

Before each flight a little ritual is performed called the "preflight or walk-around inspection." This is the first of a number of very important safe flying habits which you should develop. An aircraft is a mechanical device which should be looked over carefully before you trust it to carry you aloft. During the flight training phase you will be trusting the judgment of your instructor as you perform the walk-around inspection. Listen carefully to his comments, and if time at the flight line doesn't permit a thorough inspection, ask him for an appointment when there is time to be guided through a very complete preflight inspection of the plane. The time will soon come when you are flying solo or pilot in command, and then the responsibility is yours to see that the plane is airworthy.

The preflight inspection is a personal thing. It is the individual responsibility of the person contemplating the flight as pilot. You shouldn't trust this responsibility to a friend. You shouldn't even trust it to an aircraft mechanic.

I once left my Travelair 6000 at an airplane shop for a yearly inspection and servicing. When the job was completed I went to the shop, paid for the work, and was told the plane was ready to fly. Since it was almost sunset I was in a hurry to get started on the forty-mile flight home to the Skyport. I walked hastily around the ship, noted that the tires weren't flat, and that the oil and gas were up, so I removed the chocks, strapped myself into the seat, and started the engine. The instrument readings were proper and as I pushed the rudder pedals to the full extent of their travel, I looked back and noticed the rudder was responding properly. The ailerons also responded in proper sequence and travel to the wheel movement, and so did the elevators. The thought flashed through my mind that the work order had indicated one elevator had been recovered, so it must have been removed from the ship and then replaced. In my haste to get started on the flight I hadn't really examined the elevator installation job, and even though it seemed to function properly I shut down the engine and walked back to the tail. My intent was just to be sure all the attachment pins had been safetied with locknuts or cotter pins. The elevator movement is controlled by cables attached to arms on each side of the plane extending above and below the elevator. As I leaned over to check the lower-cable connecting pins I found both lower cables were not only *not* safetied, they were not even connected to the control arms. They dangled loosely beside the fuselage.

This couldn't be detected from the cockpit check of the controls because the weight of the elevator made it appear to respond as the stick

was moved forward. I doubt very much if the plane could make a successful flight without the elevator control, and I had almost *not* made a thorough preflight inspection.

Every airplane will have a detailed list of items to inspect which is tailored for that particular ship. Following is an outline of check points common to most planes.

Preflight, Before Starting Engine

1. Inspect the propeller for tightness to hub, nicks, dents, and cleanness. A prop will build up residues from smashed insects, grass blades, and dirt, which roughens the leading edge surface and causes loss of efficiency. Most residue will wash off with water.

2. Every nut on the aircraft should be safetied by one of three methods: (a) Safety wire; (b) cotter pin; (c) fiber friction nut. Inspect the engine for loose bolts, safety wires, ignition wires, and old leaks. Take a close look at the carburetor and manifold attachments. Don't be afraid to grasp the engine parts firmly and give them a smart shake to test for tightness. If you finish examining the power section and your hands are still clean, the chances are you did a poor job of inspecting. Carry a rag with you for wiping hands during the inspection.

3. Check the fuel supply by removing the gas cap and observe the fuel quantity, or check with a calibrated dipstick. If you add gas, don't let the gas hose rub on the plane or plexiglass windshield because instant scratches will result. Be sure to replace the cap securely. The rule for fueling is to carry at least twice as much gas as you expect to

need for the intended flight. Drain some fuel from the sediment bowl or quick-drain fitting. This should remove any accumulated sediment or water from condensation within the tanks.

4. Check the ground area under the propeller for loose pebbles. It is best to start over grass or a clean hard surface. The rotating propeller causes a tiny whirlwind to develop below the blade, and debris and pebbles may lift right off the ground and into the whirling prop tips.

5. Next to the engine, the landing gear takes the most abuse. Examine tires for proper inflation. The full width of the tread should contact the ground, but unusual bulging on the lower sidewalls indicate underinflation, which could cause damage to the inner cords of the tire during use. Look for exposed cords, and cuts or breaks in the sidewalls. Look for signs of leaking brake fluid. Grasp the top of the tire firmly and rock the plane from side to side to test for looseness in the wheel bearings or looseness anywhere in the landing gear shock struts or fittings.

6. Inspect the tailwheel for inflation, bearing looseness, lubrication, and security of attachment. Check the leaf springs for tightness.

7. Walk around the entire aircraft examining all strut and wire attachment fittings, condition and cleanness of fabric. Check aileron, rudder and elevator control cables, pulleys, and attachment fittings. All hinges should be safetied and free moving, but not loose. The pitot tube should be uncovered and the windshield cleaned. Use only soap and water or Mirror Glaze plastic cleaner for cleaning plastic windshields.

One stroke of a gritty rag will do irreparable damage to a plastic window.

Starting

If you need to reposition the plane before starting, be sure to use proper ground-handling technique. You will need two people: one at the fuselage ahead of the stabilizer to steer and help push; the other next to the fuselage under the wing supplying the main push force on the wing strut close to the strut attachment point at the fuselage. Don't lift, stand on, push, or pull the struts in the outer unbraced area. Also don't push or pull a plane by the propeller.

You are now ready to board the plane, fasten the seat belt, and set the altimeter to field elevation. Next, check that the controls move freely and in the proper direction. It is quite possible for the control linkage to be inadvertently connected backward by a mechanic. Turn the gas selector valve "on" to the fullest tank, set the mixture to "rich" position, and crack the throttle about ⅛-inch.

If you have an electric starter, there is a precaution you should always take. Shout loudly the question "Clear?" Don't turn the prop until you have heard the acknowledgement "Clear!" from someone who can see that your propeller area is unobstructed.

I have the further precautionary habit of engaging the starter and turning the engine over a couple of revolutions before turning on the magneto switch. If a person or object did get in the way of the prop, the starter force would do little damage. This habit paid off for me once when I had left a short step ladder ahead of the plane. The prop bumped it at the first turn of the starter and I had only a red face to live with instead of a pile of kindling and a bent propeller.

Figure 114. Propping Cub

Swinging your leg forward when propping an engine is a commonly practiced mistake.

Turn the master switch "On," turn the magneto switch to "Left" or "Both" as recommended by the engine manufacturer. Hold the brakes on and engage the starter until the engine is running.

If you have overprimed, an accumulation of fuel in the carburetor could become ignited by a backfire. If this happens, open the throttle half way and keep the starter turning to draw the flames into the induction system.

If your plane doesn't have an electric starter, you should use the following routine of hand propping. In this method one person in the cockpit handles the controls, brakes, and switches while the other spins the prop. The pilot at the propeller is in command of the starting routine, and he will give instructions to the man in the cockpit. A sample starting routine would be as follows: Pilot says, "Switches off and prime." Student checks that the magneto switch is off, repeats the commands verbally, and makes two or three strokes of the primer (on some engines the throttle can be used as a primer). The pilot pulls the propeller through a few revolutions to distribute fuel to the cylinders. Pilot says, "Switches on and brakes on," or "Contact and brakes." Student turns the magneto switch on, holds the elevator up (stick back), holds the brakes on and cracks throttle open ⅛-inch, and then repeats the commands. The pilot spins the prop. As soon as the engine starts, the student pulls the throttle back to idle and watches for an oil pressure indication.

If you are the man in the cockpit, it is critically important that you respond properly to the starting signals. When the prop man says "Brakes!" be sure you are holding brake pedal pressure. If the engine starts without brakes on, the prop man could find himself being chased by a whirling meat cleaver. If he survives, you might find yourself being chased by a madman with a club.

Now turn the carburetor heat from "cold" to "hot" position for idling and taxi operations.

Occasions arise when a solo pilot doesn't have a helper available, so he should take one or more of the following precautions to see that he doesn't provoke an accident when he flips the prop. Set the parking brake, chock the wheels, or tie the tailwheel securely to a post. After starting, retard the throttle, remove the chocks, and board the plane.

Before hand-turning a propeller to start the engine, always examine the ground beneath the prop. Loose gravel, oil, or slippery wet grass, could cause a problem. Move the plane, if necessary, to a place which will give you a good footing. A tired back would be much better than a broken one. Stand at a 45° angle to the propeller with your right shoulder pointing toward the hub. Most of your weight should be on one foot (your preference) and as you pull the blade through its compression point, step backward onto the other foot.

Grasp the trailing edge of the propeller with both hands one-third to one-half of the way in from the tip and thrust downward with a quick positive stroke. Follow through each stroke with a full arm swing, which gets your hand quickly out of the plane of propeller rotation.

Always treat a propeller as though the switch were on and ready to fire. Don't ever handle it in a way which could cause you an injury if the engine fired unexpectedly. Many pilots swing their right leg forward toward the propeller, then back again as they pull down on the blade. This gives them additional power and balance for pulling the blade down on larger engines. I know a one-legged pilot, though, who will give you a real sales talk on the hazards of this habit. When propping larger engines, I simply grasp the blade closer to the tip where I get more leverage.

If the blade stops in an awkward position, turn the switch off and reposition the prop.

Taxiing

Before taxiing out to the runway, determine the direction and velocity of the wind. Airports have three common types of wind indicators:

1. The wind sock is the most universally used. A sleeve-shaped cylinder of cloth is mounted on a ring which swivels freely to allow windflow to inflate the sleeve. The open mouth of the sleeve always faces the wind and the tail trails downwind. By noting the degree of inflation of a wind sock you can determine roughly the wind velocity.
2. The wind tee is an airplane-shaped board structure which is mounted on a pivot so that the tail of the tee always points downwind.
3. A tetrahedron is a large four-sided pointer which looks like an arrowhead from the air. It is also on a pivot so that the pointer faces upwind. The tee and tetrahedron are useful for telling the direction of the wind, and aircraft traffic pattern, but they don't help you determine velocity.

The reason for finding the wind direction is to help you pick the proper end of the runway to taxi to. You should always taxi to the downwind end of the runway because landings and take-offs are made into the wind.

Taxiing in no-wind conditions is fairly simple. Use a small burst of power to get the plane started, and then use rudder pedals to steer. Taxi speed is controlled with the throttle and should be a slow walking speed in congested areas around other planes, and a fast walking speed while on a taxiway. When taxiing, be ever conscious that your wings project fifteen feet or more on both sides, and that the propeller stirs up a small gale behind you, even at low throttle settings. A courteous pilot will avoid directing his prop wash toward other planes or persons.

A student during his first experience at the controls once said to me, "Gee, this thing steers like a rubber band." The springs in the linkage cause the spongy feel to the rudder pedals, and it takes a little experience to get the feel of steering. It is easy to overcontrol, and anticipating helps to prevent this. Apply rudder a moment before you need it, and also release rudder a little early. Forward visibility in tailwheel-type airplanes is not too good, and if you see a plane zigzagging down the taxiway it is not really a tipsy pilot at the controls. Shallow S turns are the approved solution to the visibility problem while taxiing.

Tricycle gear aircraft are more responsive to steering, have better forward visibility, and are relatively free from the effects of wind gusts during taxi.

The flight controls are very functional during taxiing, and the position of the elevator is important. Prop wash is wind generated by the propeller, and it can cause the tail to lift right off the ground if the elevator is not properly positioned. Normally the stick is held back (elevator up) during all ground operations. Occasionally when taxiing with a strong tail wind the relative wind against the elevator could be from behind in spite of the prop wash. In this event you should hold forward stick (elevator down) to help keep the tail planted.

Taxiing crosswind sometimes presents some real problems in a tailwheel-type plane. The wind force against the tail and fuselage will often force the plane to weathervane into the wind in spite of your corrective rudder pressures. Applying the downwind brake is sometimes the only way to maintain your course. If that doesn't work either, you had better taxi back to the hangar and wait for better flying weather.

Brakes

Aircraft brakes are not designed for heavy duty use as on an automobile. Older planes, especially, are prone to brake "fade" when overused. They were designed primarily to stop the plane from slow speeds, to hold the plane at a standstill, and to assist with slow taxi maneuvers such as tight turns. Don't taxi with excess power and don't hold your speed down with the brakes. Remember, planes were flown for years without brakes at all.

If you develop the habit of taxiing as though your plane had no brakes, you will never suffer serious consequences from accidental brake failure. One final reminder—don't jam on both brakes quickly. You may get away with it in a tricycle gear plane, but a tail dragger will simply tip up on its nose and the prop will throw chunks of sod on your windshield.

Pre-takeoff Check

On the preflight you determined that the plane appeared to be in proper condition. The purpose of the pre-takeoff check, or "runup," is to be certain that the engine and instruments are operating properly. It is your last opportunity to find something wrong before flight, so the runup should be taken seriously.

Park facing into the wind so that the engine cools properly, and with the area clear to your rear. Set the throttle at about 1000 rpm and scrutinize each instrument. Airspeed should read zero or a little above. Altimeter should read field elevation. Read both hands, because it is easy to mis-set the short needle. The tachometer should read steady. Oil pressure should be in the normal range. Oil temperature should be creeping upward. The ammeter should show a positive charging rate. The compass should read approximately your aircraft heading. The gas gauge reading should be about the same as your visual inspection of fuel quantity. The gas selector valve should be on the fullest tank.

Change the carburetor heat from "hot" to "cold" position. Now advance the throttle to 1800 rpm. You may need extra brake pressure to prevent creeping. Turn the magneto switch from "both" to "right," and observe the tachometer needle for a drop in rpm. Switch back to "both," wait two or three seconds until engine rpm's stabilize again, and then switch to "left" and again watch the tach for an rpm drop. If the spark plugs, magneto, and wiring are all in good condition, the rpm loss on either left or right mag will not exceed 50 or 75 rpm's below that shown for both mags. If the drop is over 100 on either magneto, or if the engine sounds audibly rough, then something is wrong and you shouldn't fly.

While still at 1800 rpm, apply carburetor heat and watch for an rpm drop of about 50. This proves that warm air is entering the carburetor because a small power loss always occurs with the carb heat on.

Reduce throttle to idle and make a final control check. Move elevator, aileron, and rudder from stop to stop and visually check to ascertain that the control surfaces are moving in the proper direction. Don't just wiggle the controls and conclude that they move freely so they must be all right. While the elevator is up, look at the trim tab and see if its position corresponds with the trim handle setting. Normal takeoff trim setting is about neutral.

If you are flying from an airport with a traffic control tower, you will get radio clearance for takeoff. You should still examine the runway and traffic pattern, however, before proceeding to take off.

Landing aircraft have the right of way over you. Sometimes you need to make a 180° turn to get a good look at the traffic pattern. When you have determined that there is no landing traffic, taxi onto the runway centerline and face into the wind. If the taxiway connects to the runway some distance down field from the actual end of the runway, then make your taxi pattern and turn so that you have no runway behind you when you are faced into the wind and ready for takeoff. This is called "using all the runway," and it is a safety habit which could

pay off some day if you should have to abort a takeoff and stop before running off the other end.

CONTROL DURING FLIGHT

Takeoff and Climb

By taking off into the wind the ground roll will be shortened. This way the aircraft already has some airspeed even before it starts rolling. Takeoffs are surprisingly easy. You simply push the throttle to a wide-open position and wait. A lightly loaded plane takes only a few seconds to accelerate to 50 mph. If properly trimmed and balanced the plane will leave the ground and begin climbing by the time the speed reaches 60 mph. The stick and rudders are held neutral during the takeoff roll. On tail wheel airplanes some right rudder may be needed if the nose of the plane tries to yaw to the left. If the plane isn't airborne at 60 mph, apply a gentle back pressure to the stick. The nose will move upward a few inches and the plane will leave the ground smoothly.

Every plane has a "best climb speed" which has been determined by engineers and testing studies. Seventy miles per hour is approximately right for most light airplanes. The elevators are the controls used to keep the speed at 70 mph. If forward or back stick pressure is needed to hold the speed at 70, then rotate the trim adjustment until the stick feels neutral. Usually a slight right-rudder pressure will be necessary during climbs to compensate for torque. This right rudder won't be necessary after you level off and reach cruising speed, which is about a third faster than climb speed. The climb should continue straight ahead after takeoff. A crosswind will cause you to drift sideways from the runway center line. Set up a crab angle to compensate for drift by turning slightly into the wind.

It is best to make shallow banked turns after leaving the airport traffic pattern of 800 feet. Your visibility is better while turning.

Keep the throttle wide open during climb unless your plane has a reduced power setting recommended for climb. At 2,000 feet above the ground, level the aircraft by gentle forward pressure on the stick. The nose should now point slightly below the horizon. As the airspeed increases you can stop holding right rudder and retrim the elevator to fly "hands off" at cruising speed. Do not reduce throttle until after reaching cruising speed.

Straight and Level Flight

This should be easy, but surprisingly it takes a lot of knack to maintain straight and level flight. Some pilots never do get completely away

Figure 115. Level Flight (bank, wingtip)

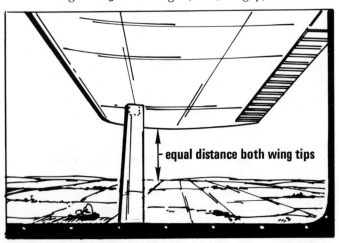

equal distance both wing tips

from the "Chinese" approach (Won Wing Lo) to level flight. Coordination in level flight requires that the fuselage be aligned with the direction of travel, and the wings must be horizontal. Any deviation from this will cause a loss in either airspeed or altitude. To practice straight flight, monitor visually the position of your wingtips to the horizon. They should be the same on both sides. This gives your neck a lot of exercise, but it is the only way to develop a feel for wings-level flight. Looking out the nose and trying to relate the instrument panel or windshield frame to the horizon simply doesn't work for beginners. You will, however, use the nose-to-horizon relationship for pitch reference, and a bank reference during turns. If the air is bumpy from convection currents, which are common on a sunny day, you may become very frustrated in attempting to hold level flight. Don't fight the bumps. Precision is impossible in unstable air. Relax and be content with the wings approximately level.

If airspeed, altitude, and heading stay constant, you are in level flight. If you find one changing, feel for the pressure you are holding on the stick and rudders, and remove that pressure.

The throttle, not the elevator, is your primary altitude control. However, from a practical standpoint the elevator is what you use when making small altitude corrections during level flight.

To hold a constant altitude you must frequently refer to the altimeter and to the nose-to-horizon reference. As a student you should think of altitude control as a series of corrections. You will be above or below your selected altitude most of the time. The important thing is that you detect the error and correct for it. You correct for being too low with a little back stick

LEFT TURN (start)

LEFT TURN (established)

**A left turn is established by applying left aileron together with left rudder.
During the turn controls are neutral except for slight up elevator which is
needed to prevent the nose from dropping.**

Fiugre 116. Left Turn. (1) Start; (2) Established

pressure. When too high, a little forward pressure will begin your return to the desired altitude. Don't just stab the control. Apply a gentle pressure and hold it. Note from the nose reference that your pitch has changed, and then check the altimeter to see the effect. If you are more than fifty feet too low, it is best to add a little throttle to assist your climb back to correct altitude.

As your proficiency increases you will find your altitude corrections becoming smaller and less frequent. If the altitude creeps off consistently in the same direction, check to be sure you have the trim set accurately. A mis-set trim tab can cause you no end of pilot fatigue and frustration when trying to hold an accurate altitude. Remember, for every change in your weight or airspeed, you will need a new elevator trim setting.

The plane needs very little, if any, help from you to maintain straight and level flight. Thirty seconds at a time is enough to spend concentrating on level flight. You should, however, space these half-minute practice periods frequently. Put one between each turn and before each climb or glide.

Turns

Before making a turn, "clear the area" by looking in the direction of the intended turn to be sure it is clear of other aircraft.

To turn efficiently the airplane must be banked, just as a bicycle or motorcycle banks during turns. I have already explained that bank, or rotation about the plane's longitudinal axis, is regulated by the ailerons. However, simply applying left aileron to establish a left bank will not result in a proper turn. The delicate balance of forces acting on a plane can be upset by applying left aileron. Moving the stick or wheel left causes the left aileron to bend up and the right aileron down. A downward-moving right aileron develops more drag than the upward-moving left aileron. The excess drag on the right wing causes the plane's nose to yaw to the right. You can prevent this only by applying left rudder together with the left aileron. When banking to the right you must apply right rudder together with right aileron.

The yaw which is induced by the ailerons is called "adverse aileron yaw." Its effects have been reduced in modern designs by giving the

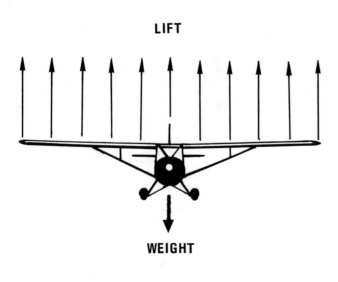

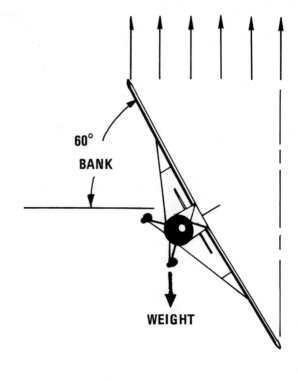

Figure 117. Loss of Lift during 60° Bank

up-moving aileron more travel than the down one. Aileron yaw is still present, however, and it is every pilot's responsibility to learn just when and how much rudder to apply together with the aileron when banking. Once a desired degree of bank is established the rotation must be stopped and the controls neutralized. To stop the bank from progressing steeper, apply just a slight touch of opposite aileron, and then hold rudder and aileron neutral. The plane will now be turning at a constant rate in a fixed degree of bank. The turn will continue indefinitely except for the loss of lift which results whenever a plane is banked. In level flight the wings have 100 percent of their area acting to offset gravity. During a turn, lift is acting perpendicular to the wing, but because the wing is banked only a portion of the lift is offsetting gravity, so a loss of lift and consequent descent will always occur when you bank.

The diagram illustrates this with a 60° bank which yields only half as much lift in an upward direction to offset gravity. A 60° bank is a rather extreme example, but the loss of lift will be noticeable during a bank of only 10°. To compensate for this loss of lift and to maintain altitude during a turn you must increase the plane's pitch altitude with up elevator. You will need back stick pressure anytime your bank angle exceeds 10°. This nose-up altitude will cause the airspeed to diminish, so if you want

to keep a constant airspeed during turns you will have to manipulate the throttle as well as the elevator.

In practice the airspeed loss during turns is ignored unless you are making steep turns with a 45° or greater angle of bank.

Explaining a simple turn has developed into quite a complex description of control movements. Perhaps if I summarize it will sound less complicated: To turn right from level flight, apply right stick pressure and simultaneously apply foot pressure to the right rudder pedal. As the angle of bank increases you should gradually apply back stick pressure. When the desired bank angle is reached, stop the bank with a touch of left aileron, and then hold rudder and ailerons neutral. To roll out of this right bank and return to level flight, apply left aileron and left rudder. As the bank angle decreases, gradually release the back stick pressure. When the plane is level all controls should be neutral.

I like to have a student begin turn practice with 20° banks and 360° turns. After he gets the idea I have him make 180° turns and finally a sequence of 90° turns. Always use heading references on the ground, such as fence lines or roads. You will find that to roll out on a given heading you will have to anticipate or "lead" by starting the rollout before reaching the desired heading. After gaining some confidence in

20° turns, work on turns with a 30° bank, and then 45° banks. The steeper the bank angle, the more you should lead the rollout.

You can easily detect if your rudder and aileron are not properly coordinated. The ball indicator on the turn-and-bank instrument will be centered only when a bank and turn are properly made. Too much rudder will cause the plane to skid and the ball will be off center to the outside of the turn. Too little rudder causes a slip and the ball will be off center to the inside of the turn. Watching the ball can become discouraging, especially if you are a perfectionist and inclined to be impatient with yourself. As a student I remember the only time I could get the ball to stay centered was after a landing.

I would like to emphasize that the control pressures I talk about should be thought about as pressures and not movements. The stick and rudders do move a little, of course. However, for a pilot to become smooth and proficient he must avoid abrupt movements with the con-trols. Thinking "pressures" instead of movements is often a helpful tip when a student is striving for smoothness.

Climbs

To begin a climb, establish a nose-up pitch attitude and apply throttle to the recommended climb power setting. Climbing airspeed is usually about one-third slower than cruising speed. Your forward visibility is reduced during climbs, so it is best to keep the plane turning. During climbing turns you will find that banks in excess of 15° will cut down the plane's rate of climb. It is best always to make climbing turns shallow. The right rudder you must hold to correct for torque during climb has an interesting effect on climbing turns. For climbing turns to the left, the torque is giving you the same effect as left rudder, and you may be able to make a coordinated left turn by just easing off the right rudder as you apply left aileron.

Figure 118. Normal Turn 20° Bank

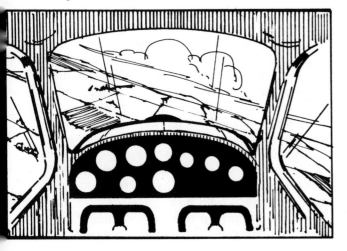

Figure 119. Normal Climb

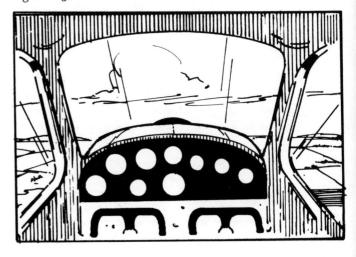

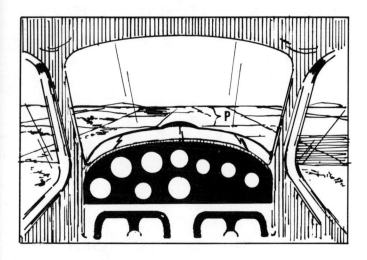

**Distance P is the pilot's pitch
reference during all attitudes of flight.**

Figure 120. Level Flight (pitch, nose)

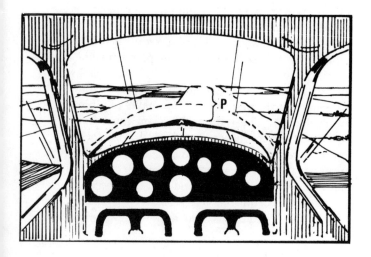

**During glides, distance P is slightly
greater than during level flight.**

Figure 121. Normal Glide (pitch)

During right-hand climbing turns an extra amount of right-rudder pressure will be needed. A small amount of back stick pressure is necessary during all climbing turns to maintain a nose-up attitude.

Glides

The glide is made with a power-off or idle throttle setting. The best glide speed is that which gives the maximum forward travel with the minimum loss of altitude. In light planes the best glide speed is usually about the same as the best climb speed. Seventy miles per hour is an overall average. This will yield about an eight- or ten-to-one glide ratio.

The beginner often believes that any time the power is off the plane will have to "dive" to keep up its flying speed. It is true that gravity provides the thrust to keep the plane moving forward whenever the engine power is off. However, you don't need a steep nose-down attitude to maintain proper gliding speed.

During a glide the attitude is very nearly the same as during cruising flight. The nose is allowed to drop slightly from the level flight position, and held there with *back* pressure on the stick. It would seem as though you would need forward stick pressure to hold a nose-down position. However, with the power off there is no slipstream effect past the stabilizer and the plane then balances in a nose-low condition. The up-elevator requires considerable back stick pressure which may be trimmed out during sustained glides. If you do trim for a glide, be prepared for the nose to pitch up when you finish the glide and apply power.

Be sure to apply carburetor heat at least ten seconds before starting a glide. Make throttle changes smoothly, and "clear" the engine periodically during the glide by running the rpm up to 1500 momentarily. This keeps the engine from overcooling or "loading up" from an over-rich mixture.

To recover from a glide, open the throttle to about 50 rpm less than the cruise setting. Keep the nose straight with rudder and prevent the nose from pitching up with properly timed forward stick. Remember, the propeller slipstream will exaggerate the effects of deflected elevators. Return the carburetor heat to cold position. This will give the engine the additional 50 rpm.

Gliding turns are good coordination practice because your attention will be focused on the elevator and rudder. Without the benefit of the slipstream the rudder will require greater deflection when rolling into or out of a turn. If you are holding back stick for a glide, it will take more back stick to make a gliding turn. A common error is to hold insufficient back stick pressure. This will cause the nose to drop and airspeed to build up, resulting in a spiral. Spirals are a good way to lose altitude in a hurry. Our jump and towplanes at the Skyport often utilize the spiral to get back down fast. Be cautious during a spiral or gliding descent to lead the level-off altitude. That is, apply power fifty feet *before* reaching the desired altitude. Your downward momentum will use up some altitude, and altimeters "lag" behind your actual altitude slightly during glides.

Orientation

During the first few hours of dual instruction you will undoubtedly become disoriented frequently. It takes practice and experience to be able to relate your position to the earth below and maintain your sense of direction. After three or four hours of dual you should begin to be able to relate your position and altitude to the airport. Test yourself frequently by asking yourself, "Which way is the town? The airport? North? How high am I now?" Remember, your altimeter tells you how high you are above sea level, and you must subtract from that figure the height of the terrain below you to arrive at your altitude above the ground. With practice you will finally develop an awareness of altitude, distance, and direction without concentrating on instruments or landmarks.

Instruments

Look first, interpret later. Ninety percent of your attention should be outside the cockpit. This means that you must be able to see and interpret instrument readings very quickly. Even as a beginner you can practice a technique which will help you keep your attention outside the cockpit. Instead of reading and studying the instruments until you understand their meaning, give yourself half a second to look at the altimeter or airspeed. Then immediately look outside the cockpit again. You can ponder the instrument reading and make control corrections, if needed, from the mental image that remains after a quick glance. Then glance back for a quick look at another instrument. In time you will be able to read three or four instruments in one quick glance.

Stalls

As explained earlier, a plane will stall if the wing is made to meet the air at too great an angle of attack. The common stall occurs in a nose-high attitude when the airspeed dwindles to below minimum flying speed and airflow over the wings can no longer create enough life to sustain flight.

Accelerated stalls may be brought about at higher speeds by abruptly pulling back the stick. When the angle of attack becomes great enough, the air will no longer flow smoothly over the wing, but will tumble into turbulence. To restore flight in either normal or accelerated stalls you must decrease the angle of attack by forward stick pressure. With a normal nose-high stall some altitude is always lost during the stall recovery. This is why stalls should be avoided at low altitudes.

It is very important for a pilot to know when his plane is flying close to stall speed. As a student you must learn to recognize a stall approach before the stall occurs. There are several clues you can use to indicate an impending stall. The airspeed indicator is one reference. The stall warning indicator used on many planes flashes a red light and toots a small horn when airspeed is a little above stall speed. The pilot's best stall indication of all is the behavior and feel of the plane and its controls. The plane will seem unresponsive to the aileron and elevator movements. The stick will feel loose and sloppy even though the control surfaces are responding normally to stick movements. The plane's nose will be high, which means that the pilot must hold back stick pressure in order to bring about a stall.

A "nibbling" wobble in the control stick or rudder pedals indicates the beginnings of the breakdown of smooth airflow. Some planes will shudder before they stall. Every airplane design has its own unique stall behavior. For this reason a safe pilot flying a different plane for the first time will always make a few stall approaches to acquaint himself with the plane's behavior before and during a stall.

Modern designs will maintain aileron control even though the wing is partially stalled. One thing always happens in a stall. The nose drops in spite of up-elevator pressures on the stick and you lose some altitude; perhaps only 100 feet or less, but a stall recovery always means that you must regain flying speed at the sacrifice of altitude.

Engine thrust alone will not overcome a stall, but it will hasten recovery. Applying full throttle together with a release of back stick pressure is the recommended technique for stall recovery.

STALL PRACTICE WITHOUT POWER

Have at least 1,500 feet of altitude. Make a 90° left and then a right turn to make sure your practice area is clear, and line the nose up on a horizon reference point. Apply carburetor heat and reduce throttle to idle. Raise the nose to about 15° up, which is approximately a landing altitude. As airspeed decreases you will need an increasing amount of back stick pressure. Maintain your heading with the rudders. Look to the sides rather than straight ahead over the nose. This will also help you to keep the wings level.

The stall "break" will occur by the time your stick has reached the full limit of its backward travel. The nose will begin to fall in spite of your up-elevator position.

STALL RECOVERY

Release back pressure on the stick and smoothly apply full throttle. Return the carburetor heat to "cold." Retard throttle as you reach cruising speed. You will find very little rudder control is needed until you apply power during the recovery. The torque and gyroscopic effects will then yaw the nose left unless you correct with right rudder.

Don't try to prevent losing altitude by abruptly pulling back on the stick after the power application. You may induce a "secondary or accelerated stall. The power-off stall is particularly helpful to practice because the stall approach is amost the same as that performed during a landing approach.

POWER-ON STALLS

Make clearing turns, but leave the throttle at a cruising setting. Raise the nose to 20° above the horizon and hold it there with gradually increasing back stick pressure. You will need right rudder and a bit of right aileron to maintain a fixed heading. Even with a higher pitch attitude the stall will take longer to occur because of engine thrust. Also, power-on stalls occur at a slightly slower airspeed because prop wash across the wings, and the upward component of propeller thust in a nose-high attitude, will help support the plane.

When the stall occurs and the nose drops, relax your back stick pressure and apply full throttle. Use coordinated rudder and aileron to level the wings and control your heading. Many vintage light planes without washout (twist) built into the wings will lose aileron effectiveness during a stall. In this case rudder is the next most effective means for roll control.

TURNING STALLS

Your instructor will demonstrate a variety of turning stalls with and without power, and with various bank angles. The important thing to remember about turning stalls is that they will occur at higher speeds than wings-level stalls. Furthermore, the steeper your angle of bank, the higher will be the stall speed. This is because centrifugal force during a turn makes the plane behave as though it were heavier. The steeper the bank and sharper the turn, the heavier the plane becomes. This is called "load factor."

In a coordinated turn with a 60° bank the plane will be about double its normal weight and the stall speed will increase by forty percent. If the stall speed is 45 mph in wings-level flight, it will be about 63 mph when making a 60° turn.

Turning stalls are almost sure to cause a wing to drop when the stall occurs. Usually it is the high wing that stalls first because the plane begins to slip sideways as you approach the stall and some of the lift is lost on the inboard area of the higher wing. Turning stalls will give you good practice in using rudder and aileron to level the wing after the stall.

STALL SPEED INCREASES WITH ALTITUDE

The thin air at high altitudes provide less lift at a given speed, so it is reasonable to expect a plane to stall at higher speeds. One clear summer day our Travelair 6000 was carrying six jumpers to 10,000 feet. I was watching from two miles below. As the pilot slowed the plane down on the jump run, suddenly the big bird seemed to go out of control. I thought my eyes were deceiving me, but it appeared as though the plane rolled onto its side first one way and then the other. Finally it was level again and the jumpers began to dot the sky as they left the plane in a group.

The plane landed a few minutes later and the pilot did not seem disturbed over anything. I queried him anyway. "Did you have any problems with the plane up there? Once I thought I saw you almost on your back." "Oh, ahhh, that. Well . . ." He seemed willing not to discuss it, but finally he said, "You know, I'd almost forgotten how easy you can stall at those high altitudes."

Slow Flight

Flying the airplane at about 5 mph above stall speed is called "slow flight" and it is one of the best exercises for developing your feel and control of the plane. It is also a procedure fre-

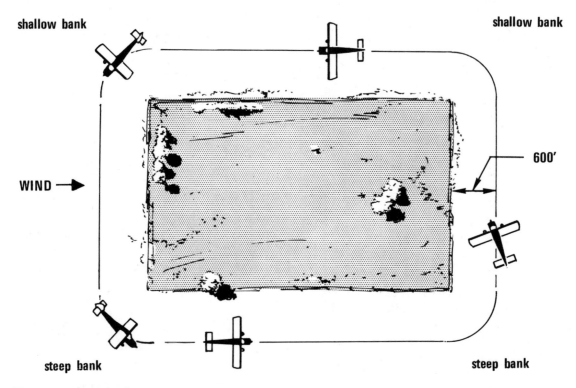

shallow bank   shallow bank

600'

WIND →

steep bank   steep bank

Figure 122. Rectangular Course

quently used by an FAA check pilot on the pilot license flight exam.

To practice slow flight, first reduce throttle to about 1500 rpm. As your speed diminishes, apply back stick pressure to raise the nose. As you approach slow flight speed, add throttle to maintain a constant altitude. You will find it takes a surprisingly high power setting to maintain level flight at this slow airspeed. This is because at the high angle of attack induced drag is very high and it absorbs considerable horsepower.

Be sure to maintain your heading by using right rudder as needed to correct for torque. It is best to reset the trim rather than fly by holding a constant back stick position. The throttle is adjusted to maintain your altitude, and elevators are manipulated to keep the slow flight airspeed constant.

When you feel fairly at ease in slow flight, try a shallow, banked turn. This will require a small power increase and some additional back stick pressure to maintain altitude. Practice climbs and glides at minimum airspeed also. Try to maintain a constant airspeed during the transition from glide to climb to level, etc. You can easily overheat the engine while slow flying, especially during climbs, so make them short.

Wind Drift

An explanation of how wind affects your flight path is given in the soaring chapter of this book. Here I would like to describe an exercise which is good for presolo students to practice if they have a flight lesson while the wind is blowing. It is called the "rectangle course," and it will help the student learn to control his flight path over the ground.

Choose a field or group of fields on the ground with well-defined sides, half a mile long by one-third to one-half mile wide. Approach the field with 600 feet of altitude and make a turn so that you are flying a counterclockwise course parallel to the field boundary about 600 feet away. At this altitude and distance from the field boundary you can watch out the left window and easily detect any drift in your flight path caused by the wind.

To keep your course or track parallel to and 600 feet outside the rectangle you will have to crab your heading into the wind. Otherwise you will drift off course unless the wind is directly on your nose or tail. With a direct head or tailwind your ground speed will be altered, but you will have no drift. Follow the example course in the

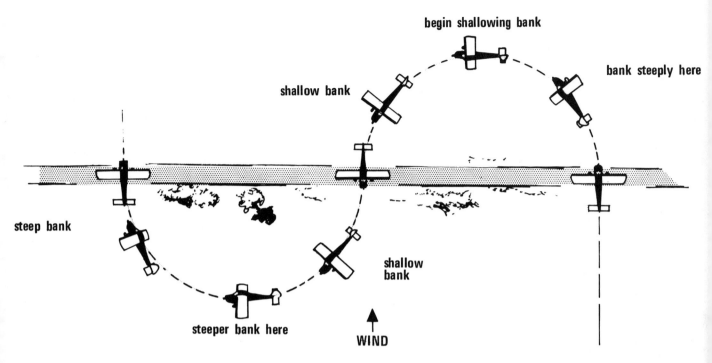

begin shallowing bank

bank steeply here

shallow bank

steep bank

shallow bank

steeper bank here

↑ WIND

Figure 123. S Turn across Road

diagram and you will find that on two legs of the rectangle a crab angle must be used. If the wind blows at a diagonal to your rectangular pattern, you will need a drift correction in your heading on all four legs of the course. The required amount of crab depends on wind velocity and direction in relation to your course. You will need the most crab when the wind is 90° to your course.

On the first trip around the course you have to guess at the crab angle and correct it by visual reference to the field. By the second time around you should be rolling out of the corner turns with about the right crab angle on each leg.

Your angle of bank during turns should also account for drift. When you have a headwind your groundspeed is slow and your turns can be shallow. If you have a tailwind your groundspeed will be faster and a steeper bank is necessary.

S Turns Across Road

Another exercise called the "S turn" is excellent for helping the student relate his control of the plane to movement across the ground. It is simply a series of alternating left and right 180° turns with a road or fence line for a ground

reference. Approach the road at an altitude of 600 feet on a right angle. As your wings pass directly over the road, begin a left turn with a 30° bank. When you have almost completed a 180° turn, roll out so that the wings are level as you pass over the road. Your track on the ground has prescribed a semicircle. Immediately begin a 180° right turn and again level the wings as you pass over the road. This maneuver does not become a challenge until you try it with a wind blowing 90° to the road. When drift is influencing your track, you have to compensate with a constantly changing angle of bank.

For best results, make your first pass across the road downwind. Begin an immediate steep bank to the left. Begin gradually shallowing the bank so that you have a 30° or medium bank when you reach the 90° point in your semicircle. Continue to shallow the bank gradually and cross the road with wings level. You are beating upwind now and have a slow ground speed. The rule for bank angle is, *shallow for slow ground speed, steep for fast ground speed.* Slowly start a shallow-banked right turn until you reach the 90° point, with a medium bank. The wind is abeam on your left now, and ground speed will start picking up due to drift. Increase to a steep

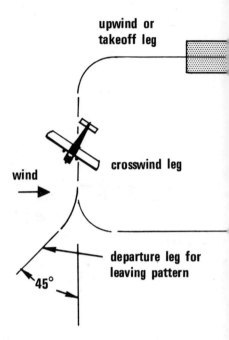

upwind or
takeoff leg

crosswind leg

wind

departure leg for
leaving pattern

45°

Figure 124. Airport Landing Pattern

bank and roll out quickly to cross the road with
wings level and ready to repeat the series of
turns. The student frequently makes too slow
and too shallow a turn during the moments when
drift is strongest. Remember, high drift speed
means to use a high bank angle.

The rectangular pattern and S turn practice
will teach you how to correct for wind drift,
which is especially important when flying the airport traffic pattern.

Airport Approaches

In the early days of flying an airport was a
huge grass field, and planes could come and go
from any direction. Now it is necessary for pilots
to follow an orderly pattern as they arrive and
depart from paved runway strips.

The typical traffic pattern is rectangular with
curved corners. It is flown at a prescribed altitude, which is usually 800 feet above the runway
surface. The diagram describes the important
parts and legs of the typical pattern. Many airports display a marker on the field called a
"segmented circle," which shows the pattern
prescribed for that field. If no field markers can
be found, you can presume the traffic pattern is
of the normal left-hand type, where all turns
within the pattern rectangle are to the left. Anytime I approach an unfamiliar airport, I cruise
over it about 2,000 feet high and look over the
traffic pattern in use. This also gives me a

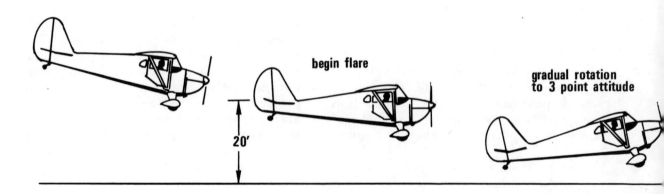

begin flare

gradual rotation
to 3 point attitude

20'

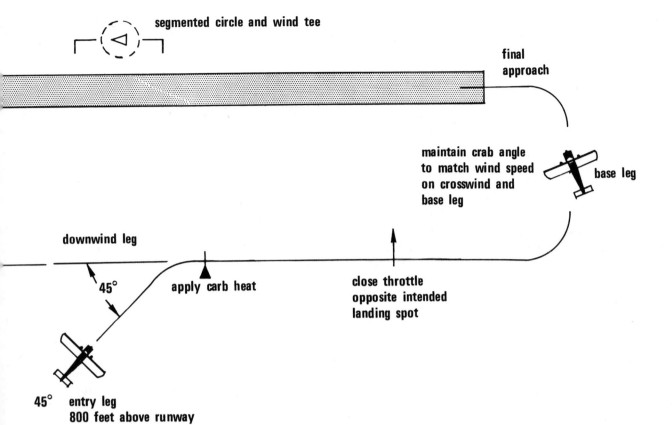

segmented circle and wind tee

final approach

maintain crab angle to match wind speed on crosswind and base leg

base leg

downwind leg

45°

apply carb heat

close throttle opposite intended landing spot

45° entry leg 800 feet above runway

chance to study the runway and taxiway layouts.

From the air you can read an unfamiliar airport like a map, but on the ground it is another story. On a large airport you could get lost trying to find the gas pump.

Normal Landing

If you have practiced power-off stalls you will already have some of the knack required for landing. A normal landing is made from a glide, with a stall approach made as you near the ground so that stalling speed is reached just as your wheels touch. The stall landing, commonly called the "three point landing," is used because it requires the minimum of ground roll after

touchdown. Under certain conditions a higher landing speed is recommended.

As a student you may carry misconceptions about landings. They don't require some masterful technique in coordination. Anybody can learn to land. Some people require more practice than others, but even a slow student, if willing to continue practicing, will learn to make safe landings.

The transition from normal glide to stall begins at about twenty feet above the runway by gently easing back on the stick. The idea is to slow down your descent rate by sacrificing airspeed. You are gliding at, say 70, and your stall or touchdown speed is 40. You have 30 mph to use up in the transition, or "flare." A continual,

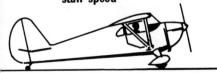

plane settles onto runway when airspeed drops to stall speed

Figure 125. 3-Point Stall Landing

Figure 126. Tricycle Gear Landing

smooth back pressure should bring you to a nose-up stall attitude about one foot above the ground. Hold this three-point attitude with back stick pressure and you will find the main and tail wheels will all start rolling along the ground together.

You can look out over the nose as you glide toward the ground, but after you begin the flare your visual reference to the ground should shift to beside the nose on the left. Look approximately 20° left and down. Look far enough ahead of the plane so that the ground is not blurred. Don't fix your gaze on one spot, but rather shift it about from horizon to a 20° downward angle. Don't try to check your instruments such as airspeed during the flare. A moment's inattention to your altitude can mean a sloppy landing.

After touchdown, control heading with rudder. Coast off your speed and avoid using brakes, if possible.

If you always had perfectly calm air, landings would be a cinch. However, nature has a way of keeping us guessing and the whim of the wind can play havoc with your best laid plans on a landing approach. This is why you watch your altitude closely during the flareout and use varying stick pressures to compensate for wind gusts, thermals, down drafts, etc.

A plane with tricycle gear is landed in exactly the same nose-high altitude. After the speed slows during the landing roll, the nose can no longer be held up with elevator, and the nose-wheel will contact the runway.

For three or more hours of flight lessons before your solo you will practice landings and takeoffs almost entirely. During these lessons you will be confined to the traffic pattern and will encounter many conditions that vary from the normal. In the following discussion, I will try to acquaint you with some of the variety of pattern and landing situations you will encounter.

Crosswind Takeoff

A crosswind during takeoff will require that you hold the upwind wing down with aileron and use rudder with determination to keep the fuselage aligned with the runway. Keep the wheels well planted on the runway until you have plenty of flying speed. This is done with forward stick pressure, which holds your tail high. If you take off tail-low with minimum flying speed, you could make some awkward sideways skips or bounces.

Takeoff Leg

Rarely do you find a zero wind condition or a headwind exactly on the nose during takeoff, so as you climb away from the runway, look back at the runway every few seconds to be sure you are tracking out along the runway centerline. If you can't see the runway on either side of the tail, then you are in a good position. When you reach 300 to 400 feet high and at least ¼ mile past the end of the runway, look back and to the left to clear yourself and make a medium bank 90° left climbing turn. This puts you on the crosswind leg, and if you had a headwind on the takeoff leg, you will need a right crab during the crosswind leg.

The length of the crosswind leg will vary with wind conditions. In brisk winds the downwind leg should be closer to the field, perhaps 1,200 to 1,500 feet out. Fifteen hundred to two thousand feet is about normal for zero or light winds. Clear your left side and bank left onto the downwind leg. Continue climbing and use whatever crab angle necessary to keep your track parallel to the runway.

Downwind Leg

Watch for other air traffic. Keep your head on a swivel, especially on downwind leg because traffic entering the pattern will be approaching from your right. When you reach 800 feet, throttle back to cruise rpm and complete your prelanding checklist. On a trainer this is simple: (1) gas to fullest tank; (2) mixture "full rich"; (3) carb heat "on." On a more complicated aircraft there might be a dozen items on the prelanding checklist.

When you are opposite your intended landing point, close the throttle and establish a normal glide. The left turn onto base leg should be slightly more than 90° if you are correcting for wind. Clear the engine by running up to 1500 rpm momentarily.

Look up and down and all around for other airplanes. Start the turn onto final approach so that you roll out from the turn aligned with the runway centerline. On a normal landing you would continue the glide until twenty feet above the runway and then start the flareout procedure already described.

On the vast majority of landings you will need to correct for one or a combination of the following:

TOO LITTLE ALTITUDE ON FINAL

If the wind is stronger than you expected, or if you flew too far on downwind leg, you could be low on final approach. If it is apparent that your glideslope will not carry you to the runway, don't harbor any hopes of stretching the glide by pulling up the nose. It won't work. A momentary power application should do the trick and will also clear your engine. Leave the power on long enough to assure you of gliding to the runway and then reduce throttle again. Be sure to maintain the proper gliding airspeed during such a power-on approach.

TOO MUCH ALTITUDE ON FINAL

This could result from not reducing power soon enough on downwind, an early turn onto base leg, less wind than expected, or encountering updrafts during the glide. You might think a simple lowering of the nose would remedy this problem. It won't because your speed would build up and you would still overfly the runway. When a beginning student finds himself too high on final approach, he should not hesitate to apply full throttle and fly along above the runway and make another complete pattern. This is called a "go around" and every student gets to make some for practice or for real.

Flaps are an excellent device for getting rid of excess altitude during your landing approach, especially Cessna flaps which are very large and effective. Planes without flaps can still slip and thereby effectively steepen their approach without increasing speed.

Forward Slips

During all normal flight the plane presents a rather clean or streamlined profile to the wind.

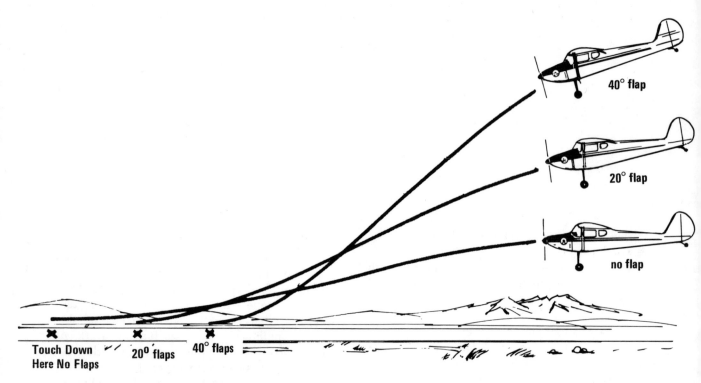

40° flap

20° flap

no flap

Touch Down
Here No Flaps   **20° flaps**   **40° flaps**

Figure 127. Effects of Flaps on Glide Angle

But it is possible to use the controls in such a way that the plane is flown sideways with perhaps a 10° or 15° yaw angle. During such a slip the drag is increased considerably and at normal glide speed the plane will descend much faster. To make a forward slip you use "crossed controls." Lower the left wing and apply right rudder. Or lower the right wing and apply left rudder. In either case the fuselage is banked as in a turn, but you prevent the plane from turning by applying opposite rudder. In a forward slip you should still use elevator to control your airspeed. Usually the nose tends to drop, so be sure to hold it up with back stick pressure.

Some planes may need slight forward elevator pressure for proper airspeed control during slips. In a forward slip your direction of travel is not altered, only the rate of descent is influenced.

Crosswind Landing

Frequently the wind will be on a diagonal to your final approach path and this is one situation where a crab angle is not the best solution. I have already described a forward slip for making steep descents and by a slightly different technique you can make a side slip to compensate for wind drift. Use crossed controls as in the forward slip to lower the upwind wing and apply just enough opposite rudder to keep the fuselage lined up with the runway. With a wing down the plane would begin to turn except that you prevent the turn with opposite rudder. The result is a sideways sliding of the plane, which will offset the wind drift.

Maintain this wing-low slip throughout the approach and flare. If the wind is diagonal to the runway you can keep the upwind wing low right down to the touchdown, which will be on one main wheel and the tailwheel. A tricycle geared plane will touch down on the upwind main wheel, and the other two will be eased onto the runway as your speed diminishes. This is the "wing down" method of making a crosswind landing and once you catch onto it, you will really be impressed with how well it works.

An alternative method for crosswind landing is sometimes practiced, which is to crab down final approach and then quickly line up with the runway immediately before touchdown. I have witnessed some bad experiences with this method when it was improperly timed and I believe it is a risky technique which can often cause a ground loop.

Common Landing Errors

GROUND LOOP

A tailwheel plane must be pointing in the direction of travel when the wheels touch the runway. If you touch down in a yaw, the plane's center of gravity or momentum is no longer aligned with the center of frictional force which is midway between the wheels. The result is an unstable condition which tends to pivot the plane in a circle to a tail-first heading. By diligent use of throttle, brakes, and rudder, a ground loop may be prevented if caught early enough.

Tricycle-geared planes are much more forgiving. They have a center of friction located behind the CG and they tend to straighten themselves out if landed in a crab.

FLARING TOO LOW

This is also known as "flying into the runway." It is frequently caused by trying to look over the nose during a landing. You resist getting the nose up into a proper stall attitude and the main wheels hit while you still have flying speed. This bounces or pitches the nose up, and the new high angle of attack will give you some quick altitude, maybe fifteen feet of it. This is a poor way to start a landing, so I always recommend a student to go around if his first contact with the runway results in a high bounce. A more experienced pilot will ease the nose over and apply enough power to prevent a stall, and then he can settle into a new flare and touchdown.

FLARING TOO HIGH

Sometime during your presolo landing practice you are sure to make a flare and stall the

A forward slip may be used to increase the glide angle when you determine your position on final approach is too high

Figure 128. Forward Slip

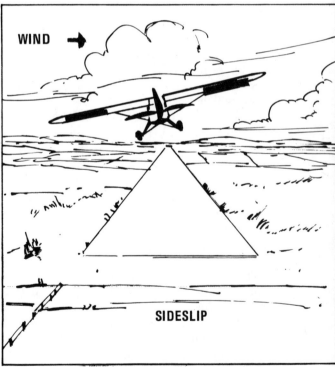

The slideslip is often used to correct for wind drift during landing approaches.

Figure 129. Side Slip

plane when you still have a few feet between you and the runway. In pilot vernacular this is called "dropping it in" because that is exactly what happens. When the stall occurs, the plane falls to the ground, and the resulting thump can be rough on the plane and your instructor's nerves. A student who has committed the other mistake of flying into the ground may be particularly prone to flare too high.

Another cause is from trying to gauge altitude during the flare by watching the ground too close to the plane. The ground is thus blurred and you simply cannot get an accurate fix on your altitude. "Ballooning" from an updraft over a hot runway or a sudden wind gust can also place you in a stall attitude with too much altitude.

The best way to recover when you recognize the plane is about to stall while you are too high is to apply power. This probably won't prevent your ground contact, but the slipstream and thrust will help to soften the landing. I don't propose that you ram on full throttle. Never jam the throttle forward. You can be quick with the throttle and still make it smooth. As soon as you have touched down, retard the throttle again and make a normal roll out. If you make a second bounce that was as high as the first, apply power and go around.

Gusty Air Approaches

When you are landing with headwinds over 10 mph you should carry extra speed on final approach. There are a couple of reasons for this. Often the wind diminishes near the ground, and if you fly down the approach path with a normal 70 mph, you could glide into low level calm airs and find yourself suddenly short on airspeed. The other condition frequently prevails here at the Skyport where winds may be gusting at 20 mph one second and nearly calm the next. An

unwary pilot could be starting a normal landing flare at fifteen or twenty feet high when the wind gust fades out and to his amazement, he is suddenly stalled.

A good rule is to fly the final approach at a speed which is normal glide speed plus half the estimated wind velocity. If our normal glide speed is 70, and the wind is 20, fly the approach at 80.

Wheel Landings

The normal three-point or stall landing is fine for most landing conditions. However, there are times such as with unpredictable gusty winds when you will want to make a "heel landing." Use the proposed extra speed on final approach and keep a little power on, perhaps 1200 rpm during the flare. Start the flare at a lower altitude, about ten feet high, so that you will touch down with a slightly tail-down attitude. "Wheel landing" means main wheels only, with the tail up, and at least 10 mph of excess airspeed above stall. In a tricycle gear ship the nose wheel should touch together with, but not before, the main wheels. As soon as the wheels touch the runway, apply slight forward stick to keep them down and retard throttle. Keep the tail up with forward stick until your speed has diminished and the tail comes down anyway. Remember, wheel landings use more runway because of higher landing speed and longer roll out.

Clouds and Visibility

Student pilots fly only under FAA Visual Flight Rules (VFR). This means that the horizontal visibility in the flight area must be at least one statute mile. Also the plane must be kept at all times a minimum distance from clouds as follows: 500 feet vertically below, 1,000 feet vertically above, and 2,000 feet horizontally. In addition the plane must not be flown nearer to the ground than 1,000 feet over populated areas, or 500 feet over unpopulated areas.

Logbook

Beginning with your first flight under dual instruction you should record all pertinent information in a pilot's logbook. Facts such as date, registration number of plane, duration of flight, and location of flight are recorded and verified by the signature of a licensed instructor. Preserve this book carefully because it constitutes the only official record of your flight experience.

Flying Publications

Aero Magazine, 599 S. Barranca St., Suite 583, Covina, California, 91722. Free to FAA registered aircraft owners; nonowners, $6 for 12 issues (2 years)

Air Progress, Box 1711, Des Moines, Iowa 50306. $6 per year, $10/2 years, $14/3 years

Antique Airplane Association News, Route 5 Industrial Airport, Attumwa, Iowa 52501. $12.50 per year includes membership, $6.00 per year subscription only

AOPA Pilot, P.O. Box 5800, Washington, D.C. 20014. $19 per year includes membership

Flying Magazine, Portland Place, Boulder, Colorado 80302. $6 per year

Plane and Pilot Magazine, P.O. Box 1136, Santa Monica, California, 90406. $6 per year

Private Pilot Magazine, 116 E. Badillo St., Covina, California 91722. $5 per year, $9/2 years

Sport Aviation, Publication of the Experimental Aircraft Association, P.O. Box 229, Hales Corners, Wisconsin 53130. $10 per year includes membership in EAA

Sport Flying Magazine, Challenge Publications, Inc., P.O. Box 1334, Canoga Park, California 91304. $9.50 per year, $17.95/2 years

The Flyer, 4267 E. 17th Ave., Port Columbus, Columbus, Ohio 43219. $3 per year

POWER PLANE GLOSSARY

ADVERSE AILERON YAW—The tendency for a plane's nose to veer or yaw in the direction of the downward-moving aileron because it causes more drag than the upward-moving aileron.

AILERON—The movable section of the outboard trailing edge of each wing which controls a plane's movement about its roll or longitudinal axis.

AIRFOIL—A structure such as a wing or propeller which is shaped to take advantage of the differential pressures which develop on an object that is moved through the air.

AIRFRAME—The main structure of an airplane such as the wing fuselage and tail, but excluding the engine and accessories.

AIRSPEED—A plane's speed in relation to the air through which it is passing.

AIRWAY—An air route designated and controlled by the FAA and provided with radio navigational aids.

AIRWORTHY—An aircraft's condition of being mechanically sound and safe to fly.

ALTIMETER—An instrument which indicates the altitude of an airplane above sea level by measuring the atmospheric pressure.

ALTITUDE—Usually given as height in feet above mean sea level (MSL). Sometimes quoted as height above the ground over which a plane is flying.

ANGLE OF ATTACK—The variable angle between a wing's chord line and the relative wind.

ANGLE OF INCIDENCE—The fixed angle between the wing chord line and the plane's longitudinal axis.

ANNUAL INSPECTION—A required yearly inspection by

an authorized mechanic to verify an airplane's airworthy condition.

APPROACH—The final stage of a flight whereby a plane is guided in to a landing.

ATTITUDE—The position of an airplane in flight in relation to the horizon.

AXIS—The three theoretical lines extending through the plane's center of gravity and extending fore and aft (longitudinal or roll axis), up and down (vertical or yaw axis), side to side (lateral or pitch axis).

BANK—To roll or tilt an airplane about its longitudinal axis to accomplish a turn.

BASE LEG—A segment of the landing pattern lying perpendicular to the final approach.

CARBURETOR HEAT—A control handle in the cockpit used to direct heated air through the carburetor to remove or prevent ice formation.

CEILING—The altitude of the base of the clouds above the ground. Sometimes given as altitude above sea level.

CENTER OF GRAVITY—Commonly called "CG," this is the balance point of the aircraft.

CHECKLIST—Sometimes an airplane ground or flight operation is performed by following a written list.

CHORD—The distance measured in a straight line through the wing between the leading and trailing edge.

COCKPIT—The area of an airplane within the fuselage where the pilot sits and where the controls and instruments are located.

CONTROL STICK—The vertical shaft positioned between the pilot's knees and linked by cables and levers to the control surfaces.

CONTROL SURFACES—The movable parts of an airplane's wings and tail which the pilot controls to maneuver the plane.

CROSS CONTROL—To apply right aileron and left rudder, or vice versa, which results in a slip.

CROSS-COUNTRY—A flight to a destination twenty-five or more miles away.

CROSSWIND—When the wind is blowing at an angle to the airplane's direction of flight.

CROSSWIND LEG—A segment of the traffice pattern perpendicular to the runway.

DOWNWIND—When the wind is blowing the same direction as the airplane's flight path.

DOWNWIND LEG—A segment of the landing pattern lying parallel to the runway.

DRAG—The resisting force which the air has to the passage of the plane.

DRIFT—The change in an airplane's flight path over the ground caused by a crosswind.

DUAL INSTRUCTOR—Flight training in an airplane by a licensed instructor.

ELEVATOR—The movable horizontal control surface used to raise and lower the tail during flight.

FEDERAL AVIATION AGENCY—The U.S. Government agency which has the responsibility to supervise, regulate, and encourage aviation.

FINAL APPROACH—Same as Approach.

FLAPS—The hinged portion of a wing's trailing edge inboard of the ailerons, used to give the wing more lift during slow flight, thereby allowing steeper landing approaches and slower speed landings.

FLAREOUT—The moment when the plane's nose is raised and the flight path is leveled to allow a smooth contact with the runway.

FLIGHT SURFACES—Wings and tail of an airplane.

FORCED LANDINGS—Any time a plane is forced to land due to unforeseen circumstances such as engine failure.

FUSELAGE—The portion of an airplane's airframe to which the flight surfaces are attached. Usually contains the engine, cockpit, and controls.

GLIDE—The forward flight of a plane whereby speed is maintained by a loss of altitude and not by engine power.

GLIDE RATIO—A figure which represents a plane's forward travel in relation to its vertical or descent travel when gliding.

GROUND LOOP—When a plane makes an uncontrolled turn of 90° or more while taxiing or landing. Often results in damage to the landing gear and wing tips.

GROUND SPEED—The speed of an airplane in relation to the ground over which it is passing.

HEADWIND—A wind blowing from ahead of the airplane, thereby slowing its ground speed. A crosswind blowing from a forward direction which slows the plane's ground speed may also be called a headwind.

INCIDENCE—See Angle of Incidence.

LANDING—The act of bringing a plane from flight to a standstill on the ground.

LANDING GEAR—The wheels, axles, and struts which support an airplane while on the ground.

LATERAL AXIS—The theoretical line running from wingtip to wingtip. Nose up and down or pitch movements are about this axis.

LEADING EDGE—The forward edge of any airfoil or flight surface.

LETDOWN—Losing altitude, usually in anticipation of a landing.

LIFT—The upward force which acts on a wing and sustains a plane in flight.

LOGBOOK—A personal record of flights kept and maintained by every pilot.

LONGITUDINAL AXIS—The theoretical line running from nose to tail of the airplane. Banking or rolling movements are about this axis.

MAGNETO—Also called "Mag." A generator which supplies a high voltage current to the engine's spark plugs.

MIXTURE CONTROL—A control handle in the cockpit by which the pilot can adjust the fuel-air mixture supplied to the engine by the carburetor.

NOSE WHEEL—The forward, steerable wheel on a tricycle-geared airplane.

OVERCONTROL—To move the airplane's controls more than the desired amount.

OVERSHOOT—To fly past the desired point, such as running off the end of the runway after landing.

PATTERN—Usually a rectangular flight path around an airport intended to assure the orderly arrival and departure of air traffic. Also called "traffic pattern."

PITCH—Refers to a plane's nose-up or nose-down attitude.

PITCH AXIS—See Lateral Axis.

PITOT TUBE—A tube projecting into the airstream which measures impact of ram air pressure and is converted to airspeed on the airspeed instrument.

PREFLIGHT—An inspection of the mechanical condition of the airplane by the pilot prior to flight.

PRIVATES—Short for private pilot's license which is issued by the FAA. Sometimes called "private ticket."

PROPELLER—A pair of solid wood or metal airfoils or blades attached to the engine crankshaft. When rotating, the propeller blades convert engine power to thrust by accelerating a large mass of air rearward.

PROP WASH—The area of fast moving turbulent air driven back by a rotating propeller.

PUSHER—Refers to an aircraft design which has the propeller mounted behind the engine.

RAM AIR—At flight speeds the air at the front of the plane will have greater than atmospheric pressure when trapped by openings and scoops. It is useful for cooling the engine, ventilating the cabin, and pressurizing the airspeed indicator system.

ROLL AXIS—See Longitudinal Axis.

ROLL OUT—The leveling of the wings after a banking turn.

RUDDER—The movable vertical control surface on the airplane's tail which controls the plane's movement about the vertical axis.

RUNUP—Before each flight the engine, magnetos, propeller, and instruments are tested for proper operation.

SKID—Sideways movement of the airplane which results from using rudder without ailerons.

SLIP—A sideways movement of the airplane achieved by banking one direction and applying rudder in the opposite direction. A slip puts the plane in a high drag position which causes a faster than normal loss of altitude. See Cross Control.

SLIPSTREAM—Same as Prop Wash.

SLOW FLIGHT—When level flight is maintained at a speed slightly faster than stall speed.

SOLO—When a plane is flown with only the pilot aboard. Also refers to a student pilot's first flight by himself.

SPAN—Usually means wingspan, or distance from a plane's wingtip to wingtip.

SPIN—When a plane is maintained in a stall by holding up elevator and caused to rotate or spin by holding full rudder deflection. Sometimes used as a training maneuver.

SPIRAL—A steeply banked, prolonged, descending turn.

STATIC—Usually refers to atmospheric air pressure at flight level, but in an undisturbed state, such as within the cabin, or beside the fuselage.

STICK—Same as Control Stick.

STABILITY—The tendency of an airplane to return to and maintain an upright and level flight attitude.

STABILIZER—Used to help stabilize the airplane on its lateral axis, the stabilizer is the horizontal flight surface at the tail to which the elevators attach.

STALL—A condition where the airplane begins to lose altitude and stability because of insufficient speed of airflow across the wings.

TACHOMETER—An instrument which tells the revolutions per minute of the engine. Also called "Tach."

TAILWIND—A wind blowing from behind the airplane, thereby increasing its ground speed. A crosswind which increases the plane's ground-speed may also be called a tailwind.

TAKEOFF—The act of bringing a plane into flight from a standstill on the ground.

TAXI—Moving the airplane on the ground under its own power.

TAXIWAY—Airports usually have roads called taxiways intended specifically for aircraft use while taxiing.

THRUST—The forward force generated by the engine acting through the propeller.

TORQUE—The tendency for an airplane to bank in a direction opposite to propeller rotation.

TOUCH-AND-GO LANDING—A landing where the throttle is opened following the touchdown and another takeoff is made.

TOUCHDOWN—During landing the moment when the main wheels contact the runway.

TRAFFIC PATTERN—Same as Pattern.

TRICYCLE LANDING GEAR—A three-wheeled landing gear with one wheel under the nose (nosewheel) and two under the wings (main wheels).

TRIM TAB—The small hinged part of an airplane's control surface which is connected to the trim lever in the cockpit.

UNDERSHOOT—To fall short of an intended mark. To undershoot a landing would mean to land short of the runway.

VERTICAL AXIS—The theoretical line running vertically through the plane's center of gravity. Yawing or turning movements are about this axis. Also called Yaw Axis.

WEATHERVANE—The tendency of an airplane on the ground to face into the wind due to lateral wind pressures on the tail.

WIND SOCK—A large cloth sleeve mounted on a metal hoop and supported on a pole near the airport runway. Used by pilots to determine wind direction and velocity.

WING—The large horizontal flight surfaces designed to support the plane in flight.

WING CHORD LINE—A theoretical line running from the wing's leading edge through the trailing edge.

YAW—To turn the nose of the plane so that the longitudinal axis is not aligned with the flight-path.

YAW AXIS—Same as Vertical Axis.

YOKE—In place of a control stick some airplanes use a control wheel (controls ailerons) mounted on a tube called a "yoke" (controls elevators).